Little Stories
of
Frontier Denison

OTHER BOOKS FROM
THE HISTORY GALS

Frontier Denison, Texas
by Donna Hord Hunt
edited by Mavis Anne Bryant

Images of America: Denison
by Donna Hord Hunt and Mavis Anne Bryant

Two Schools on Main Street:
The Pride of Denison, Texas, 1873–2007
by Mavis Anne Bryant and Donna Hord Hunt

Donald Mayes of Denison, Texas:
An Architectural Legacy
by Mavis Anne Bryant

Lives in Photography:
Denison, Texas, 1872–1999
by Mavis Anne Bryant

My Life in Print
by Donna Hord Hunt
edited by Mavis Anne Bryant

LITTLE STORIES
OF
FRONTIER DENISON

Bredette C. Murray

Edited by
Mavis Anne Bryant

3

ISBN-13: 978-1516945528
ISBN-10: 1516945522

Library of Congress Control Number: [LCCN]

Contents

Section Two: Little Stories of the Past   *147*

Chapter

Fig. 1. Bredette C. Murray, 1910. Photo by George W. Moore. Courtesy of B.C. Thomas Jr.

Editor's Note

In 1910 and 1911, newspaperman Bredette C. Murray published in his *Sunday Gazetteer* two series of remembrances of early days in and around the frontier town of Denison, Texas. He called these two series "Little Stories of Denison" and "Little Stories of the Past." In these delightful essays, quite useful to the local historian, Murray mused upon the early days of his North Texas community, which was founded by the Missouri, Kansas & Texas Railroad in 1872; and the nearby Indian Territory across the Red River.

In addition to providing much factual information about his subjects, the writings collected here, as a group, show Murray himself as a vigorous, adventurous man in his thirties and forties. Now in his mid-seventies, he looks back with evident longing for "the good old times." He tells of lively encounters with frontier characters of both sexes, local gambling and sporting diversions, social events in and around Denison, and lengthy camping and hunting trips in the wilderness across the Red River.

The reader senses that Murray, having spent many years filling columns of newsprint with details about local events and people, was asking himself what it all amounted to. What was the big picture? And, now that most people were gone who had lived those times with him, what had been omitted that needed telling? What—and who—would be lost forever if he didn't recall them? These stories were his responses, his legacy.

This book begins with a biography of B.C. Murray written by his oldest daughter, Dulce (sometimes spelled Dulcie). She was born July 27, 1867, at San Antonio, Texas. In that Spanish-speaking place, playmates called her "sweet," and the name fit so well that it stuck. She came to Denison as a small child, when the newly minted town was merely a tent village. She studied with the nuns at St. Xavier's Academy and with George L. Harshaw at his Gate City Literary and Commercial Academy.

Occasionally Dulce wrote articles for her father's newspapers,

Fig. 2. The first home built by B. C. Murray in 1873 at 300 W. Morgan St. Seen are: Helen Owings (widow of L. S. Owings), Roxana West Murray (mother of B. C. Murray), Dulce Murray, Helen West Murray Thomas. Courtesy of B. C. Thomas Jr.

including feature articles on a trip to Mexico and coverage of an early World's Fair. After B.C. Murray passed away, she became the caretaker of the bound files of his *Denison Daily News* and *Sunday Gazetteer*. She used them to produce regular columns for the *Denison Press*, recapping events in Denison many years in the past. These ran in the 1930s, 1940s, and 1950s. In the early 1940s Dulce sold the files of her father's newspapers to the *Denison Herald,* which drew on them for its long-running "Frontier Diary" features and other historical pieces.

Ms. Murray grew up in the Murray family home at 300 West Morgan Street, then moved with her father to 1031 West Main. After her father's death, she lived at 601 West Monterey Street. She was an active member of St. Joseph's Catholic Church until passing away on August 7, 1947.

Closing this volume is the obituary published in the *Sunday Gazetteer* when B.C. Murray's voice was stilled forever. Included in that document is the eulogy that Judge Walter Stephenson

Pearson (1860–1928) delivered at the funeral of his former employer and long-time friend. Helen Johnson kindly shared with me her biographical research on Pearson, whose life story Murray surely would have wanted told.

In the mid-1880s, Walter S. Pearson and his uncle, Peter Lee Pearson, a teenager, left the family farm in Hunt County, where their families had relocated from Georgia after the Civil War. The 1886 Denison City Directory found both working for Murray's *Denison Daily News*, Peter as printer and Walter as bookkeeper.

In 1889, Denison had five newspapers. By that year, Walter had purchased the *Gate City Guide* from Thomas J. Crooks, who had started it a year or so earlier, with offices at 100 West Woodard Street. The *Guide* lasted only a short time. On May 17 that year, Walter married Henrie Ann Messenger and purchased a house at 419 East Gandy Street, where he would live for the rest of his life. In 1891 Walter became associate editor at the *Denison Herald,* while also serving as a correspondent for *the Dallas News.* In 1893, Walter was city editor at the *Sunday Gazetteer.*

At this point, Walter switched professions, becoming an attorney and judge. The 1896 City Directory listed his occupation as justice of the peace. Whether he began to study law after he was elected justice of the peace or before, he was admitted to the bar in Sherman in February 1899. He held the position of city judge in Denison for more than ten years. Walter served as secretary of the committee selected to write a new city charter for Denison in 1907.

After leaving office in 1913, Walter continued with his private law practice on Main Street until tragedy stuck in 1928. On May 1, Georgia Pearson, Walter's youngest daughter, who worked in his office as a stenographer, died of a brain tumor at the young age of 24 years. He was inconsolable. Three months later, still consumed with grief, he took his own life, hanging himself in the family garage. He was 68 years old.

Pearson's eulogy alludes in numerous ways to the principles that guided the life of B.C. Murray. A sample paragraph suggests what these were:

> Our departed brother was . . . an admirer of nature—a student of the grand and unchanging principles of the universe. . . . He was singularly free from the blight of

> superstition and the effects of an erroneous early education. . . . He was no slave to mistaken dogmas, antique fables, or mythological fictions. He accepted the teachings of science as the most reliable facts within the grasp of the human mind.

In embracing such principles, Murray formed part of a group of like-minded Denison leaders who formed such organizations as Denison's Liberal League and its Philosophical and Social Club. Led by Thomas Volney Munson, these groups debated scientific and philosophical questions.

Scholar Steven R. Butler, in his article, "The Infidels of Denison," points out the members' distrust of organized religion, advocacy of strict separation of church and state, love of nature, and adherence to scientifically based truth as opposed to Biblical revelation (*Legacies: A History Journal for Dallas and North Central Texas,* vol. 27, no. 2 [Fall 2015]: 32–49). Murray's newspapers gave full coverage to the group's programs and debates, as well as to local criticism of their beliefs and activities.

Between Dulce's biography and her father's obituary, this book presents all the items comprising Murray's two "Little Stories" series, each with its original publication date. The one exception is a missing story where the entire issue of the newspaper was unavailable. The stories did not carry titles, so a descriptive headline has been added for each one.

Murray's newspaper articles employed spelling, capitalization, and grammar that differed in some ways from what is standard today. I have made minor editorial changes silently, to avoid distracting today's readers. Also a few editorial clarifications have been added to the text; these are enclosed in brackets.

Mr. Murray's texts contain some racial references that would be considered offensive in newspapers today. These expressions have been transcribed as printed in the original articles, as they show attitudes prevalent at the time of publication.

The stories presented here are numbered sequentially, in the order in which they were published. The "Little Stories of Denison" were numbered somewhat differently when originally printed, apparently due to errors. In those cases, the original numbers are provided in brackets. The "Little Stories of the Past" were not numbered in the original newspapers.

I discovered the two series and typed a digital transcription of them from newspapers that Grayson County Frontier Village made available on the University of North Texas Library's Portal to Texas History. Readers are urged to explore further the many issues of Murray's newspapers to be found on the Portal.

Many thanks go to B.C. Murray's great-grandson, Bredette C. Thomas Jr., for photographs and information related to his ancestor. Helen Johnson and Donna Hord Hunt aided publication of this book in numerous ways. I am most grateful to a former Denisonian, James K. Sears, now of Bloomington, Illinois. Jim unearthed information on Murray's travels and on one of Murray's subjects, Joseph E. Bozarth, and his family.

Mavis Anne Bryant
Sherman, Texas
December 2015

Fig. 3. The Murray children (L-R): Dulce, Helen, Edith, Edwin, Bredette, Corrie. Courtesy of B. C. Thomas Jr.

Fig. 4. Sunday Gazetteer *office, 112 West Main, ca. 1890.*
Murray is the man on the right. Courtesy of B.C. Thomas Jr.

Bredette Corydon Murray

Dulce Murray

[Presented to the Red River Historical Society at
Sherman, Texas, on December 11, 1926.]

Bredette Corydon Murray was born in Allegan, Michigan, January
14, 1837—the year his native state was admitted to the Union.
B.C. was the only child of Edwin A. and Caroline Roxana West
Murray. His father was a joiner by trade, and much of the inside
finishing work of the early homes in Allegan was his handiwork.
The boy's mother was a lineal descendant of Miles Standish.

B.C. entered the printing office of Elisha Bassett, a cousin of
his mother, at the age of thirteen years. He graduated from the
Allegan Seminary and a business college in Kalamazoo. After
graduation he held a clerical position in the Recorder's Office in
Kalamazoo. He was fond of travel and adventure; when a lad of
about seventeen, he volunteered to carry the mail, horseback, from
Allegan to Lansing, the state capital, to relieve the regular mail
carrier. It was a lonesome ride through miles of country with no
sign of human habitation. One trip was enough.

At the age of twenty years, B.C. left Michigan and went by
way of New Orleans to San Antonio, Texas. In New Orleans he did
reportorial work for some time. In San Antonio, he became
associated with Dr. L.S. Owings in the mercantile business. Later,
when Dr. Owings was appointed governor of the New Mexico
Territory, Murray purchased a printing press plant and freighted it
by wagon train from San Antonio to Mesilla, New Mexico. He
established the *Mesilla Times* about 1859.

At the outbreak of the Civil War, when it became apparent
that the Mission would fall into the hands of Federal troops, he
buried his plant for safe keeping; after the evacuation of the troops
he resurrected the plant and resumed business at the old stand. The
adobe office of the *Mesilla Times* was in a state of perfect

preservation as late as the fall of 1919.

Soon after the beginning of hostilities between the North and South, Murray assisted in mobilizing a regiment of cavalry in the vicinity of Mesilla and served throughout the duration of the war on the side of the Confederacy. After the surrender, this company preserved order in San Antonio and vicinity until the Federal troops arrived to take charge. Once during the war, B.C. was compelled to swim the Rio Grande. Another time, he and two or three companions became separated from their command. They had been hiding in the brush for several days and were without food, when they saw a commissary train approaching. Not knowing whether the train contained friends or foes, they resolved to reach it and ask for food. As the famished men staggered into the road, the Negro driver jumped from his seat and ran, believing them to be ghosts. They had been given up for dead. The train proved to be their own commissary.

After the close of the war, B.C. remained in San Antonio and became identified with the *San Antonio Express*. In that city he was united in marriage, on October 7, 1866, with Miss Amanda Swisher. She was a grandniece of Milton and Monroe Swisher, pioneer Texans; a distant cousin of General Sam Houston; and a sister-in-law of his old friend, Gov. L.S. Owings. Dr. Owings would become the first mayor of Denison in 1873–75. Five children were born the Murrays, four daughters and one son. One daughter died in 1903.

In 1868, Murray went to Topeka, Kansas, and for a time was employed as compositor on the *Topeka Commonwealth*. Not liking that cold climate, he again returned to Texas, taking up residence in Austin where he, Charles Deffenbach, and one other gentleman in 1870 bought the plant of a defunct Republican paper, changing its politics and giving it a new name, *The Democratic Statesman*. This was during the administration of Gov. E.J. Davis, referred to by the Texans of those days as the "carpetbag executive." Against Davis, Murray wielded his pen unceasingly, with the result that that gentleman was retired to civil life by an overwhelming majority. In the fall of 1872, having disposed of his interests in Austin, B.C. came with his family to Denison, known as "the Gate City" and more often referred to as "the Infant Wonder."

Here Murray established the *Denison Daily News,* in a small room built of unseasoned upright boards in the 300 block of Skiddy Street (now Chestnut Street). About the only equipment he had was a few fonts of type and a Washington hand press.

Initially the family was domiciled in a tent at the corner of South Austin Avenue and Morgan Street. For over thirty years, this was the home place, the dwelling itself being added to as the family increased. The house was destroyed by fire of incendiary origin after a hard-fought battle of a political nature in spring 1907. Murray then moved to 1031 West Main Street.

On December 27, 1872, the first issue of the *Weekly News* was printed, and this was followed on February 22, 1873, by the publication of the *Daily News.* For eight years, the *Daily News* never failed to greet its patrons in time for breakfast. Murray never left the plant until the last paper was off the press, ready for the carrier. I say "carrier" advisedly, as one was sufficient for the circulation of that early paper; the editor and the printer's devil (alias the carrier) were the whole force in those prehistoric times. In 1876, the two-story brick building at 112 West Main Street was erected, and the plant of the *Daily News* was moved to the second story and enlarged, as to both equipment and staff. A city editor was added, the devil was promoted to pressman, and a new devil was installed.

In 1881, Murray sold the circulation of the *News* to the proprietors of the *Herald* and devoted his time to job printing, which included posters and show printing. It was about this time that he established the Murray Power Printing Plant, which became one of the leading printing houses of the Southwest. Specializing in theatrical and billboard printing, the firm received and filled orders from as far away as St. Louis and Kansas City; Houston, Galveston, and San Antonio.

In the spring of 1883, B.C. began publishing another newspaper, the *Sunday Gazetteer,* which was referred to by the newsboys as "Your Sunday Glass of Beer," a very significant name in those days. This paper made its regular weekly visit not only to local patrons and nearby towns, but also across the continent to California, and across the ocean to foreign countries—China, Germany, France, and England.

Finally, in 1913, Murray sold the plant to J.E. Wall and retired from active newspaper work. At the earnest solicitation of the new purchaser, B.C. edited a column of "reminiscences of early days" each week up to within a few weeks of his death.

Bredette C. Murray died at the family home on February 6, 1924, at the age of eighty-seven. Forty of those years he had devoted to the development of the community in which he lived.

Murray was a tireless reader and a student; even as a boy, a book was his greatest treasure, and he would find something to trade for one he had never seen before, thinking it rare or out of the ordinary. This hobby of book collecting remained with him through life. He amassed an extensive library, and his books covered a wide range of subjects. Many of the books were rare and valuable, especially to the book lover and student. His shorthand library is believed to be the largest privately owned collection in the State. In recognition of his work along that line, he was awarded a medal and a life membership in the Willis-Byrom Club of the Gregg System.

Murray helped to organize the Texas Press Association, became a charter member of that group, and remained an active member as long as he continued in business. As a member of the Typographical Union, he held a working card as long as he lived and attended its meeting regularly. He was a member of the Confederate Veterans Camp, and the Sons of Confederate Veterans named their camp in his honor.

Early in the history of the city of Denison, B.C. was elected to the City Council and was untiring in his efforts to quell disorder and rid the city of vice. He always kept the pages of his paper clean, refusing to print objectionable matter of any kind, whether advertisements or otherwise. His columns were always open for the discussion of legitimate questions.

Murray was always ready with his time, his space, and an open pocketbook to further the best interests of his hometown and adopted State. He was equally ready and fearless in denouncing wrong and mismanagement in high places. He was of a quiet, retiring disposition, loving home life and his books. His wife died in 1894, and he never remarried. He was a man among men, a representative citizen and a gentleman.

The Good Old Times

Sunday Gazetteer, April 4, 1909

Thirty-five years ago, the country around Denison northeast was a veritable wild strawberry bed. On Sundays the hills were dotted with parties of merry young people gathering the rosy-cheeked berries. They were the most plentiful about where the Frisco track now runs. On one occasion the writer gathered a quart of berries in that vicinity. The people who lived there then were of that class who confined their lives to the city limits. The strawberry pickers were principally the few young people of the city.

There were jolly times in Denison in the seventies [1870s]. Wildflowers grew all around the town in great profusion, and the boys and girls would go to the prairies and woods and gather bouquets and bring them to town. The Pawpaw [Creek] had not yet been polluted by the filth and trash of the city, and the woods along its banks were clean and sweet, and the water in it as clear as crystal. It was delightful to sit in the shade of the great trees, and it was always pleasant in the bottoms in the hottest weather. At the Pawpaw the city limits ended, and the forest began. Wild turkeys and deer were sometimes seen there, and squirrels would bark at you from the cottonwood trees.

Another place very popular in pioneer days was Miller's Springs. Picnic parties of happy school children would pass the day at the springs, which was considered quite a walk then. Now the city has pushed beyond. A vivid and dramatic change has come over the old Miller Springs site, the railroad and the oil mill having swallowed it. Rural felicity has virtually gone.

The whole country thirty-five years ago was mostly woodland, clear spaces were in the minority, and forest ruled supreme. Just where the old Ed Perry residence at present stands [North Houston Avenue or East Main Street], a deer was killed in 1873.

There was another resort, more modern (the Boulevards), that has gone, too, like the rest. That whole section on Sundays was alive with people, and the streetcars, propelled by mules, ran to and fro. The beer gardens flourished, and there were baseball games and amusements of all kinds. Young people danced, flirted, and had a good time out there. Many pretty faces looked out from sunbonnets. Twenty years ago, the Boulevard was the most enjoyable place in suburban Denison. Some beautiful homes were erected out there. We had an exhibition pavilion built after the belt line was completed, in which was collected for exhibition the resources of the surrounding country, including the Indian Territory. Many public gatherings were held out there, and some of the most noted men in the country let loose floodgates of eloquence in the spacious hall. There were some swell balls given in the pavilion, and the people of Denison took great pride in conducting strangers to the Exposition Building. It was destroyed by fire, and now that country out there is almost as silent and melancholy as Goldsmith's "Deserted Village," the Haynes tragedy ["Denison's Night of Terror," May 18, 1892] having cast a shadow over the spot.

Between here and where the Cotton Mill now stands, and west of the Interurban, there were many pleasant walks, and the people of the city would go out there and spend the day in the cool shade of the trees. In 1875-76 there was a beer garden where Engineer T.Z. Williams of the Katy has built so many houses. Thousands of people would go to this place. Then it was considered in the country, but now it is within the city limits.

The Pawpaw hills (dear old Paradise Heights) attracted many parties of pleasure-seekers. There is nothing more exhilarating than hill climbing, as it is work that is healthful. Excursions to these hills were very popular twenty years ago. People walked then more than they do now. Wild grapes used to grow in the Pawpaw hills, and wild plums took on purple tints in the thickets, while sumacs reddened the rocks and the woods and at a distance looked as if on fire. Goldenrod, cardinal flowers, sunflowers, purple and white asters, and myriads of other wild flowers sprang up at your feet. People used to wander up from the Pawpaw with great strings of fish caught in that stream.

Beyond the Pawpaw hills was the racetrack. To new Denison,

this place is not well known, but the Howard Racetrack was a great resort at that period, and thousands of people used to gather there. Some of the owners of the best horses in Texas were patrons of that turf, but that, too, is among the things that have gone with the rest. That was the best cultivated section of country near Denison, and fields of ripening corn, sensuous autumn days of grain, luscious grapes, scarlet plums, and the honey bee made the country east a farming community well worthy of a visit.

About the only place left now is Woodlake, the old [Denison Driving Park and Fair Association] racetrack west of the city [off Morton Street] being a thing of the past. The grandstand from which so many people looked down on some of the finest sport in the Southwest has disappeared, and the fence has been leveled. The Exposition Hall [built in 1900] is about all that is left of a melancholy failure that has attended so many Denison enterprises.

Woodlake is a pretty place, but somehow or other there is something lacking. The modern idea of outdoor life prevails too much and when two or three thousand people are gathered, the city is merged into the country. Woodlake is all we have left, but it never will take the place in memory of the good old days.

Fig. 5. Swimming and boating at Woodlake, between Denison and Sherman.

Section One

Little Stories of Denison

No. 1
Patsey Pecor, Newsman

Sunday Gazetteer, January 16, 1910

In pioneer days there was a unique character in newspaper circles known as "Patsey Pecor, the Blue Jay of Texas." Patsey did newspaper reporting, and his ready wit made him many friends, and he was a mixer. Patsey at the wind-up of his career was stricken with the white plague, and died in the home of A.R. [Alpheus Remember] Collins on Fannin Avenue near Main Street. He was sick and broke, and A.R. Collins provided him with a home. One winter morning Patsey was found dead in bed.

He was the one who named that portion of town on South Armstrong Avenue as "Sugar Bottom," a name which has clung to it ever since. In his day Patsey was known to every man, woman, and child in Denison.

The funeral of the Bohemian was unique. The body was placed on the hook and ladder truck and the coffin wrapped in an American flag. The fire department followed the body to Fairview. At the grave, singular as it may seem, there was just one woman mourner; the lady is still alive and a resident of Denison. Patsey was laid to rest in the northeast part of the cemetery. The spot is now forgotten and unmarked. No tombstone was ever placed there. The question of a headstone was agitated, but nothing ever came of it. Big-hearted John Cox, who is also dead, offered to head the list with $20, and that was all.

Pecor was a paragrapher but not a writer of much talent. But for offhand and ready wit, he was never surpassed in the early history of Denison. He had a brother, E. Forest Pecor, who for a long period clerked at the old Star Store, of beloved memory, but the two brothers were estranged. He, too, is dead. Patsey at the time of death was 37 years of age.

No. 2

Mineral City Fraud

Sunday Gazetteer, January 23, 1910

But very few present residents have ever heard of Mineral City, one of the biggest fakes that was ever pulled off in Texas, or the Southwest for that matter. Mineral City was incubated and hatched in the city of Cincinnati. The location of the magic city was north of Denison, about where the Munson Park is at present. A map with blueprints showing parks, business and residence streets was gotten out, and with the map was a description of the location of the future great city of North Texas. The location and advantages were pictured in glowing colors. If we recollect right, the business lots were offered at $1 and the residence lots at $2.00, $2.50, and $3.00, according to location.

Mineral City was a myth, having existence only in the minds of the rogues who conceived the grand fraud. They were very careful to avoid all publicity in Texas papers, but used the leading journals of the West, for instance, the *Cincinnati Journal.* Hundreds of lots were sold before the fraud was exposed, and the district clerk of Sherman was a very busy man recording deeds.

A map of Mineral City fell into the hands of H. [Harrison] Tone, who started an investigation, and the fraud was soon thoroughly ventilated. The people who had been duped wrote letters of inquiry, there was a sudden collapse, and the great fake tumbled like a house made of cards. There is no telling how much the rogues cleared, but it must have been considerable, thousands of dollars probably. The exposé came sooner than was expected. No arrests were ever made that were heard of.

No. 3

The Star Store

Sunday Gazetteer, January 30, 1910

The most prominent business house in the pioneer period of Denison was the Star Store. It was named after Sam Star [1842–1899], who came here in 1873 from Kansas. The original firm was Waterman, Weil & Star, at present all dead. The senior member (Mr. [Charles] Waterman) left the firm in the eighties [1880s] and located in New York, where he committed suicide in rather a romantic manner. Dressed in his best, he stood before a mirror in a hotel on Broadway and, placing a pistol at his forehead, blew out his brains. Mr. Weil was the next to withdraw from the firm. Max Grundstein, who was long the leading spirit of the firm, became a member, and it was known as Star & Grundstein.

In the seventies and eighties [1870s and 1880s], the Star Store was virtually the head center of all the general merchandise of Denison. All of the southern portion of the Indian Territory, west as far as Paul's Valley and north into the Choctaw country, and the whole of the Chickasaw Nation; and a large portion of North Texas were patrons of the Star Store. It was the most popular place of business in the history of Denison. It was for many years the meeting point of all the leading citizens of the Indian Territory. They frequently visited Denison then, and about the first place they landed at was the old Star Store. It absolutely controlled the trade of this section, and no inducements, however flattering, ever impaired that patronage. The Star Store was always first in the affections of the Indian people. At that period the cattle trade was largely in the hands of the white men who had in many instances taken Indian wives. Their meeting place was at the Star Store, and many thousands of dollars exchanged hands under that roof.

The Star Store was never ungrateful to its patrons, and once in a while a prominent Indian and cattleman got on a whiz and started out

Fig. 6. 100 block West Main Street, north side, looking west. See "Original Star Store" sign, ca. 1895. Courtesy of B.C. Thomas Jr.

to paint the town "red." The Star Store helped that class out of their troubles. They frequently went dead broke, and the first place they went to for a loan was the Star Store. No business house in Denison had a more romantic history, and we might add, at the wind up, a more pathetic history. It was their generosity and immense credit to their patrons in the Indian Territory that drove them to the wall and precipitated a most disastrous failure. There was, at the time the Star Store closed its doors, over $100,000 owing the firm. We once heard Mr. Grundstein say that there was sufficient to meet all obligations. Of the above indebtedness, only about $20,000 was collected.

The Star Store building was the property of Alex Rennie, a white man who married a most estimable woman of the Chickasaw

Nation, who is at present in the city, visiting her son, John Rennie. The old Star Store building was burned in the eighties and Mr. Rennie erected on the site the present building occupied by the Hall-Leeper hardware house. The old Star Store was a three-story brick building. The firm first opened up at 203 [West] Main Street. When the building at the corner of Main Street and Austin Avenue was burned, Mr. Rennie purchased the property, and the firm of Waterman, Weil & Star moved in. Watt Smith, Lee Kone, and Simon Hirsch, who contributed so much to the popularity of the Star Store, are still alive and doing well. We have Mr. Hirsch with us at the present time, with Yeidel & Son. Dear old Watt Smith is at Fort Worth and is still a subscriber to the *Gazetteer*. Max Grundstein, who has as many friends to the square inch as any man in Texas, is at Dallas and still reads the *Gazetteer*. He must be over sixty years old, but retains all the buoyancy of a young man. When he was here about a year ago, he said: "What is the use of grieving; why, I feel as well as I ever did."

Sam Star, the master spirit, is dead. A better man never lived, and those who knew him personally will always love his memory. He was foremost in every movement to advance Denison. The strongest ties bound him to this city. He was one of the best friends that the newspapers here ever had, being a most liberal patron of printer's ink. In his long business career, a paper seldom appeared that did not bear his announcement. It was hard for him to say "no" to the newspaper solicitor.

The Star Store has disappeared, but it will ever be held in grateful remembrance by the old-timers that are left.

No. 4

The Old Grand Southern

Sunday Gazetteer, February 6, 1910

One of the most notable landmarks in the early history of Denison was the old Grand Southern [Saloon], where the Red Front [Clothing Store] now stands [200 West Main]. The Grand Southern was usually referred to as "The Old Grand Southern." It was built on the first lot sold on Main Street by the Town Lot Company to Sam Cook, who disposed of it to Mr. [Martin] Chichet. It then passed into the hands of one Rohaberg and was last owned by Justin Raynal, the public school benefactor, whose name is not yet rescued from oblivion by a memorial.

The Grand Southern was a two-story wooden building. On the first floor, a saloon was conducted until it was destroyed by fire in the early eighties. The building was erected in the fall of 1874. A keno game was run by one of the best-known citizens of Denison, who is now dead. There were sleeping rooms upstairs also. Chichet, Raynal, and Jim Leaverton conducted the saloon business for many years. Chichet and Raynal made considerable money. Leaverton was a free and easy sort of man, a generous giver and liver, and left Denison in a comfortable manner.

The Grand Southern was a noted resort. It was very natural for a cowman or a resident of the Territory to drop in there. The location was favorable, and it was always popular with people who lived here. Every lover of field sports, the man who owned a good gun and bird dog, made it his headquarters. The members of the famous Denison Gun Club held their meetings there, and what a set of men! Of that invincible club that never went down to defeat, only three are left that we can recollect—J.D. Yocom, T.W. Dollarhide, and [J.G.] "Top" West. The rest, where are they:

> "Their guns are rust,
> Their souls have gone
> To the saints, we trust."

For years the boys used to gather there, around the old stove on winter nights, and tell thrilling stories of the chase. Hundreds of hunting parties left there for the Indian Territory, and the best dogs that a hunter ever shot over could always be found at the Grand Southern. The Grand Southern was the first to serve soup to patrons under the Chichet regime.

It was the scene of one of the most terrible tragedies in the pioneer period. Officer [Charles] Patman was shot and killed by Major [A.S.] Doran, a noted desperado, who had several notches on his gun. The trial was one of the most remarkable in the criminal history of Texas. It was prolonged for years. Only influential friends, money, and the best legal talent in the state saved Doran's neck. Major Doran was a gunfighter. When under the influence of liquor, he became a terror and was usually hunting trouble. At Hot Springs, Arkansas, Major Doran was the star in a street vendetta that cost two or three lives. The end came. Major Doran was killed at Fort Smith by "Pink" Fagg. Pink was a noted character in Denison in the seventies. A brother of his, "Bud" Fagg, was also a bad man, and the community was generally afraid of "the Fagg Boys." They were professional gamblers. The writer saw Bud Fagg at the Grand Southern grab Bill Hardwick, then chief of police, and force him to the bar and take a drink. The Fagg Boys always went armed and would fight at the drop of a hat.

Tandy Fulsom, an Indian desperado of national reputation, who frequently painted the town "red," had a running account at the Grand Southern bar. One night, Willie Jones, son of Governor [Wilson N] Jones of the Choctaw Nation, went into the Grand Southern with a crowd of Indian friends, and they smashed the bar fixtures, broke glasses, mirrors, etc. The next morning they called and settled the damage bill. Willie Jones was shot and killed on Blue Prairie by a companion in a drunken bout. Tandy Folsom committed suicide near Durant by shooting himself through the heart with a Winchester. Of all the "bad men" in the early history of Denison, Fulsom was probably at the head of the class. For years he ranged throughout the Chickasaw and Choctaw nations. Every officer in the Territory carried papers for his arrest, but none dared execute them. The U.S. government finally made peace with him, sending him a commission as U.S. marshal.

When the Choctaw council met at Tuskahoma, the bootleggers used to supply them with mean whisky, which precipitated many a row and several killings. Just before the council met on one occasion, Tandy Fulsom was commissioned to proceed to Tuskahoma and lay for the bootleggers, and spill the contraband stuff which the Indian lawmakers always seemed so amply provided with. It was a dangerous undertaking, as many members of the council only recognized as law the .45 dangling at the hip. It was predicted that Fulsom would die with his boots on. He arrived at the Choctaw capital and started an investigation, breaking the private bottles of members, and found a jug or so in the cellar, which he smashed. No other officer in the Territory would have escaped with his life. That was the soberest council convened in many years. Fulsom was present until the body adjourned.

The best man we ever saw behind the Grand Southern bar was Tony Stauffacher. He was a grand old man, with a tender, sympathetic heart. Under no circumstances did he ever lose his temper, and there were many trying circumstances. Everybody loved and respected him. He was the soul of honor. There were many occasions when drunken men would turn their money over to him, not having any idea of the amount, and when they sobered up and called for the money, every cent was returned and good advice thrown in. At all times and under all circumstances he was a perfect gentleman, and when he died there were many expressions of grief.

Mr. Raynal died in the second story of the Grand Southern. He was a staunch Catholic, and an effort was made to have him, on his death, give his money to the church. The sisters visited and administered to him in his sickness, but in his will he left the Raynal Building to the public schools of Denison, and thousands of dollars have been realized from that bequest, and yet this generous donor sleeps in almost an unmarked grave, to the shame of Denison. Adam Hornbeck, our old friend down on Duck Creek at present, was long associated with Mr. Raynal, and was guided a great deal by his advice. Mr. H. [Harrison] Tone prepared the Raynal will, in which he left his property to the public schools.

The Grand Southern was destroyed by fire.

Fig. 7. The Boulevards. From 1886 Denison Bird's Eye Map, Amon Carter Museum.

No. 5

The Boulevards and Exposition Hall

Sunday Gazetteer, February 13, 1910

If the reader will go southwest on Scullin Avenue until he reaches Texas Street and follow that street due west for several blocks, he will arrive at a section that was in the eighties the play-grounds of Denison. It was known as The Boulevards. The streetcar, propelled by mule power, and the old Dummy Line that was operated by "dinky" engines, used to run out there and carry thousands of people who sought the beautiful woods for rest and pleasure. There were a dancing pavilion, baseball, and gun club tournament grounds. There were beer halls with lunch counter attachments. The free, untrammeled life of the pioneer period was in full sway, and people were not particular as to who were their associates. The most respectable people of Denison could be seen on the Boulevard promenades. Society was mixed. We have seen strange men walk up to a girl they had never seen before and, without the formality of an introduction, invite them to the dance. Sunday was a gala day. Life was never dull out there. How the vivid memory of it all comes back to us, intensified rather than faded by the years. The pleasure grounds were covered with noble, majestic forest trees. In fact, Nature had been disturbed but little out there. It was a great resort for pleasure and picnic parties. It was the spot of sunshine, wildflowers, and sunbonnets. When the first breath of pure spring pervaded the land, people's thoughts turned lovingly to the beautiful woodland retreats of The Boulevards.

Go out there in the spring months and there were entrancing visions of female loveliness flitting through the woods, and up through the green vista came the merry laughter of happy hearts. It was just as fashionable to go out to The Boulevards as it is to go to Woodlake at present.

The greatest gun club tournaments in the state were held out there, and the crack baseball teams met in hot combat. There never was in the past or present history of Texas such a peerless set of sportsmen as faced the traps out there. The logical result of this activity was the wild dreams of speculators, and The Boulevard lands commanded gilt-edge prices and did not go begging for purchasers.

Many beautiful homes were erected at The Boulevards, surrounded with spacious and luxurious grounds. Dr. [W.F.] Haynes lived out there, and there his beautiful wife was murdered [in 1892]—a tragedy the most horrible in the history of Denison and which has never yet been cleared up. Davis, a traveling man, was killed out there while mistreating an adopted son.

Exposition Hall, a magnificent building that cost thousands of dollars and in which was collected a splendid exhibit of the products of this section and the Indian Territory, was erected near The Boulevards. It was an imposing structure. Many public functions were held out there. Hundreds of distinguished men from all portions of the United States were entertained at Exposition Hall. Strangers who came here to look for investment were always taken there to be impressed with our resources and advantages, which lay before their eyes. Grand balls were given out there, and the floodgates of oratory were turned loose in the vast amphitheatre.

There has never been gathered under a roof since such a vast and interesting collection. Men would look over money-making propositions from what they saw, and visitors were so impressed with the Exposition Hall exhibits that many real estate deals were consummated. Exposition Hall was one of the inspirations of the great boom which was the most memorable page in the history of Denison; and when the boom collapsed, it was then that the decadence of The Boulevards commenced. The building was burned. It made a magnificent conflagration. The streetcars were taken off to The Boulevards, and that hastened the catastrophe. Old Pap Tobin's beer hall went up in smoke, the fence to the baseball and gun club grounds was torn down, the dancing pavilion removed, and The Boulevards, the former gathering place of all

Denison, was a thing of the past—deserted and silent, a melancholy spot; and there are many people in Denison at the present time who do not know that such a place existed.

No. 6

Denison Artillery Company

Sunday Gazetteer, February 20, 1910

In 1880 to 1883, this city maintained the crack military organizations. The Denison Artillery Company was one. Major L.L. Maughs, a distinguished artillery officer of the Confederate cause, was in command of the artillery company. In the early spring, the company proceeded to the Pawpaw Heights, overlooking Red River, for target practice. The occasion was always marked by immense crowds, sometimes as many as 2,000 people swarming the surrounding hills. A point was selected, usually a sandbar, as the object to fire at, and there was some fine shooting. The guns were furnished by the state. The gun practice was regarded as a holiday, and there was a great string of vehicles, [as well as] men, women, and children on foot, down through the Munson pasture.

As a side issue there were fish fries, and Al Hall prepared his famous Brunswick stews. There were swings erected and many games in vogue. A great many parties used to linger at night in the woods on the banks of the river, and sweet strains of music floated over the waters. On the greenswards the young people danced and made merry.

The announcement of artillery practice was always hailed with delight and never failed to attract immense crowds of people, who would leave the city early and eat their lunches in the woods. Lemonade and refreshment booths were opened to the public, but the greatest points of interest were the fish fries and the Brunswick stew booths.

For a period of about three years, in the spring the artillery practice was carried on at the river heights. It was a great place for flirting, and the young maids and men used to hie there for that purpose. One or two pulpit orators inveighed against the Sunday desecration, but they never diminished the size of the crowd.

The Artillery Company was at last disbanded and the guns returned to the state capital, and that was the end of the hegira to the Red River heights. The leaders of the movement are all dead, but there are many yet in Denison who recall with pleasure the sunny days on Red River heights.

No. 7
"Jew" Jackson

Sunday Gazetteer, February 27, 1910

Every city and town has its strange and unique characters. In the early history of Denison there were many such. We recollect one in particular, known as "Jew" Jackson. He was one of the first to locate here and until he died was known by almost every citizen of Denison. "Jew" was a sporting character and something of a philanthropist. He lived in the alley just back of the Muller Block [204–206 West Main]. It was a one-room house where a woman used to do his cooking and looked after his wardrobe. He was a little squatty fellow and not very cleanly about his person. He was a professional gambler and also loaned money. He never did anything, but always had plenty of money. He was known to have befriended a number of persons.

What made "Jew" Jackson particularly notable was that he was on intimate terms with all kinds and conditions of people, and there was an individuality about the man that made his presence agreeable, and everybody had a friendly feeling for "Jew" Jackson. He was a power in local politics and exercised considerable influence among a certain class of people counted on Election Day. In the seventies there was no better known character in Denison than "Jew" Jackson.

Things were getting better in Denison, and the city was growing out of its wild and woolly conditions. The gambling houses went from the ground floor to the second story, and the old man used to lament the change that was apparent, and said that he intended to go farther west where the old frontier conditions still held full sway. But "Jew" Jackson never went.

He was taken ill and died in the little house in the alley, and was laid to rest in Oakwood Cemetery, where so many of his class sleep. The funeral was a large affair, many being present who, in this present day, would have never attended. "Jew" Jackson was reputed to have had considerable money, which, as he left no will, was sent to a brother across the sea. This was probably fiction, as his death indicated a man who lived from hand to mouth, and the woman who shared his fortunes declared he had hardly enough money to give him a decent burial. But he had plenty of warm friends who stood ready to give his body a good shift.

No. 8

Alamo Hotel

Sunday Gazetteer, March 6, 1910

The most notable hostelry in the pioneer history of Denison was the Alamo Hotel that stood where the new, magnificent Union Depot is at present in course of erection. The opening of the hotel was a red-letter day in the history of Denison. The Alamo was ready for the reception of guests on Washington's birthday. A grand ball was given in honor of the event. A special car containing a number of the leading citizens of Parsons, Kansas, came down to hold a jollification and trip the light fantastic. The

Alamo was in a blaze of glory. Gnase's band furnished the string music. The structure was two-story. The dining room, office, and bar were on the first floor. The second story contained sleeping rooms and the parlors. The Alamo was destroyed by fire in 1882. The several proprietors of the old Alamo are all dead, with the exception of Charley Schmucker, who has lived in Mexico for a number of years.

No hotel in the early days of Denison had such an eventful history as the old Alamo. It was the gathering point for all the notables of the city, and more business was transacted there than any other public place. At that period it was the only hotel of any importance in Denison. Denison was the open gate through which thousands of people poured into the state in search of homes and investments, and the hotel was always crowded with guests, for many people stopped off to see what this section offered.

The cattle barons all made their headquarters at the Alamo. If you wished to see anyone, you were directed to the Alamo. The opening of the Missouri, Kansas and Texas railway system increased the business to a great extent, most of the officials stopping there; while hundreds of railway men who roomed elsewhere ate their meals at the Alamo, and we wish to remark that the table d'hôte at the old hotel was the very best at that period and there has never been any as good since.

What distinguished the Alamo more than any other feature was the social gatherings. There were no public halls as now, and the pendulum of social life was ever swinging there. If the days were dull, the nights made up for it at the old hotel.

The joys were there. At night the spacious dining room fairly blazed, some social event being always on tap at the Alamo. The ballroom and the bar-room were generally crowded with hilarious people. The bar did a rushing business, and once in a while a fight was pulled off—to enliven the carnival occasion.

Queer characters were met at the Alamo, wrecks of dissipation, derelicts from other states, seeking nothing save oblivion. The old hotel was an eddy which caught odd bits of driftwood, such as only the frontier knows. We have seen men in the Alamo bar-room and corridors (well-dressed men, too) ask for the loan of sufficient money to buy a meal, and in those days the money was usually shoved out to them.

There were many "scenes" at the old Alamo. When John Taylor was proprietor, "Texas Charley," a bogus bad man, swaggered into the bar-room one night hunting trouble. He pulled his six-shooter and asked a tenderfoot to dance, pointing his gun at the man's feet. John Taylor was notified and ran into the bar-room, and discovering Charley, grabbed him by the seat of the pants and pitched him into the street. Charley blustered about and swore vengeance, but that was the last of it.

When Max Grundstein was married to Miss Eppstein at St. Joseph, Missouri, and returned home, his friends gave them a reception and grand ball at the old Alamo Hotel. It was perhaps the swellest social event that had ever taken place in the town, and cost a great deal of money. Guests were present from all over Texas and the Indian Territory.

The railroad men gave all of their balls at the Alamo in the seventies. It was the hub of the social world in this section

When the old hotel went up in smoke, there was a pang of sorrow felt by many at the loss, because of the pleasant associations connected with it. While it lasted, it was full of color, excitement, and picturesqueness. Many of the old landmarks will escape memory, but the old Alamo, never.

Fig. 8. Alamo Hotel, looking west on Main Street from railroad tracks.

No. 9

"Deaf Jack"

Sunday Gazetteer, March 13, 1910

One of the most unique characters who lived in Denison in the seventies was "Deaf Jack" [Lynch].

He probably used more morphine than any man in Texas. His body was literally honeycombed when he died, and after the remains were examined by the attending physicians, they declared that the body was so badly punctured that there was no place left for the needle to enter.

Deaf Jack used enormous quantities of morphine, and it was said he had been under the influence of the drug for many years. He drifted into Denison from Nevada and in his prime was one of the best-known sports in the mining camps. The man is reported to have killed a gambler and was obliged to flee, coming to Texas. He came to Denison from San Antonio. He was very deaf, consequent upon the use of the drug.

Deaf Jack was a mystery. At times he seemed to have plenty of money but haunted the gambling houses, getting a little stake now and then. He lived on Skiddy Street, the home of every derelict in Denison in the wild and woolly days, when this was the jumping-off place for all creation. Sometimes he lived with an old woman. It is strange, but this class of men always have their female affinities, and they will stick to their man even to sharing the last crumb of bread.

Deaf Jack's morphine is said to have cost him one dollar per day, and the money was always forthcoming. There was a story after his death to the effect that he had received remittances from a brother in San Francisco who lived in affluence. At any rate, there were periods when he was flush. He hung around the gambling house, but we never saw him turn a card.

At last the man died. It was then discovered that Jack was penniless. So, as was the custom in those days, a paper was started among the sporting men, and in a few hours sufficient money was collected to give the old fellow a decent shift. He was laid to rest where every man of that character went—Oakwood Cemetery. There were many tales about the man, but the majority were probably pure fiction.

No. 10
The Old Jail

Sunday Gazetteer, March 27, 1910

Probably the oldest landmark, or what is left of it, is the jail in the 200 block West Chestnut Street. The building, two stories high, was erected shortly after the city was incorporated in 1873. When the jail was completed, it was considered a structure strong enough to hold any of the bad men that were very plentiful in this section at this period. Still, there never was a jail built strong enough to prevent occasional escapes. In 1873, every man was his own law and the gun the arbiter of destiny. The city marshal moved here and there amid the chaos of 1873, tireless, undaunted, seeking merely to exercise some slight restraint. The bagnios and dance halls were ablaze, the bar-rooms crowded with hilarious or quarrelsome humanity, the gaming tables alive with excitement, the cowboys rode into open saloon doors and drank in the saddle— and the jail was full every night. It is true that we had courts of justice, and there was an endless grind.

From 1872 up to the 1880s, no town in Texas had more bad men for citizens than Denison, and the women—women worthy of the name there were few. The nights saw flitting female forms in plenty, and the lights of the saloon displayed powdered cheeks and painted eyebrows. Tragedy was always in the air, and many now sleep in unmarked graves, who in the frontier vocabulary died with their boots on.

Many of the most desperate men that have ever figured in frontier history have passed some of their days in the old jail. Many were brought in from the old Indian Territory—murderers, horse thieves, train robbers, and whatnot. This section then was fairly redolent with bad men.

How many, many graves at Oakwood were filled by violence.

The most picturesque officer of that period was Captain Tom Wright, at present city jailer. What stories and episodes he could tell of the old jail. How many men he has put behind the bars. Into those wooden jaws and behind those iron teeth passed many a man who left all hope behind. There were fearless gunfighters in those days, and Captain Tom ranked with the bravest.

It is a most singular fact which cannot be refuted that the Denison jail from early in 1873 until 1880 harbored more bad men than any jail on the western frontier. Officers of the border counties often stopped in Denison with their prisoners. The prisoners were largely horse thieves and cattle rustlers and a few murderers.

The writer used to visit the jail and talk with the prisoners, and on one occasion we were particularly impressed with a handsome young man who had been captured in the Cherokee Nation after a running fight in which an officer was shot and killed. The young fellow was wanted for cattle stealing in Jack County, Texas. His parents resided in New York and had sent their son to Texas to live on a ranch. He drifted away and in a few years became the leader of one of the most noted gangs of horse thieves that ever operated from Texas up to the borders of Kansas. He was tried and convicted but later escaped from the Jacksboro jail. However, we learned afterwards that he had been shot and killed in the Cherokee Nation while following up his old games. It is said that his mother and sister had the body taken up and conveyed to the old homestead in New York for burial.

Money was plentiful and human life mere sport in the seventies, and the bullet and cold steel settled more disputes than the courts. The old jail was in reality a roaring hell. Night after night it was truly a raging bedlam over there—women were screaming and men cursing. Women who had fallen so low that they could go no farther, were tumbled in with the men. Dante's Inferno had its counterpart in the old jail.

People who live in this day and generation might picture the situation, but they could never color too highly the Denison jail as it existed in the seventies.

An interesting phenomenon was the change for a better condition of things, which was working out through the leaven of better citizenship. The change came on very slowly, but it was irresistible. A new jail was demanded, and work was soon begun on the present one. The old jail, as bad as it was, will always be surrounded with a halo of romance, as it was a part of the "Wild West" which, even as early as the eighties, began to pass away. Looking backward, what memories are evoked from the misty past! It is at present but a crumbling ruin and yet remains the oldest landmark of pioneer Denison.

In those early days, Sherman was in about the same condition as the new town of Denison. They were wild and woolly times. They were both frontier towns. Gambling was as open at the county seat as at the "Infant Wonder." Faro and other gambling devices were run "on the ground floors" right on the courthouse square, and the keno rooms were crowded every night. The notorious "Red Light" reservation was about as tough a place as you can well imagine, and it rivaled anything in that line existing in the new town in the sand hills.

But all this soon became a matter of history. The better elements in both cities soon gained the ascendancy—and at about the same time. Reformation followed. First the gamblers were driven into secluded rooms in the second stories, and most of the sports dropped out. The familiar sound of keno, with the accompanying echo that all the old-timers will remember so well, no longer floated out on the night air. In a few years the two towns were sufficiently purified to take positions in the class of respectables.

No. 11

Dance Halls

Sunday Gazetteer, April 3, 1910

With the incorporation of the city came the dance halls. They were confined principally to what was Skiddy Street, but owing to the bad odor of the street, the council changed the name to Chestnut. The 100 and 200 blocks of old Skiddy Street were devoted principally to dance halls and brothels. It was for many years the toughest section of Denison.

There was a dance hall on [225 West] Main Street about where the [J.G.] Reynolds drug store now is. There was a row there one night, when McDowell, chief of police, shot and killed a man who, after receiving his death wound, ran to the middle of Main Street and fell dead. At that period, gambling was wide open and conducted on the first floor, in plain view of people passing on the sidewalk. You could get any game that you wanted, from Mexican monte to chuck-a-luck. The dance hall on Main Street didn't last long after the tragedy and moved to more congenial surroundings on Skiddy.

There were three and sometimes four dance halls in full blast on Skiddy Street. The two most notorious were kept by Sallie Miller and Mike Langley. Langley was shot and killed by Policeman William Mitchell at the dance hall. The policeman was exonerated. Langley was a dangerous man when in his cups, but while sober, he was a very agreeable man and had many friends, even among decent people. At one end of the dance hall was a platform on which the fiddlers sat and called out the number of the dance. After a set was over, the girls would march their partners up to the bar and call for drinks. This was the principal source of revenue to the proprietors, and they made lots of money.

The dance hall never languished for want of patrons—they never had a dull night—men taking their turns to go on the floor with the girls. Never in the wildest days of the frontier town had there been a more dissolute or more desperate class of inhabitants than during the dance hall regime. There were cowboys galore, for this was one of the principal shipping points for cattle in Texas.

At all hours of the night, the dance hall section was crowded with men, and female forms were seen flitting here and there in plenty. It was a strange, commingled congregation of cowboys, Indians, gamblers, saloon keepers, and occasionally respectable people who went to see the sights—Denison by gaslight.

The dance halls were wooden structures, the Sazarack being the only one of that character that was two stories. The bar was at the entrance, and from the bar you passed through a door into the dance hall, which was a large room capable of accommodating twenty-five sets on the floor. In the eighties, the dance halls disappeared. Denison was awakening to a better life, and public sentiment had driven the gambling houses to the second floors. The bullet that killed Mike Langley marked the decadence of the dance halls. They occupied a large part of the pioneer days, and this short story has not told the half. Very much that was picturesque, bizarre, and romantic belongs to old Skiddy Street days.

Fig. 9. Dance hall in Denison. From Edward King, "The Great South," ill. by J. Wells Champney.

No. 12

[The *Sunday Gazetteer* for April 10, 1910, was not available on the Portal to Texas History. Presumably it contained No. 12 in the "Little Stories of Denison" series.]

No. 13
Wild Game Markets

Sunday Gazetteer, April 17, 1910

From seventy-two [1872] until the early eighties [1880s], Denison was one of the greatest markets for wild game in North Texas. The writer has seen displayed in front of the markets on Main Street, deer, turkey, antelope, [and] bear meats; while ducks, geese, squirrels, prairie chicken, and quail were always to be had, and now and then buffalo meat was offered. Great displays were made during the holidays. The markets then presented a very pretty effect, the wild game being adorned with many colored ribbons and evergreens. We have seen as many as twenty deer and wild turkeys galore displayed in front of the markets. There never was a period in the seventies that wild game was not procurable at the markets. A few hours' travel in the Indian Territory would put the market hunter in a hunter's paradise.

We can recollect on one occasion when George Black, now a resident of Cale, brought to Denison two wagonloads of deer and wild turkeys. It was the biggest hunt pulled off in that period. George refused to tell the section where the game was found.

Indian hunters brought a great deal of game to the city which always found a ready market.

Choice venison cuts could be had for 10 cents per pound, and fat, plump wild turkeys were offered at 50 cents each. Bear and antelope steaks were a luxury and commanded a good price.

In the early seventies, deer and wild turkeys were killed within sight of Denison. Major [Leonidas L.] Maughs killed a deer in Munson's pasture. Colonel Tom Lipscomb used to hunt deer and turkey in the Hudson Quarters. At Warren Flats, every season thousands of jack snipe were shot, and ducks were slaughtered by the thousands and sold at the markets.

There was a great plethora of wild game in the early days of Denison, and many hunters made a good living with their rifles and shotguns and did not have to go very far either.

Beaver and otto [perhaps a type of catfish] now and then appeared in the market. In 1878 beavers had extensive dams on Red River, Allen Bayou, and other contiguous affluences near the city.

There were great roosts of wild pigeons in the Indian Territory, and thousands of birds were sold in Denison. In the early gun club tournaments, the wild pigeons were used at the traps. There was a roost east of Stringtown in the McGee Mountains that covered the mountains for a distance of twelve miles. Millions of the birds were killed or trapped and shipped, principally to St. Louis.

In the eighties, wild game began to disappear from the Denison market, although venison was quite plentiful, but the price was usually 15 to 20 cents per pound.

In the seventies, many game dinners were announced, and the bills of fare were always spotted with venison, wild turkey, and small game.

The writer can recollect on one occasion when a number of live wild turkeys were trapped and a shooting tournament took place in the southeast suburbs. The turkeys' heads were displayed just above the ground and a target rifle was used, and it was ten cents a shot. There were many misses, and it proved very profitable to the party or parties who conducted the tournaments.

The only kind of game seen in the Denison markets for many years past are ducks, rabbits, and fat o'possums and a few squirrels. This period, like many other features of the old times, is gone— forever gone.

No. 14
New Year's Calls

Sunday Gazetteer, April 24, 1910

The habit of making New Year's calls has gone out of practice in Denison. In the seventies and eighties, New Year's calls were a great social event, and all the young bloods and many who had passed the meridian exchanged the social courtesies of the day at the leading mansions in the city. All of the prominent families of the period kept "open house."

It sometimes happened there was snow on the ground and the calls were made in improvised sleighs, and until a late hour of the night you could hear the merry jingle of the sleigh bells.

At that period there was something stronger than lemonade served. The fair hostess treated her guests to wine and frequently champagne. All hours of the day and frequently late at night there was a steady stream of callers. How vividly the memory of it all comes back. The social distinctions that have come with the growth of the town did not exist. It was hail fellow well met. "Come, boys, let's have a good time," was the spirit that ruled the holidays. The spirit of enjoyment was abroad. The ladies, young and old, received their guests in the most gracious manner and made the stranger feel as much at home and at ease as if they had been old friends.

It sometimes happened that the caller was a little "boozy" after his many rounds, but no attention was paid to the incident.

There was published in the papers a list of those who would keep "open house," and it was a long array of names. As the city grew, it seemed to affect social conditions, and as early as the latter part of the eighties, making New Year's calls was almost a thing of the past. It is true that a few were at home to their friends, but the general spirit of the social function was gone.

Those were happy days—and the participants, where are they? Seventy-five per cent are dead, and many are scattered in every state in the Union. Denison will never again see such days. The spirit has departed, the conditions have changed, and the men and women who extended the warm hand of hospitality are not here.

No. 15

Military Telegraph System

Sunday Gazetteer, May 8, 1910

If a person walked down Main Street in the eighties, his attention would have been attracted to strange-looking flags flying from the windows of the *Sunday Gazetteer* office. They were weather signals that were obtained from the United States military telegraph office. The U.S. military telegraph system, starting from Denison, extended to all the military posts in Texas and Indian Territory, with its other terminals at Brownsville on the Rio Grande and San Antonio. The weather reports were flashed to all portions of the country.

Lieut. [Adolphus Washington] Greeley, the famous Arctic explorer, was at one time in charge of the station here. Greeley was a tall, austere man with Burnside whiskers. He was not much of a mixer. During our early newspaper career, the news arrived in Denison that the line had been destroyed west of Jacksboro by a war party of Comanche Indians and that a stage had been held up and the driver killed and a passenger carried into captivity. The story of the holdup was fiction, but the line had been interrupted. We called on Lieut. Greeley and requested the particulars. He waved us away and said no such news had been received and that newspapers must be careful of what they printed. The chilling reception prejudiced us against Greeley, and when we wanted news of Indian raids we avoided Greeley and "pumped" his subordinates.

The first office was at the corner of Main Street and Austin Avenue, where the Hall-Leeper hardware store is located. This was removed to the second story of the McDougall Building, this side of the Ford Block, and one day lightning struck the flag pole on top of the building, knocked off the whirligig that registered the velocity of the wind, tore a hole in the roof, and entering the telegraph office did considerable damage to the instruments.

Greeley did not stay very long, and was succeeded by Lieut. Myers, as fine a man as ever wore the livery of Uncle Sam. The military telegraph was later removed to the corner of Gandy Street and Rusk Avenue. They occupied the second story of what is now the home of W.B. Munson.

The line was frequently put out of business by Indian raids. At that period, the Kiowas, Comanches, and Apaches were still raiding Texas. The linemen were sometimes killed. There was a vast scope of country, treeless plains, extending for thousands of miles, where the government had military posts, and it was through the telegraph line that they kept in touch with the Indian situation. The Indians were bad, especially the Comanches, and it frequently happened that troops were dispatched to guard the line. The line was maintained at a great expense. An immense immigration soon poured into this country and towns springing up, it was abandoned. Two or three of the frontier forts were also abandoned, and the warlike Comanches had retreated forever beyond the Red and Canadian rivers to their ancient homes near Fort Sill, to be cooped up in a reservation, which is now a part of the prosperous State of Oklahoma.

There was a great scandal in connection with a Lieut. [Charles A.] Tingle, who commanded here. Tingle was a very gallant and courteous gentleman and immensely popular with the people. He fell in love with a beautiful girl who was an inmate of a bagnio and married her. This created such a stir that the matter was carried to Washington, and the lieutenant was dismissed from the service. It is said that the marriage turned out unhappily and that he procured a divorce from his wife at Dayton, Ohio.

The weather predictions, as furnished the *Gazetteer*, were much sought after and eagerly looked for. But the flags were furled and the military telegraph line became a thing of the past. It cost the government a great deal of money to build, equip, and maintain it.

The attachés of the office at this point were genial, sociable fellows and very popular with the people in society circles. The military line was one of the most notable landmarks of pioneer Denison.

* * *

[Related Item]

AN INTERESTING STORY.

Denison and the U.S. Frontier Telegraph Lines.

[Letter to the Editor, in Response]
Sunday Gazetteer, May 22, 1910

West Palm Beach, Fla.,
May 12, 1910.

Editor Gazetteer:

As an old friend of yours and your paper, and of Denison, I have somewhat enjoyed reading the "Little Stories of Denison" you are publishing. Some of them seemed a little stretched, while others came nearer the facts as I know them, as I was there at the time and even helped make some of the stories. This is true especially of the "story" in your issue of May 8, about the government telegraph line.

I lived at one time at Galveston, but the first time I hit Denison was in November 1874, when I came there in charge of 25 U.S. Signal Service men to build 1200 miles of telegraph line for the government, starting from Denison. The only part of the line not in Texas was the line from Red River to Fort Sill in the Indian Territory.

Lieut. Allyn Capron was in charge, and our first office was in what was known as the government freight depot—a large freight warehouse belonging to the MK&T, and north of the warehouse the railroad used. In the south end of the warehouse, Col. A.J. Strong, the U.S. Quartermaster, had his office with Thos. Richardson as clerk; Graham & Co., contractors for hauling government freight out to the different posts, also had an office there with Charlie Converse in charge, and I had the U.S. Military Telegraph office there and was in charge of it—that is after I came in from the front.

The line was started from this building, and I stayed with the men to oversee the building and show them how, as out of the 25 men brought down, probably only 3 besides myself knew anything of the business and I had to break them in. We also had Co. G, 24th Infantry, a colored company of 45 men, to help in the work, and 10 teamsters to haul our supplies and material, and of these latter Wood McMillin was in charge and a good wagon boss he was.

I remained at the front until the line was about to Pilot Point, and then I came in to Denison and took charge from that city, leaving Schermerhorn, a first-class operator and telegraph man, at the front.

About this time Lieut. Capron got tired of the job and was succeeded by Lieut. A.W. Greely of the 10th Cavalry—now known as Gen. Greely—and the office was moved up to the corner of Main Street and Austin Avenue, over the Leeper-Lingo wholesale grocery, and opposite Jerry Nolan's saloon. Here we stayed until the line was nearly built. In the meantime the men had learned how to build the line, and Lieut. Greely had divided them up, sending some to every post and having them work toward one another, getting assistance from each post. This hurried the work. Lieut. Greely, it is true, was not a "mixer" but was a fine and friendly man with those who knew him, but he was suffering from dyspepsia nearly all the time; besides this, he was a great student and often "burned the midnight oil." His health was such that he was obliged to get leave of absence, which he did just before the line was completed, and he was succeeded by Lieut. Heintzelman, a son of Gen. [Samuel Peter] Heintzelman, in charge of the Department of Texas. The office was now moved up over McDougall's. To make a change of operators, I went out to Jacksboro (Fort Richardson) and sent the operator from there up to Fort Sill, running the office myself till the operator came down from Fort Sill. While I was there, a desperado who was confined in the Jack County jail was liberated one night by his friends, and they cut the wire; but I went out and repaired it in time to get a message to Graham City and have the fellow caught. He was taken to Austin, I think, for safekeeping. At this time also, heavy rains carried the line away over two or three rivers, and it took a little time to fix them up. The same rains carried some of the MK&T bridges away, and among the passengers marooned were Lieut. Heintzelman and his bride, who were on their way to Denison. They spent their Fourth of July [1876] in the Nation, while I spent mine at an old-fashioned barbecue and celebration, the like of which we will never see again.

The line was finished, repaired and all in good working order, soon after, and I left the service while at Jacksboro—Aug. 4, 1876—and came back to my home in Denison.

Lieut. Greely finished building the line and secured material and supplies in full sufficiency, all within the appropriation of $100,000 which Congress had granted, and even carried a few thousand back into the Treasury. This was before the days of graft.

During my connection with the line, from start to finish, I heard once in a while of an Indian raid, but I never saw one; nor did I ever hear or know of the Indians cutting or molesting the line or killing any of the linemen. Such fairy tales we used to tell for the benefit of amateur reporters and tenderfeet, but the only Indian raids I remember were north of or near Decatur, about or just before the time we began to build the line, and out on Lost Creek, northeast of Jacksboro. In both cases, if I remember right, one or two cattlemen were killed by the Indians who were said to be of the Comanche tribe.

The wires were cut and trouble given, but mostly by cowboys shooting at the insulators or by horse thieves and desperadoes trying to head off messages for their arrest.

The line from Fort Concho to Fort Stockton was only a branch line at that time and went no further than Stockton. This line got in trouble once—in the fall, I think, of 1875—when the buffalo, in emigrating, used the rough cedar poles for scratching posts and sprung them over so their horns caught in the wire, which they carried away for quite a distance.

I knew Lieut. Myers, who was a nephew of Gen. [Albert J.] Myers, but if he was in charge of the U.S. military telegraph line, it was after Lieuts. Greely and Heintzelman. I also remember Lieut. Chas. Tingle and his marriage. It was after the fire that he offered me a position on the line up at Fort Supply, I.T., and I accepted and left Denison in March 1881, and have never been back since, much to my regret though possibly Denison has been no loser.

The original U.S. military telegraph line ran from Denison via Pilot Point and Decatur, to Jacksboro (Fort Richardson). From this point a branch ran through Henrietta to Fort Sill, I.T., but the main line went down through Graham City to Fort Griffin in Shackelford County, then through Colorado City to Fort Concho, from which a branch line ran out to Fort Stockton, the main line going on down through Fort McKavett, Boerne and Fredericksburg to San Antonio. From this city the line ran out to Clarksville and down to the Rio Grande, taking in Fort Laredo and Ringgold Barrack, on its way to Fort Brown (Brownsville), where it ended.

After that the Fort Stockton branch was extended to El Paso, where it joined the U.S. military telegraph line that ran to San Diego, Calif. The Fort Sill branch was also extended through Fort Reno, the cantonment on the north fork of the Canadian, Fort Supply, all in the Indian Territory, and out to Fort Elliott (Mobitee) in the Panhandle of Texas, and while I was there I saw a branch line built from Fort Supply, I.T., to Dodge City (during Bat Masterson's regime) and Fort Dodge, Kansas.

I remained at Fort Supply until about Dec. 1, 1881, then went up to Fort Dodge and ran that office for a couple of weeks or so. From there I went to Chicago and have never been back to Texas or the B.I.T. since.

Now, friend Murray, I have given you, not a "Little Story of Denison," but quite a big story of the U.S. military telegraph line that had its headquarters in Denison for a long time, finally moving to San Antonio and at last abandoning the line entirely.

Tell the writer of those stories to look out and try to remember things straight or others besides myself may think that his age is ruining his memory—none of us are as young as we were in those days, but we can still remember many things, including fake spirit rappings and a coon and o'possum hunt down in the creek bottom east of town.

Yours for more little stories,

GEO. W. ROWLEY.

* * *

[Related Item]
Sunday Gazetteer, May 19, 1910

Tom Wright, city jailer, the best posted man on the early history of Denison, in speaking of the Geo. W. Rowley letter in the last issue of the *Gazetteer*, states that in his history of the military telegraph line, he (Rowley) stumbled into several errors.

No. 16
Denison's Amazing Growth

Sunday Gazetteer, May 15, 1910

On the 23rd of September, 1872, the first sale of city lots was made in Denison. The first lot offered was at the [southwest] corner of Main Street and Austin Avenue, and was knocked off to Sam Cook at $250. There was quite a crowd at the sale, but people were cautious, thinking that Sherman was in the way of Denison; in fact a number went over to our sister city looking for locations, but returned to Denison and invested. The crowd present at the sale, however, purchased thirty-one lots; the price paid for the bunch was $4,791, or an average of $154.60 each. That was a good starter for what was then called "the Infant Wonder." Denison was known by that name all over the country. If we mistake not, it was first called that by H. [Harrison] Tone.

In less than two hours after the sale, building commenced on Main Street.

There was a great deal of business done on old Skiddy Street, now Chestnut. The post office was there, and Mr. H. Tone was postmaster. It was a very small hole in the wall. There was some business done on Crawford Street. Many thought that Skiddy would be the trade center of Denison.

Buildings were erected under the greatest disadvantage. All of the pine lumber was hauled from eastern pineries, a distance of over 100 miles, or transported by wagon 50 and 100 miles through the Indian Territory. Native lumber was very scarce, and the mills were few and far between. The mills could not begin to fill the many orders and were taxed to their utmost capacity. While a half-dozen customers stood by ready to quarrel for each board as it dropped from the log, yet all the time the wonderful growth went on, and the more its facilities increased, the faster was the work of improvement. Tents and wagons were succeeded by houses; bundles and dry goods boxes gave place to chairs; and blankets were supplemented by mattresses, sheets, and pillows. We had at first isolated buildings, erected apparently without order or design, which developed into regularly defined and well-filled streets with tasty homes. Each day saw some new building going up or completed, and some new stock opened to the public. Money was plentiful, and as a general thing people who came here seemed to have plenty of the wherewith. At the close of the first year, cotton commenced to roll in, which inflated business. At the close of 1872, there were in Denison 450 wooden and 18 brick and stone buildings.

In our second year the magnificent high school building on Main Street was erected and became a matter of pride to the city and state. It was during this year that the North Texas Compress was completed. As a cotton market, Denison was not surpassed in North Texas. The writer has seen on Main Street cotton wagons all the way from Houston Avenue to Mirick Avenue—perhaps thousands of bales. The streets were crowded with cotton buyers, and competition was so great that the street men frequently engaged in rough and tumble fights. Every house that purchased cotton had its own buyer, and they were a tough lot, ready to fight at the drop of the hat. Sometimes the merchants took a hand at it, and about the liveliest fisticuff we ever saw was between two prominent merchants—both now dead.

Speaking of the Main Street school building, we can recollect that many thought the building was too far in the country. There is an incident we will never forget. Dr. Acheson invited us to accompany him in a ride over the city in the fall of 1875. There was not a building west of Armstrong Avenue, the woods covering that part of town. Riding through poorly lined streets, we said to the doctor: Will Denison ever build out here? "Build out here, yes, and miles beyond here." And the prophecy has been fulfilled to the letter. In the seventies, there were many substantial improvements made—the Lone Star Flour Mill, ice plant, gas works, and the song of the hammer, saw, and trowel never ceased.

No. 17

A Great Lottery

Sunday Gazetteer, May 22, 1910

Perhaps not one resident in fifty of Denison knows anything of the great lottery that was conducted here in the seventies. The lottery was engineered by a lot of businessmen. The capital prize was $100,000; and after paying off the prizes, a fund was to be set aside for park improvement. The office of the lottery was in the 100 block on the north side of Main Street. The office was in charge of a large clerical force. The lottery company advertised all over the United States, and the literature was appallingly large. The writer heard Horace Tong, chief clerk, say that the company spent at least $100,000 in general literature and other advertising, and perhaps the estimate was not exaggerated, as there was tons of printed matter sent out. The newspapers in Denison kept their job presses going day and night, and the company paid good prices.

There was a great deal of matter printed abroad.

The company did a rushing business, and sometimes their mail matter was so large that a wagon was used to carry it to headquarters. Tickets were sold in every state and territory in the Union. This lottery attracted the attention of the whole country to Denison; in fact, it was the best advertising card Denison ever had. Denison was better known abroad than any city in Texas.

The drawing took place in Forest Park, and the wheels were revolving for several days and nights, with great crowds of expectant people in attendance who held tickets.

In the shuffle, Denison ticket holders got badly left, and no prizes of any consequence were drawn, and the state people did not fare any better. The capital prize was drawn by a man in San Francisco, who was brought here and paraded around the streets in a carriage. He gave out that he would invest largely in Denison dirt, but never spent a cent. The writer heard Horace Tong say that the dummy was paid $3,000 and all expenses to come to Denison. The truth of the matter is that the lottery company started in with honest intentions, but the business got dull at the wind-up, and one of the leading spirits declared that they did not make a cent.

The lottery company put a great deal of money in circulation in Denison, and it was a good thing from a financial standpoint. After the drawing was over, many people denounced it as a huge swindle, and a charge of this kind resulted in a savage fight between the secretary of the company and a well-known sporting man in the 200 block of West Main Street.

Fig. 10. Forest Park, 1886. From Bird's-Eye Map, Amon Carter Museum.

No. 18

Forest Park

Sunday Gazetteer, May 29, 1910

Forest Park, the playground of Denison, was a gift from Mr. R.S. Stevens, one of the fathers of Denison. The tract was transferred from the Denison Town Company, the consideration being one dollar. It was stipulated in the transfer that the city should keep the park in good condition and that it should ever be used only as a park, and in case of failure should revert to Mr. Stevens or his heirs, or words to that effect.

Until the young men of this city took charge of the situation, assisted by the present city government, the park had been shame-fully neglected. As a popular resort, the park was well patronized in the past twenty years. A great many public gatherings have been held there, consisting of public speaking, barbecues, ball games, picnics, etc.

A number of years ago, largely at the instance of Joe Euper and Ex-Mayor Yocom and the City Council, the grounds were enclosed by an iron chain fence. About twelve years ago, bicycle grounds were established, Walter Nevins being the principal promoter.

It is said that Forest Park was responsible for the cholera in the seventies which carried off so many people. There was a barbecue held in the park attended by hundreds. The grounds were like a beehive. It rained while the meat was being barbecued, and a good deal of it was eaten which was only partially cooked. The next day or two, a disease broke out, the symptoms of which resembled those of Asiatic cholera, and many died very suddenly. Whether it was the result of the rain, meat, or real cholera has always been an open question. Anyway, the sickness was confined to Denison, and there were a good many deaths.

A number of attempts have been made to make the park an inviting place to visit, but the efforts have never been successful for some reason. Even now, with the many beautiful improvements, the park is not a popular resort, and but few people go there. The *Gazetteer* attributes the reason largely to the location; considering the geographical situation, it is really in the center of the city. The park should have been northwest of Main Street. Somehow or other our people are not park loving citizens, and thousands go to Woodlake who never visit Forest Park.

When the park was first laid out, it contained hundreds of majestic forest trees. Many have died, and many have been cut down. It is said that the dense volumes of black smoke which envelop the park, from the Katy machine shops, will eventually kill all of the forest trees. At the present time they look dingy, and many are decaying. There is a chemical substance in the smoke which is absorbed by the leaves, affecting the healthy growth of the trees. The late C.P. Parrish told the writer, as long ago as sixty years, he had seen troops of deer standing in the shade of the trees fighting off flies in the summertime and that he once killed a deer near the center of the park grounds. Col. Tom Lipscomb, now dead, had hunted on the same grounds many times, and no doubt the clamor of hounds in full chase of the wild deer and the notes of the hunter's horn have awakened echoes in Forest Park before Denison was even thought of.

There never was a real hearty effort to make the park presentable until within the past two years. Considerable money has been spent, and the park is really a beautiful spot to visit, but somehow or other the people do not go there.

It was very popular on concert nights, and great crowds patronized the occasions. It would be a good idea to revive the concerts, but in a prohibition town it seems hard to get up public attention or public enthusiasm. Some people may decry this statement, but it is a fact nonetheless.

It is very natural for people to want to get out of town, and Woodlake has drawn attention from our beautiful park. It takes a great public occasion to draw people to the park, and the question is now up to the park commissioners to induce people to go there. The paved avenue to the park will be a factor to this end. In the language of Loving & Glackin's business house motto, "Get the Habit" and go to the park; take your families there; let the children play on the grassy swards. The touch of Nature will make them healthier and prettier. Revive the night band concerts. The tennis games are worth viewing. Hold picnics there, and do not let public interest languish, but stir up things and make Forest Park a popular resort.

No. 19
Billy Sims

Sunday Gazetteer, June 5, 1910
[Original newspaper labels this No. 14]

There have been as many bad men (professional desperadoes) in Denison as in any city in Texas. In the seventies and eighties, when the gambling houses were on the first floor and dance halls and bawdy houses in full blast, Denison was an ideal frontier town; there was no factor lacking, it was all here. At least 50 per cent of the people toted guns, and many died with their boots on. The writer at the time was young in journalism—young in years and overflowing with the exuberance of spirits. Ambitious to get ahead of his competitors, he was always on the alert, and those who knew us in our first advent into journalism will bear witness to the fact that we always got there, and such a thing as "a scoop" was out of the question.

One of our first experiences was when Billy Sims killed J.V. George, who was at the time a clerk in a grocery house. George was killed at a house of ill repute on old Skiddy Street, near Rusk Avenue. When the newspaperman arrived at the house, the body had not been removed. It had been placed on a bed with the feet hanging over and almost touching the floor. George was a very handsome man: black wavy hair, eyes that scintillated like diamonds, and a fair complexion; the upper lip curved with a black moustache. Where he came from was never known, and the mystery was not cleared up after his death. He was a good dresser. A peculiarity was that he always wore his pants in his boots. He always took particular pains with his footwear. He had a small, pretty foot as well shaped as a woman's.

George was considered a dangerous man. He was very insulting and overbearing when drunk, which was quite often. The demimonde were afraid of him. He had a habit of going down to the houses at night and kicking the doors open if refused admission.

There was in the city at that time a boy sport by the name of Billy Sims, who afterwards acquired a national reputation by killing Ben Thompson at San Antonio—the man who had terrorized all southwest Texas. Sims was a quiet, manly young fellow, and, like every sport of that period, had his mistress. While Sims was asleep in a Skiddy Street resort, he was aroused by a man who, with many oaths and threats, demanded entrance. The man was George. The door was finally opened; and George, with pistol in hand, jumped into the room, when he was shot and killed by Sims. The victim fired his pistol, which was clutched in his hand, but a fraction too late. The law cleared the killer. It was self-defense; an even break. "Him or me," as Sims said to the writer when he was held in a small room in the 300 block of Main Street.

The virtue of "the drop" was eminently respected in those days, and scores are sleeping over in Oakwood Cemetery who lost their lives by being too slow at pulling the trigger.

The body of George was held for three or four days. If he had any relatives, they could never be found. It is said he was a Missourian, but very few mourners paid the last respects, and there were no flowers at the little opening made in the ground. There was relief when George was dead. It was a handsome corpse, like one who lies down to pleasant dreams, and there was no expression of pain. We have seen many men who died with their boots on, and on their pallid features were depicted fright and terror.

A short time afterwards, Billy Sims left Denison and eventually became a very rich and prominent gambler at San Antonio. A year or so ago he died. He owned considerable property, but it was stipulated in his will that none of his property should ever be let for immoral purposes.

There was a big Mexican by the name of [Jacob] Coy, who was considered a brave man and a fighter, who was present on the terrible night at the theater [Jack Harris Vaudeville Saloon and Theater in San Antonio] when Ben Thompson and King Fisher were killed [on March 11, 1884]. In the struggle, Billy Sims shot him [Coy] in the leg, which made him a cripple for life. Sims supported him until his death a few years ago. Sims in firing on Thompson accidentally killed his particular friend, [Joe] Foster. It is claimed by some that Foster killed Thompson, but the majority of the evidence is in favor of Sims' gun.

All of the bad men of that period have at some time or other in the seventies been visitors to Denison. In making up a holiday edition for the *Daily News* in the eighties, a record was kept of the number of men and women who died violent deaths in this city and the number was something over 100. Some of the women were killed, but the majority went by the morphine route. Seventy-five per cent were men who died with their boots on.

No. 20

Cattle Shipment

Sunday Gazetteer, June 12, 1910
[Original newspaper labels this No. 26]

The historian who tells of the early of period of Denison, just for material draws largely on the cattle era. From 1878 up through the eighties, the cattle transactions amounted to many million dollars, and the number of cattle shipped and driven through here signified as many cattle as dollars.

When the MK&T reached here in the winter of 1873 [actually the first train arrived late in December 1872], there were thousands of cattle around here waiting for shipment, and vast herds were moving slowly down through western Texas for this point. For ten years Denison was one of the largest points for shipment in the state. There were no Frisco, Santa Fe, Rock Island, or other systems in the state as rivals in the cattle business. As railways were built, the business gradually died out, and the great cattle barons went to other points. The Gulf, Colorado and Santa Fe made Gainesville a formidable rival, and the Fort Worth and Denver controlled the vast cattle interests of the Panhandle. The Texas and Pacific and the International and Great Northern companies shipped thousands of head of cattle to the eastern markets.

In the seventies and eighties, the great cattle barons all maintained offices here, and this was one of our sources of revenue. We had the Addingtons, N.B. Carnes, the Lovings, the Rues, Matt French, Blassingame, John Taylor, and a number of lesser lights. The cattle business of that period overshadowed all other interests. We had one or two of Quantrill's rough riders in the cattle business. Lee McMurtry and John Maupin at the [Red] river were large shippers. Once in a while a buffalo calf would come in with the herds. John Boling had in the back yard of his saloon on Houston Avenue and Main Street a buffalo cow that was purchased of the Addingtons.

The cattle were all longhorns, savage beasts that were the terror and sometimes death in the stampedes. Many and many a cowboy had the life ground out of him on the western prairies; hundreds perished in that manner. They sometimes furnished amusement and excitement in the streets of our city.

You never saw a cattle town that wasn't a rough town. The cattlemen had plenty of money, and when looking around for a little excitement they got all they wanted at the poker and faro tables. Thousands of dollars were lost, and they stood the acid and never cried over spilt milk. They were the gamest lot of sports that ever shuffled a card or called a hand. If the inside history of Denison could ever be written, a thrilling chapter would be of a party of cattle barons who sat around the table in a private room on Main Street, and where in one night about $20,000 exchanged hands. Money was prodigal in the old cattle days, and the cowmen had the most of it and they spent it lavishly. Some of the barons held thousands of head of cattle around Denison. There was a great awakening in the cattle business. Then began the great exodus of Texas cattle. The government was in the market for large quantities of beef to feed the many thousands of Indians cooped up on reservations, and now that the buffalo was gone, the substitution was cattle, drawn very largely from Texas, that harbored millions of longhorns. Denison was the horn of plenty, a great chute through which there was an unceasing flow of Texas cattle to the reservations and the northern markets. The climax was reached in the latter portion of 1879 and the early eighties. In one year it is said that 800,000 head of cattle crossed Red River at or near this point bound for the new Northwest. Some idea may be formed when we state that to manage these vast herds it took 4,000 men and over 30,000 horses, for every cowboy had his several mounts. The drives ran into the millions. The MK&T was not equal to the occasion, and vast herds were driven on foot to the Indian reservations, as far distant as Montana and the Dakotas. It is no wonder that money was plentiful.

The life in Denison was free and easy, the gambling places and hurdy-gurdy saloons were the great invite to the cowboys that thronged our streets and made merry at all hours of the day and night. This was indeed the reign of unbridled license. We can recollect one occasion, when about fifty cowboys were quartered at the old Nelson House [a hotel]. They were of the Mulhall & Scaling outfit and received their money here. They were wild and woolly and hard to curry. W.B. Boss was then mayor, and some timid people went to him and advised that he put the city under martial law, and he came very near doing it. Many had their guns, and it needed only a spark to explode the magazine.

There was one man in particular whose presence we'll never forget. We went among the crowd to get pointers. They were all game men, but they seemed to stand in awe of this man. His name we have forgotten, but Matt French, chief clerk for the Carnes, said that he had a bloody record and had killed at least twenty men. He happened to be with the outfit when it was en route to the Blackfoot reservation in Montana. He was a wolf hanging onto the flanks of the cowboys. It was said he would start trouble before he left the city and perhaps put another notch on his gun. He had been driven out of Hays City, where he killed a man on an even break. We looked upon this bad man with a sort of admiration. He wore a buckskin shirt, spread his hair out upon his shoulders, and carried a bowie knife and pistol. He refused to put off his pistol, and the officers did not insist. He presented an eye-filling spectacle. That evening the crowd received orders to go north and join their outfits. It was great relief when they left, for a night in Denison would have meant murder. Inflamed with whisky, there was no telling to what extremes they would go.

The cowboys of that period had a dialect of their own, and in a crowd of them, you were at sea as to what meaning they intended to convey.

The world will never see again the scenes associated with the great movement of cattle from Texas (largely Denison) and the vast herds which crossed [Red River] near here. There was always a grim sort of romance connected with the old cattle days in Denison; not so grim after all, for the cowboys were a little rough, but they were indeed the knights of that period, hale fellows well met, big-hearted, with open purses, and a friend in need is a friend indeed. Their transactions ran up into the millions, their presence in Denison made flush times. They were men of good digestion, strong and healthy, and it was a very easy matter to know their profession when you met them on the streets.

In the eighties, the cow business in Denison went to pieces, other railroad lines having absorbed the business; the offices were closed, and the cattle were scattered. Looking back over the list, we can mournfully say that they have nearly all crossed the great divide, and the trail is cold. We don't know of one alive at the present time.

In this little story we have just skimmed the surface, for there was never a period in the history of Denison more interesting, more romantic, than the wild cattle days of the seventies and eighties.

No. 21

The Cotton Trade

Sunday Gazetteer, June 19, 1910

The two most prominent factors in the early history of Denison were the cattle and the cotton trade. Denison at one period was the most important cotton market in North Texas. We bought more cotton than Sherman or other neighboring towns or cities. At that period, all of the southern portion of the Indian Territory was a feeder to Denison. It may surprise the reader when we state there has been cotton on our streets from as far north as the Creek Nation, 150 miles distant.

The towns along the MK&T were of very small population, and the merchants bought little cotton. Paul's Valley, the richest and fairest portion of the Chickasaw Nation, had no rival in the Five Nations and in the seventies sent nearly all of her cotton to Denison—in round numbers, many thousand bales. Fifty per cent of our cotton came from the Indian Territory. All of the country northwest (Preston, Delaware Bend, Sivil's Bend) and then on the east (Warren Flats, Shiloh, and other points) contributed to the Denison market. We not only got the cotton but the trade, which amounted to many thousand dollars per annum. The present residents ought to have seen the Denison of the seventies and eighties. We had three times as many dry goods and other business houses, and the sidewalks were so crowded with people that it was difficult to get along; and the transients spent more money in one day than is spent now in a month—and Denison wasn't as large by half. The writer has seen cotton wagons on Main Street reaching from Houston to Mirick avenues, and sometimes on the side avenues. All of the dry goods houses had cotton buyers, and the foreign buyers had not as yet come in. J.H. Porter & Co. and the

Star Store were the largest buyers. The Star Store depended largely on the cotton trade, and did an enormous business with people who brought the staple here. The receipts on some days went up into the thousand of bales.

Diversified farming was hardly known then, and the staple crops were cotton and corn—mostly cotton. Cotton did not command the glittering prices of the present day, and speculation in futures was an unknown feature of the market.

The rivalry between buyers was something fierce, and street fights were of frequent occurrence. Every house had its street drummers working for trade, and as a usual thing the drummers were a tough, unscrupulous lot. There were the Saum boys— desperate men—who were always ready to start trouble, and they "toted" guns. Bill Mitchell was one of the best drummers that Denison ever had, and was for many years with the Star Store, but eventually went on the police force. He killed Mike Langley at the dance hall on Skiddy Street. The stores dropped the drummers when business began to decline. New railways and new towns took the cotton and cattle business from Denison.

There was always excitement and some romance on the big cotton days. Hundreds of excited men crowded the streets, many seated on the cotton wagons, and such a jabber of voices has never been heard on our streets since. It was in the hard-drinking period, and the saloons were always crowded with men. As soon as a sale was made, the farmer and the buyer always marched off to the saloon. The gambling houses, wide open on the first floor, had their "cappers" [middlemen in a fraud scheme] among the farmers, and many farmers were fleeced. Still, at that period, the gambling houses gave their patrons a square deal. It was not until they were forced into the second stories behind closed doors that the suckers "got it in the neck."

In 1875, the cotton compress was erected at an expense of $40,000. It was considered the finest plant of the kind in the United States. It could, and did, handle 1,000 bales per day when pushed to the limit. The building was 310 feet long by 80 feet wide. Two-thirds of the stock was controlled by the MK&T Railway Company. The plant was able to handle the entire output of this section. Ed D. Chaddick [or Chadick] was the first superintendent.

He was afterwards largely identified with railway construction in this state and the Indian Territory. Major Shallenberger, at present in Denison, was Mr. Chaddick's right bower. When J.P. Rockwell, the treasurer, was appointed superintendent of the compress, he celebrated the event by giving the newspapermen a blowout.

Millions of dollars exchanged hands in Denison in cotton deals. The commodity was the greatest feature of our commercial activity in the seventies and eighties. Cotton was in reality King. Joe Meadows, one of the best men and best friends Denison ever had, sent thousands of bales from Preston, and Joe was a liberal spender and also one of the best poker players in North Texas. The Colberts in the Territory and many others brought all of their cotton here.

The farmers did not always get a square deal; in fact, many of the buyers were cheats, and their methods were denounced by the farmers who frequently "caught on"; and one instance occurred which is fresh in our memory, where a farmer put a head on one of the leading buyers and made him hide out. When the cotton business commenced to decline, many efforts were made to bring the old times back, but conditions had so changed the situation that Denison lost her cotton trade and has not done much in that line in the past decade.

The men who were most active in the cotton market in the early days have passed away and, sorrowfully we say it, are forgotten. They, like the cattle barons, were the most liberal, enterprising citizens that Denison ever had. No man who lived through that period can look back without repining and regret to the dear old days gone, forever gone. Another class has come here, many cold-blooded and selfish people, who count a man's worth by the dollars he can jingle.

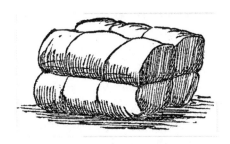

No. 22
Lee "Red" Hall

Sunday Gazetteer, June 26, 1910

The writer read in a San Antonio paper a number of years ago that Lee Hall, or "Red" Hall, was the gamest man in Texas. Hall was called Red Hall because his hair was so red that it always seemed in a blaze. He was captain of the Texas Rangers when Denison was in her swaddling clothes, and at the period when Texas harbored more bad men than any state in the Union. If a man cut up any devilment in another State, the first step was to escape to Texas. Hall probably had as many encounters and narrow escapes at the hands of bad men as any ranger that wore the livery of the State.

We heard him tell on the steps of the old Nelson House how he captured three men who were wanted for murder and had been running at large for a long period, as the officers were afraid of them and they stood in with the settlers who furnished information when the officers appeared in the neighborhood. Hall got word that the three men had "holed up" in a cabin in a dense wood in San Saba County. They were living with a woman until matters had quieted down, as they had stolen a number of horses in Kansas, and there was a hot pursuit. The cabin was a long way off of the main traveled highway, which in those days in a thinly settled country wasn't much better than a trail.

Hall took a Mexican with him. The outlaws were so vigilant that it was hard to get the "drop" on them. They took no chances, and the man suspected had to give a good account of himself, and it sometimes happened that a stranger was put out of the way on the slightest suspicion that he was a spy or an officer.

One morning at daybreak, the cabin door opened and one of the men went to the cow pen, saddled a horse, and rode away. Hall was secreted in the brush, and after the man had gone for a few moments he cut in ahead of him and made him stand and surrender. The man was conducted a short distance and the irons placed on him. The village was about two miles distant, and the sheriff lived there. Hall knew if the captured man was taken to the town that his two remaining pals would get word and light out.

Hall, the Mexican, and the bandit sat down under a tree. Hall made this proposition: that the prisoner should write a note, and the prisoner replied, "I can't write." "Well then," answered Hall, "I will send my Mexican to the cabin with a message from you, and if you don't give me your right name, I will kill you. After I capture the men, you are free, if you do as I direct." The prisoner agreed to the proposition, and the Mexican started on foot for the cabin. The message was to the effect that the bandit's horse had fallen and broken his leg and for them to come and take him to the village for treatment. The ruse was successful. At a certain turn in the road, Hall jumped from behind a pile of brush and ordered them to hold up their hands. The Mexican pulled his gun, and the two bandits surrendered and were taken in. Hall, fearing a rescue, traveled all night, never halting until he crossed the line into Lampasas County, where the sheriff was friendly to law and order.

That is only one incident among hundreds in which Lee Hall figured. Captain McDowell, also of the Texas Rangers, whose life and adventures have recently been published, was never up against it like Lee Hall.

Hall went into the Army during the Spanish-American War and was assigned to duty in the Philippines. He returned to this country, and a Chicago reporter on the *Tribune* got hold of him and published an account of his thrilling adventures, giving his photo.

Lee Hall was a man absolutely without fear, and he was captain of the Texas Rangers at a period when the state [Texas] was evolving from the rough border conditions to one of law and order. The last heard of him, he was in Old Mexico, guarding trains from the mines loaded with bullion. One of his men was recruited from Denison, but we have forgotten his name.

No. 23

Old Man Speaks

Sunday Gazetteer, June 26, 1910

Henry Speaks of Sterrett [later called Calera], Oklahoma, who was here the other day, was one of the original cowboys on the range. Speaks was lamenting the great change that has come over the Indian country. We can recollect the many days and nights that Speaks passed in our cabin on Allen Bayou, when we cut loose from civilization and was a denizen of the woods all of one winter.

Our cabin was visited frequently by cowboys, but none enlivened the occasion equal to Henry. He was the soul of mirth, and when he darkened our cabin door, the blues and loneliness made a sudden exit. Speaks was a hard rider, and even now we can hear his "whoop-pa-la" as he dashed up to the door and dismounted, and stretched himself out on the puncheon floor before the wide-throated chimney that gave forth a cheerful glow.

There never was a time that venison, wild turkey, ducks, or squirrels did not welcome our guest to the festal board, and it sometimes happened, before the banquet was spread, that a bottle was brought forth which made the spirits flow. The range riders always found the latchstrings on the outside. We used to play poker and shoot at marks, and tell stories. There was nothing to disturb the night but the cry of wolves and whoop of owls, nobody living in the neighborhood. The days and nights went and came, and our only callers were Henry Speaks and his band of cowboys.

But the white man came, and the smoke from his cabin covered both prairie and woods, the cattle disappeared from the range, and Henry Speaks went with them.

No. 24

Ghost Stories

Sunday Gazetteer, July 3, 1910

There is probably no city of any size in the United States that has not had its spooks, and Denison is no exception to the general rule. We will not speak of public so-called spiritual manifestations, as they are generally discredited. But events have happened in Denison that have baffled investigation and are still a mystery.

Here is a story that is true, and vouched for by persons at present living here. The information is furnished by the wife of the city editor, who is calculated to tell a straight story without any flights of imagination.

The manifestations happened at the home of Mrs. Brown, who was then a teacher in the public school and resided in the 500 block Woodard Street.

A little girl, who was in the primary department of the public school and had not as yet acquired the practice of writing, was stopping with Mrs. Brown. At an early hour of the evening, a noise was heard like someone knocking for admission. The front door was opened, and no one was there. The knocks were repeated on the window and at various points on the outside of the house. Mrs. Brown called in the neighbors, and the outside of the house was surrounded, but still the manifestations continued. The yard and premises were thoroughly searched, but no person could be discovered. Frequently violent knocking was heard on the roof. The little child, who had been asleep in the bed, opened her eyes and then apparently relapsed into a trance, with deep breathing. She finally called for paper and pencil, and wrote in a plain hand, so that all present could read, message after message that was signed by what purported to be her mother, who had been dead for some time. It must be recollected that the child in her normal state could not write at all. The mother did not want her little girl forgotten, as the holidays were near at hand. She (or whatever it was) laid great stress on the request that the child should receive presents. The child wrote a number of messages, her hand seeming to be under the control of some invisible power.

During the time the child was writing, the knockings continued all over the house. George Strobe (dead for many years) entered the house, and when told of the manifestations, said, "Well; it must be a d—d poor spirit that can't make more noise than that," or words to that effect. In an instant it seemed as if large stones were being hurled on the roof, and the residence fairly vibrated.

Mrs. Pollard, who resided a block distant and was a great believer in spiritualism, was sent for. When the lady appeared on the scene, the situation was explained. She declared that it was the spirit of the child's mother who was communicating.

The pencil finally dropped from the child's hand; she opened her eyes widely, and the demonstration ended. The next day she was taken to Mrs. Pollard's residence, and the "spirits" were invoked but with no manifestations whatever.

On what hypothesis the manifestations at Mrs. Brown's residence can be explained, we offer no explanation. Here was a child about four years old, that had never written a line in her life, and yet through some unknown agency she wrote rapidly and correctly, and in letters so plain that it was read without any difficulty whatever.

There used to be on Main Street, about where the [F.E.] Shaffer hardware house now stands [321 West Main], a "haunted" house. The house stood in the rear of Mr. Pollard's tin shop. Every evening about dusk, footsteps could be heard ascending the stairway which was on the east side of the building and connecting with the second story. Several people who had rooms in the second story moved out, declaring the house was haunted. Many heard the invisible steps going up the stairway.

Mr. Charles Fillmore [1854–1948], Katy cashier, who had a room in the building, made a public statement that, about midnight, something entered his room which was securely fastened, and that he could hear chairs moving and footsteps in the room. In the morning it was discovered that the chairs had been moved, and on one occasion the washbowl and pitcher had been set on the floor. Fillmore was a spiritualist, but the nightly visits caused him to vacate the room. [Later Fillmore founded Unity, a church within the New Thought movement, with his wife, Myrtle Page Fillmore.]

An old, eccentric man had died in the Fillmore sleeping apartment. He came to Denison a stranger and would never give any account of himself. He left some money at his death.

There was great excitement at reports sent out that the residence owned by the Cuff Bros., corner of Gandy Street and Burnett Avenue, was haunted. It had been proclaimed by Tom Foley, who lived there, that in the night, noise, violent knockings on the floor, prevented sleep; and Mrs. Foley declared that she had on several occasions seen a sad, pale-faced woman in the room, that, when approached, faded into the wall. The entire newspaper force of the city press spent one night there. They all got drunk and raised such a racket that, about midnight, they were invited to get out and go home, or the police would be called to eject them.

On West Texas Street there used to be an old Negro cabin occupied by a family named Yarbrough. A man was murdered there; at least the man was carried there after being murdered. This cabin was haunted, and nobody would live there. It was set on fire and burned, and the people in the neighborhood said the incendiary was the spirit of the murdered man. One of the manifestations was the pulling up and down of the well buckets; also rocks were thrown against the cabin, and heard-rending groans could be heard. Mr. Dickinson, a reliable man, stated that he spent one night on the premises, and that the reports were true. He heard the noise at the well and, in company with a friend, saw the buckets ascend and descend, and he heard the rocks hurled against the cabin.

There are other stories of haunted houses, but the one that happened at the home of Mrs. Brown was literally true.

No. 25
Lone Star Flour Mill

Sunday Gazetteer, July 10, 1910

In 1874 the Lone Star Mill was erected under the management of W. [William] B. Boss [1832-1921], who was twice mayor of Denison and several times a member of the council. The mill had a capacity of 250 barrels of flour per day. For many years the mill had no opposition, and its prosperity was not affected by any rival concern in Texas.

The mill was a three-story rock building, and was modern in every respect; the flour manufactured [was] first-class and had a market in all East and West Texas and the Indian Territory, and in the seventies and eighties it was in the height of its prosperity, hundreds of carloads being shipped from here.

The mill was situated between the Katy tracks, and that fact made it the bone of contention for a great many years. The Missouri, Kansas & Texas Railway Company tried in vain to acquire the property, as it was a stumbling block in the way of the railway people, who wished to use the ground for trackage purposes. For many years the people up north, who owned the property, maintained a watchman and refused any overtures from the railway company.

The chief miller, Chas. De Haven, was one of the best in his profession in the state, but [he] was ruined by whisky and lost his position. Charley was taken back later on probation but only to fall from grace. He owned considerable property west of the H&TC [Houston & Texas Central Railway] tracks, but it all passed from his hands. The family (a most interesting one) went to the dogs. A daughter, Stella, drifted to the Indian Territory and shot herself in a dance hall.

Fig. 11. Lone Star Flour Mill, 1891. At Owings St. and Houston Ave. From 1891 Birds-Eye Map, Amon Carter Museum.

For many years the Lone Star Mill was one of the leading factors of the city, and hundreds of people who stopped here paid it a visit. W.B. Boss, the manager, was a courteous gentleman and a royal entertainer. The first visit the writer ever made there, Mr. Boss opened a bottle of wine and conducted us personally through the mill. Mr. Boss had a wonderful success with the mill for many years, but like many other Denison enterprises, it had its day and the mill closed.

The enterprise was later revived, but it never was a success. Many new towns sprang up on the lines of railway radiating from this point, and many flour mills were built. The Lone Star Mill struggled along, but close competition and other causes closed its doors forever. There was a genuine sorrow when the "old Boss mill" closed down. It was one of the very first industrial enterprises in the pioneer period of Denison. It has had its romantic history, and for twenty years it was deserted, save for the watchman who was kept there by the foreign owners, who paid out thousands of dollars to have it guarded.

The mill was built of sandstone taken from a quarry southeast of the city. We are not sure, but it is our impression that the rock work was done by Mr. Larkins, now dead.

Mr. [John W.] Jennings was identified with the mill and furnished the money, being the first man on the ground. He died a few years ago in New York. The lumber firm of Boss, Pinto & Jennings was at the inception indirectly interested in the mill.

To protect the insurance on the old mill, Mr. [John E.] Jasperson was appointed as watchman and looked after the property for a period of twenty years. For many years his salary was a good compensation but later was cut down.

When the old mill was dismantled, the cornerstone was not removed. It contained a copy of the city newspapers, a bottle of whisky, some coins, a bottle of oil, and many other things.

The old mill was acquired by the MK&T many years ago and dismantled. The interior was virtually a wreck, the timbers rotted out, and a portion of the roof was gone; and it presented a melancholy spectacle to the old-timers who, with its downfall, realized the many changes that have taken place. *Sic transit gloria* [thus passes glory].

No. 26

City Planning

Sunday Gazetteer, July 17, 1910

No stranger visits Denison but is impressed with the beauty of its streets and avenues. The people of Denison hardly realize and appreciate the fact that Denison is the best laid out city in Texas.

The plan of laying out the city was such as could scarcely be improved upon. All the resident streets are of uniform width from one extremity of the corporation to the other, and an alley twenty feet in width extends through every block. There are no angles, jogs, or crooks in the streets and avenues. The location of the ground is such that, while the business streets occupy the heart of the city in either direction, the residence portion was mainly forest, principally post oak, affording shade such as a generation of artificial culture could not produce.

In the summer of 1872, Major O.B. Gunn, then chief engineer of the MK&T Railway, made a personal inspection of the country for a hundred miles in each direction and decided that this was the most eligible location. In September of that year, the town was laid out and called Denison after the vice-president of the MK&T Railway. The history of Denison and the MK&T Railway are inseparable and identical, for one is the petted child of the other. The wisdom of Major Gunn in the selection of the site of Denison was never questioned. The selection was eminently a happy one. Situated upon high, rolling ground above the level of Red River and far enough from its banks to be free from malaria and miasma incident to bottom lands, the location is known as one of the most delightful and healthy in the entire Southwest.

Denison was for many years known throughout the world as "The Infant Wonder." In the seventies, all the boom printed matter distributed throughout the country used that expression.

Denison is today everything of which her early history gave promise. Her geographical position, placing her at the neck of the funnel through which for nearly forty years has passed the great bulk of Texas immigration, makes her the grand depot of commerce. The same industry and energy which caused her to spring into a city of 20,000 are still at work. Her ambition is unlimited and her faith in herself and her future is unbounded, and she must ever remain the largest and most important city north of Dallas. The location and the manner in which the city is laid out are destined to make a great city.

Where Denison now stands there used to be a cornfield, and in Forest Park deer and wild turkey were hunted and killed. Even the buffalo almost pushed their excursions in sight of the city. The men who lived then are nearly all dead and forgotten, a new generation has stepped upon the stage, and Denison is still marching on to her grand destiny. The old stagecoach, the prairie schooner propelled mainly by ox power, the great herds of cattle, the buffalo trains, and all the paraphernalia of frontier life have disappeared forever. They can be revived only in memory. The men who conceived Denison have left us as a future legacy one of the most beautiful cities west of the Mississippi. The natural advantages of the city cannot be overestimated. The struggle has been a little slow, but Denison is coming into her own at last, the spirit of improvement is abroad, and there never was a period when the sky bending over the city looked so bright.

No. 27

Denison's African Americans

Sunday Gazetteer, July 24, 1910

Denison until recently has been very fortunate as to the character of her Negro population. The Negroes as a general thing were peaceful and industrious, and were property owners in pioneer days. Since the saloons went out of business and the latitude allowed them by the officers, an undesirable class has got a foothold here. Seventy-five per cent of the bootleggers are Negroes, and in the justice and city courts they are the principal offenders.

There are several sections of Denison (in the extreme northwest and southwest) where there is a large population. In the southern portion of the city there are also large Negro settlements. It is estimated that the present Negro population of Denison is not less than 6,000, and is said to be increasing more rapidly than any city in North Texas of its size. A great many Negroes own property in Denison and are among our most respectable people, attending to their own affairs and engaged in respectable and lucrative business pursuits. They have nothing to do with the disreputable class. A number are engaged in the government service, as mail route carriers on the trains, and we are told that they perform their duties in the most satisfactory manner.

The Negroes have worshipped in Denison ever since the city was incorporated, and they have at the present time no less than eight churches and all of them in a flourishing condition.

The Negro is an emotional creature, and religion strongly appeals to his nature. The majority attends church, and if they would live up to the good advice given by their pastors, they would be a better people.

The colored public schools of Denison are not surpassed by any colored schools in the state and have reached a high state of efficiency.

In the seventies and eighties, the Negroes were the dominant political factor of Denison. This was before the Terrell election laws were enacted and the restrictions that have been placed around the ballot since. Every man who ran for office counted the Negro vote. In that period, the Negro "boss" was old Dave Williams, and he was a power to be reckoned with at every city election. Williams was a very shrewd, aggressive Negro. He was a man of considerable natural ability. In those days politics was a paying business, and "Uncle Dave" was always ready to receive overtures. He was tricky and unscrupulous and did not always "tote fair." Political lines were very seldom drawn in city elections. While [he was] a Republican, Democratic money always seemed good to "Uncle Dave," and there is no question at all but that he turned the tide in many city elections. He was very muchly courted by the white politicians. Many colored bosses have popped up since "Uncle Dave" left here, but they were weaklings when compared with him. It may be truly said that he carried the Negro vote in his pocket in the seventies. He was a great organizer and, with few exceptions, could hold his men together and march them to the polls in a solid phalanx. If there were not enough in Denison, "Uncle Dave" could send to the Indian Territory after political recruits. Voters were not challenged, and it was not necessary to produce any papers.

The writer has seen Negroes herded like cattle and at the last moment turned loose, and turn the tide of battle. Every one of them received so much for his vote. The price was not much—50 cents, 75 cents, and $1.00—and we can recollect in an election in the second ward (the banner Negro ward) for councilman, the candidate is said to have turned loose $1,000.

On one occasion we saw about fifty Negroes herded to Jerry Nolan's livery stable, and the man who bought them was elected with a rush. Of course there were a number of respectable Negroes who could not be enticed by money.

There has always been a bitter strife in Denison in the colored wing of the Republican Party, and on many occasions there was a big rumpus at the city conventions, and the white element was sometimes routed. The white Republican leaders would go to any extreme to capture the Negro influence, and frequently their antics were disgusting and they might in truth be called "nigger lovers." No man who has ever appeared as a leader in the Republican ranks could manipulate the Negroes like Dr. [William M.] Nagle. He was the boss, but his power departed. The Negroes have always been loyal to the Republican Party but have been split up on state occasions. The Lily Whites were one of the entering wedges, and then, when Dr. [Alexander W. "Sandy"] Acheson [1842–1934] appeared upon the political horizon, there was another political earthquake which split up the Negro factions.

There have been Negroes in Denison of historical importance—the old-time slaves and black mammies. They are about all dead, but they carried with them to their last resting place the respect and affection of the southern people.

There has been many a bad Negro in Denison whose footsteps had been marked in blood. Charley Russell, for instance, who killed Constable Jim Nelms and an Indian [Charlie Colbert, on July 4, 1879], and many others whose names but not deeds have escaped our memory. Sin-Killer Griffin, now famous throughout the South as a colored evangelist, is a Denison product. We have had a great many colored people who are progressive and a benefit to the city, and we also have a great many who should have been "weeded out" by the officers long ago.

In pioneer days, the Negroes were not half as bad as they are at present. Here is the present great trouble: hundreds of Negroes are supported by Negro women prostitutes, and as long as this condition of affairs exists, they will never perform any manual labor.

Most all of the barber shops in the early days were conducted by Negroes, and Dave Williams' place monopolized 75 per cent of the custom, and it was there the affairs of state were discussed and where the white politicians used to get scraped.

The Negroes held many camp meetings in the woods around Denison in the good old times, and down at the MK&T stockyards the converts were immersed with much ceremony—singing, shouting, praying, etc.

The Negroes have strong lodges here, also a brass band, baseball clubs, and many societies. We must say the band music did not amount to much. They have their schools, churches, and literary pretentions, the rights of franchise, and many other things which should be conducive to their moral and intellectual growth.

No. 28

Elections

Sunday Gazetteer, July 31, 1910

The Democratic primaries that have just been held were like a churchyard affair compared with the county, state, and city elections of forty years ago. They were the most exciting political events known throughout the state. The bars were thrown down, and no safeguard was taken to protect the polls. Hundreds voted in Denison who had no right to vote, and many were not residents of the state, but crossed over from the Indian Territory. The voting boxes were suffocated, and it frequently happened that a man had to wait some time before he could exercise the privilege of elective franchise. The wards were full of "heelers" [people who worked for a political party or boss at the ward level, performing minor tasks], and men were dragged around by toughs and importuned as to whom they intended to vote for.

Fights were of frequent occurrence, and on one occasion we saw big Al Hall, then chief of police, holding at bay on Rusk Avenue near Chestnut Street at least two hundred Negroes, who had been fighting and rioting all day and at last resolved themselves into a mob. Hall used a big club freely and finally was master of the situation, after several Negroes had been laid out.

Every hack and other vehicle in the city were brought into requisition, and on them were large stretchers of canvas announcing the names of the various candidates. Laws were defied, and on Election Day, the worst element in the city seemed to have the upper hand. No doubt ballot-box stuffing was frequent, as claimed by defeated candidates.

In the seventies and eighties, Denison's legitimate voting population amounted to about 1,000, and yet it frequently happened that 2,000 votes were cast. The Negro vote was always for sale, and many white people bartered away the dearest right of an American citizen.

Denison had many bitter political feuds that culminated in disgraceful affrays. Looking over the early files of the newspapers, all kinds of charges were made against candidates. They were even charged with grafting. The city editor of the old *Daily Herald* made a speech in Driggs' hall, charging Judge [W.M.] Peck, candidate for mayor, with gross irregularities. The address was delivered Saturday night, and Sunday morning the judge happened to meet [Herman] Kuehn, the newspaper speaker, and gave him a good beating at the corner of Main Street and Austin Avenue. Judge Peck was elected by a rousing majority, and the victory was celebrated with bell-ringing, bonfires, and a noisy crowd parading the streets.

The city elections were all bitterly fought. A singular thing happened. Jim Burson, editor of the *Herald*, was a candidate for councilman in the first ward and up to a late hour in the afternoon had no opposition, and it looked like a walkover. Some of the newspaper boys, headed by Geo. Riggins and Walton Hembey, brought out a candidate; and when the polls closed, Burson was beaten by over 100 majority. We never saw a man so crestfallen and mad, and he never forgot it.

There used to be the Rawhide Party, headed by one [Major Frank] Shrader, who kicked up a big commotion. Shrader was called everything by the press, a veritable political monstrosity; but Shrader was elected mayor [1873–74] and during his term of office was annoyed by newspaper attacks.

In those days a great deal of money was used, and it was money that won many a city election. The candidates always went into an election weighed down with promises which were never carried out.

In the seventies and eighties, and we may say the nineties, there was considerable grafting in the city council. If a man wanted an office in the city government, he had to "put up," and the bosses fixed the thing. There is no doubt that grafting on a small scale prevailed, and would have been carried on on a large scale if the opportunity had offered. The Winn [1875–76] and Ed. Perry [1874–75] city administrations were fiercely attacked as being rotten, and with some truth. Perry fostered [foisted] upon the city three brick schoolhouses, the history of which is known even to the present generation.

There was a continual wrangle in political affairs in the pioneer history of Denison. The newspapers sold rapidly in those days. Weeks before the city elections, the wires were being placed, and the excitement was at a white heat. There were rings and counter rings, and the situation was always panicky.

There were many hot times in the city council, the present imbroglio being a tame affair compared with the doings of the city council in pioneer days. Two prominent city officials proved to be defaulters. We have seen a chief of police for two days in a room in the Muller Block playing poker.

The Baskin-McGregor election laws were the beginning of a better order of things at elections, and the Terrell election law was another innovation. The toughs were cut out, and at present we have very decent election laws. Elections, as held in pioneer days, were generally a farce, and we want to say right here that the present primary elections are the biggest farces of all and should be abolished. They are not an honest expression of political sentiment. There is so much claptrap about them that honest men hold aloof and do not vote at all.

Fig. 12. Ferry on Red River. Illustration by Champney.

No. 29

The Red River and Its Woods

Sunday Gazetteer, August 7, 1910

We have seen the time when Red River was at its lowest stage of water. You could wade it; you could almost jump across it. All ferry communications were cut off, and horsemen and teams crossed with impunity. This was a number of years ago. The water stood in pools in the bed of the river, and the sand bars were landing places for wild geese and ducks in the fall and winter.

A very singular thing happened at the river in the latter part of the seventies and which was commented upon at the time in the home and foreign papers. The water was at a very low ebb; there had been no rain in several weeks, and hunting parties from Denison had crossed on foot. At an early hour one day, water came surging down the river with a great rush, boiling and foaming as it came on. In the morning of the next day, the sand bars had disappeared, and Red River was a turbulent, raging stream. There was an eight-foot rise. No rain had fallen in the Panhandle clear down to Denison. The red current was filled with large trees and drifts. It was several days before the matter was cleared up. There had been a cloudburst on the upper Washita [River]. Such a volume of water never had fallen before or since. The Washita empties into Red River eight miles north of Denison. It is a stream almost as large as the Red. When the water (during a rise) reaches the mouth of the Washita, it spreads out over the adjacent lands. Many cattle and two Negroes were drowned. The water could be seen coming down, the waves writhing and tumbling over each other. The ferry boat on the Washita had been washed away. Very sudden rises in this river frequently took place.

Red River, when stage full of water, is an awe-inspiring sight. Sometimes there is a roar like thunder heard when the great forest trees fall into the water. The high water and heavy drifts have on two occasions swept our bridges away, causing a loss of over a million dollars.

When the railway bridge was swept away in the great flood of the seventies, Ed Chaddick, in charge of the [Cotton] Compress, put in a ferry boat and made thousands of dollars transferring passengers from the Territory to this side. Red River seems to have fallen out with our people. In pioneer days hundreds used to go into camp there; [and would] fish and frolic on Sunday. When the Denison Artillery Company went there for practice, hundreds of our people followed, in vehicles and on foot. Public fish fries were much in vogue, and we have seen a dozen fish fries going on at the same time, and the campfires at night illuminated the surrounding gloom. There was frequently heard the dulcet notes of the guitar, played for dancing parties.

For many years Red River had been the crossing point for horse thieves from the Territory to Texas, and some of the most notable battles between officers and outlaws have taken place on the stream. Hundreds of desperate men have perished while attempting to cross stolen stock into Texas.

The Red River woods have harbored many of the worst outlaws that ever cursed the earth, among the most notable being [William] Quantrill, the famous guerrilla chief, who came down from Missouri with his rough riders. Quantrill went into camp on the banks of Red River at Colbert's ferry. He remained there for a few days and then crossed over to Texas, proceeding to Sherman. Todd, Bill Anderson, our Lee McMurtry, and John Maupin followed the fortunes of the guerrilla chief in Texas. After killing several persons near Sherman, the arrest of Quantrill was ordered by General [Henry] McCullough, who was then stationed at Bonham. Quantrill, while confined in a room, made his escape, but his band was split up; and that was the beginning of the end.

Bill Anderson and his gang joined the regiment of Colonel Martin, who was ordered to capture Quantrill, dead or alive. About where Denison is situated, the fight was opened. Quantrill retreated but made a stand at Red River. Bill Anderson was in advance of Colonel Martin's regiment and fought the guerrilla chief, who retreated and made another stand. Colonel Martin abandoned the pursuit, for the reason that Quantrill was out of McCullough's jurisdiction. Quantrill went into camp at the old Frank Colbert farm on the north bank of Red River. That was the last time that Bill Anderson, who was the most blood-thirsty of Quantrill's band, had anything to do with his chief.

There is no river in the Southwest that has furnished so many desperate encounters. The Red River woods are truly historical grounds; for more than a hundred years, it was the fighting grounds. The painted Comanche and Kiowa with their plumes and feathers crossed it on their raids into Texas. Millions of buffalo have quenched their thirst in its waters while traveling to the rich plains of the Panhandle and where the new State of Oklahoma flourishes at present. [George] Catlin, the great Indian historian, crossed the river where Preston now is, and Generals Grant and Lee have sat in the shade of the trees that grew along its banks. General [William] Harney with his dragoons was in camp near Preston and crossed into the Comanche country at the mouth of the Washita.

Red River is destined to play an important part in the future of Denison. It will give us navigation and make Denison one of the leading factors of Northern Texas.

There are a hundred incidents in connection with the river that might be dilated upon, and are of thrilling interest. It has been demonstrated that boats have proceeded as far up Red River as Gainesville, west of Denison. [Choice] Randell, [John Levi or his son, John Morris] Sheppard, and other Texas Congressmen have secured large appropriations to improve the river, and government boats have been at work over two years improving the stream.

We can recollect thirty years ago, when the Red River woods were full of deer and wild turkeys, and many nights we have passed at the campfire in the great forests that line its bank. The presence of such a body of water must relatively affect the future destiny of our city, and Red River will always be a burning question with our people.

No. 30

Howard Racetrack

Sunday Gazetteer, August 14, 1910
[Original newspaper labels this No. 28]

About twenty years ago, there was, east of the city, what was known as the Howard Racetrack. To reach it, you had to climb the Pawpaw Hill and then detour into the Carpenter's Bluff highway, traveling a distance of about one mile. The grounds were well laid off, and there was at one point a number of beautiful shade trees in which a small house was situated.

The Howard Racetrack was a dream. It was regarded as a nucleus of a great sporting enterprise, and the future predicted for it stimulated some real estate deals. A great many races took place out there, and we have seen as many as 2,500 people present, and among the patrons a large number of ladies.

The great drawback was getting there, but the county road gang was put to work on Pawpaw Hill, and the improvement was very marked. When a man was a candidate for county commissioner, he was pretty sure to make promises to improve the road leading from the city to the Howard Racetrack. Many crack racehorses were stabled out there, and a man was hired to superintend the grounds.

The races were usually held on Saturday, and we have seen hundreds of vehicles in line and hundreds of people on foot proceeding to the races.

The enterprising liverymen used to put on hacks, and they were always well patronized. The price to the grounds was 15 cents; the more pretentious conveyances charged 25 cents. Many horses were brought here from the Indian Territory. The betting was lively and some very spirited races were pulled off, and much money exchanged hands.

When the Denison Live Stock Show was discussed and it was decided to go to the northwest suburbs of the city, the interest in the Howard Racetrack began to languish. The hill east was always a drawback and contributed as much to extinguish the interest in the Howard Racetrack as any other factor. The old racetrack finally went out of existence, and another pleasure ground of Denison was numbered with the past. Seventy-five per cent of the present population do not know that such a place existed.

The racetrack northwest [of town] was for a number of years the finest track in Texas, and some of the best horseflesh in the Southwest were patrons. That course, too, is now numbered with the melancholy past. The fair and stock show was a losing proposition, and after a five years' trial the enterprise was abandoned. The MK&T is at present using the grounds for its tie treating plant [W.J. Smith Wood Preserving Company].

No. 31
Overton~Saunders Feud

Sunday Gazetteer, August 21, 1910
[Original newspaper labels this No. 29]

You may talk about your dark and bloody grounds which have made Kentucky notorious for many decades, but the old Indian Territory will take first premium at the fair.

One of the most desperate feuds in the history of the Chickasaw Nation was transferred to Denison. We have reference to the Overton-Saunders vendetta, in which a number of men directly or indirectly lost their lives. Dr. [Robert H.] Saunders [1835–1907] was a white man. [Benjamin Franklin "Frank"] Overton [1836–1884] was a half-breed Indian, governor of the

Chickasaw Nation when the trouble first began. Dr. Saunders was principal of a national school in the western part of the Nation. Saunders allied himself with the element that was opposed to the political aspirations of Overton, and the result was that he lost his position and was obliged to flee with his family to save his life. Before his departure, the academy was fired into by a party or parties in ambush.

Governor Overton was a crafty, unscrupulous man, who wielded a tremendous influence among the Chickasaws. He was a sort of Indian [Porfirio] Diaz, and all efforts to displace him were unavailing. He was one of the most remarkable men that the Five Nations ever produced. His ambition was unbounded, and he always found plenty of means to carry to a successful conclusion his political aspirations.

Dr. Saunders was also a remarkable man. He had served throughout the Civil War in the Confederate service. He was a fighter, and so was Overton. Saunders was a man of very strong notions. and when he got his head set, there the matter rested. Saunders charged Overton with many political murders, [and] at any rate during the vendetta, a number of persons were assassinated.

When Dr. Saunders came to Denison with his family, there came with him Judge [Laban Lipscomb] Woods, who had one arm. Woods was a member of the Chickasaw government, but espoused the cause of Dr. Saunders and was also obliged to flee for his life. He took a very conspicuous part against Overton from this city.

The first thing that Dr. Saunders did on his arrival here was to start a daily paper, and no such paper has ever been published in Denison and, we might say, in Texas. The name of the paper was the *Daily Herald.* The writer was connected with it; and one of the principal factors was Captain Williams of Preston, who is very ill at the present time. The *Herald* fired broadside after broadside into the Overton camp, and thousands of papers were sent across the river to influence the political situation. Governor Overton was held up to the public eye as a monster—a Nero, guilty of every crime in the human catalogue. Such a tirade of abuse was never heaped upon a human being. Denison was in a ferment, and serious trouble was predicted at almost any time. Governor Overton had crossed the river several times into Denison, but it somehow happened that he and Saunders never net.

Saunders was a drinking man and was frequently intoxicated. He always went armed and was arrested several times for carrying concealed weapons. He was one of the prettiest writers that ever wielded a pen on the Denison press. He wrote an article entitled "A Cup of Milk," which was copied all over Texas. He was a very strong writer on any subject. Judge Woods was associated with Saunders in the publication of the *Herald*. The firm name was Woods & Saunders, publishers.

The paper was published in the second story of the John D. Ourand building, nearly opposite the *Gazetteer* office. Attorney F.N. Robertson was for some time editor of the *Herald*. He was as good a writer as speaker, and that is saying a good deal.

The Saunders-Overton feud came very near putting Denison under martial law by Mayor W.B. Boss [he served 1881–84]. It was intimated that Governor Overton with a large party of followers was coming across the river into Denison to clean up the Saunders faction. Saunders heard of this and sent for his adherents. A front room in the Muller Block was filled with Winchesters and ammunition. It was good [as] a fortress, as there were but two entrances, and a storming party would have all been killed before they could have reached the second story. Dr. Saunders and his faction waited all of one day for them, but the Overton party failed to show up. It was on this occasion that Mayor Boss was urged by the businessmen to put the city under martial law.

Saunders and Woods published the *Herald* for about two years, when it went out of existence.

Judge Woods was killed under tragic circumstances at a sawmill near the mouth of Washita River. He was the proprietor of a large mill. In a trouble with a man he was shot, receiving a wound which proved fatal. After being shot, the judge grabbed his pistol and fired at his assailant, who was just disappearing through a door. The man staggered and fell over dead. It was a wonderful shot, as the judge had only one arm and was wounded to the death.

Governor Overton was finally voted out of power, and Saunders, having no paper, remained in Denison only a short time and then left with his family, locating at a town on the H. & T. C.

[Railroad], where he commenced the practice of his profession, and was still alive a few years ago.

The Saunders-Overton feud embroiled the whole Chickasaw Nation. Overton was the strongest man that country has ever had, and Saunders was no match for him in political strategy. He made and unmade men. The writer spent several days at his camp near Oil Springs. The governor was very hospitable and gave his version of the trouble with Saunders, putting his side of the question in the best possible light. He said that he was always sorry that he did not kill Saunders and Judge Woods, and when he said this, we never saw a more devilish looking face, and with an oath, he clenched his fist and yelled: "I made Saunders, and you see my reward."

The Guy-Byrd trouble is another exciting chapter in the political history of the Chickasaw Nation, which we will try to touch on at some future period. The two rival candidates for governor [William Malcolm Guy and William Leander Byrd] were frequent visitors to Denison and did their trading here.

No. 32
The Woods Brothers

Sunday Gazetteer, August 28, 1910
[Original newspaper labels this No. 30]

It is singular how misfortune follows some families. The presence of a man named Ben Woods who passed through here Saturday recalls the unfortunate ending of his two brothers, George and Drew. George died in a madhouse in Tennessee; and Drew, poor and forsaken, was cared for in his last days by the Confederate camp at Dallas.

Drew and George Woods arrived in Denison about twenty-five years ago. They were handsome brothers, both having black curly hair, fair complexion, and black eyes that were soft and pensive. They engaged in the saloon business and made friends and prospered. Drew finally obtained a half-interest in the White Elephant and acquired money so fast that he purchased a number of houses and several vacant lots.

The tide turned, and a moral wave put the White Elephant out of business. The Woods brothers left here but returned and again engaged in the saloon business. Drew was established in a little cubbyhole on North Rusk Avenue near the Mathes Livery Stable. He gradually frittered away his property in Denison, and his luck seemed to have deserted him. He was a desperate drinker, but of all the saloon men we have ever met in our thirty-six years' residence [in Denison], he was the most generous, and excessive drink didn't seem to sour his kindly feeling toward his fellow man. He gave away a great deal of liquor, and a poor unfortunate never appealed to him in vain. When a man commences to go downhill, the descent is often hurried by persons who should be his warmest friends. Many of those whom he had befriended in his prosperous days would hardly treat him with common courtesy. The little saloon closed its doors, and the brothers again left the city, only to return again.

The Oklahoma fever was on, and all eyes were turned toward the promised land. The brothers determined to cast their lot with the great crowd which, like the tide, ebbed and flowed across the border. They raked together sufficient money to purchase a poor span of horses and a covered wagon, and with a faithful dog following, they turned their faces toward the river, and that was the last ever seen of them. Their going was sad, and as George turned to a few friends to say "Good-bye," the tears started to his eyes. The brothers acquired some land near Duncan, Oklahoma, and settled down for a year or so, but the crops failed and they pulled out to face the wide world again.

A woman's love and past misfortune wrecked the mind of George, and he died in an insane asylum. Drew drifted from place to place, broken in health and spirit, and was unable to earn a living. He wrote to Mike Collins, explaining his condition. Joe Meadows of Preston, who would share his last penny with an old friend in distress, took up the matter, but the old-timers who knew Woods in his days of prosperity had scattered, and Meadows and several others made up a purse and sent it to Drew at Dallas. Meadows gave $20 and others small amounts.

As a last resort, Drew Woods appealed to the Confederate camp at Dallas. He was a member of Pickett's division which stormed the heights at Gettysburg. He was with Lee until the flag was furled at Appomattox. He was a Virginian by birth and came from a family of wealth and culture. J.W. McMillin, who resides near Bells, went side by side with Drew up that fatal hill. Had "Mac" known of the distress of his old comrade, he would have taken him to his old home. The camp at Dallas provided for him until death closed his eyes, and provided for his last resting place.

Many days and nights have we sat at the campfire with the Woods brothers in the old Indian Territory. They were generous spirits, hail fellows well met; grand entertainers, good storytellers, and the life of the camp, training in the woods for nearly forty years. We can truthfully say that we never met two more congenial spirits than the Woods brothers.

No. 33

Fox Hunting

Sunday Gazetteer, September 4, 1910
[Original newspaper labels this No. 31]

In the seventies, one of the most popular of rural sports was fox chasing in the country around Denison. Many businessmen, after working hard all day, would go to the woods and pass the night in the exciting sport of chasing the fox. The sporting spirit has died out, and the famous trailers of pioneer days have either moved away, grown too old, or are dead. There are at the present time plenty of foxes in the country around Denison, but such an event as a fox hunt is never heard of.

Jack Sims and Col. Tom Lipscomb were the great foxhunters

of the pioneer period, and there were many others of less repute. It is the sport of all sports and, before the war, throughout the South was considered the gentleman's pastime. Southern literature contained a great deal about fox chasing. Every southern man of affluence had his pack of blooded foxhounds. There used to be many good dogs in this city, dogs of blue strain whose pedigree extended back many generations.

There is nothing more exciting or more exhilarating and healthy than following a pack of hounds in full chase of a fleeing fox on a warm trail. The fox is a most cunning animal and will frequently baffle and escape the pursuing pack. We can recollect a night spent in the Hudson Quarters woods with Col. Tom Lipscomb. The dogs opened in grand style, and the colonel said that they had the red of the fox in sight several times. Over hills and down into the dense bottoms of Red River went the fox, closely followed by the dogs. The chase was prolonged for several hours, and yet the fox escaped. The colonel sat around the campfire that night with his head in his hands, almost weeping. The conclusion he arrived at was that the fox had taken to water, swam Red River and escaped, and thus the dogs had lost the scent. Many years after, discussing the night's experience, the colonel declared that it might have been a cat, wolf, or spirit fox. A fox will double, circle, climb a fence, and run along it many yards, jump to the ground, and escape. The dogs are at a loss, become bewildered, and their clamor ceases—the great woods are silent.

We believe that the greatest foxhunter in the South is Captain Ellison, who is at present manager of the Sporting Club at Beaumont. We could tell some stories of the exploits of the little captain that would beat any woodland romance ever published. Ellison was our companion for a number of years in our forays into the Choctaw woods. He never went out without bringing his fox home. He has more fox scalps hanging to his belt than any single hunter that ever followed a pack of hounds. He once chased a fox through three counties in the Choctaw Nation and "holed" the quarry at last in a rocky gorge of the mountains. The chase consumed one whole night of hard riding, including the day following. The fox was a wonder. Time and again he shook the dogs from the trail. That little red fox led the captain a merry chase of many miles through a country noted for the rugged hills which sometimes approach the dignity of mountains. There is nothing more exciting and picturesque than on a crisp autumn night to see the riders getting ready for the chase. Anon come the sweet clarion notes of the hunter's horn, which is answered by the music of the pack that is clamoring for the prey, and men and dogs disappear into the dark arches of the night and are lost to view. The pack has struck a warm trail, the scent streaming up from the moist earth; the pack opens up, and the greatest sport in the American forest is on. He who takes a part at once finds himself longing for similar experience until the habit becomes fixed, and another foxhunter is born.

A foxhunter would pass a deer or wild turkey any time and give Raynard the preference. There is a fascination about the sport that is indescribable. We all know or have seen illustrated in brilliant red colors the famous fox chaser of merry old England, where men and women could be seen leaping fences in the mad pursuit, and the climax of bringing the quarry in—holding it by the tail down toward the yelping pack.

An old-time foxhunter is a great storyteller, and we have passed many a night at the campfire listening to their narratives. Jack Sims, who lived in Denison thirty years ago, was a great foxhunter, and he could give his experience in a piquant, vivid narrative. Jack was a hard rider after the fox and always had a pack of staunch hounds around his home. It was very seldom that a fox ever escaped him.

The pleasures of fox chasing are many, and one that stands out most prominently is the gathering at the campfire in the cool, autumn nights. Old "Cap" Ellison was the best narrator we ever listened to. He was originally from Tennessee and had chased fox over the mountains ever since he was big enough to be lifted into a saddle. He had hunted fox in the old Indian Territory for a great many years. He was a fearless rider, and as long as he could hear the yelp of the hounds, stuck to the business.

A few years ago a party composed of [Tom] Reardon, [Fred] Bogar, Williams of the post office, Will Senter of Bokchito, Capt. Impson, and the writer, went over to Clear Boggy on a hunting frolic. While in camp, another party of hunters joined us. In the party was a Dr. Rutherford, one of the most formidable men physically that we have ever seen. He was a giant in strength and status. This man was a veritable ranger of the woods, passing days and even weeks chasing with his pack of hounds. By profession he was a horse doctor; by practice he was a foxhunter. He loved his dogs better than his wife, who lived neglected at Bokchito. He had dropped into that country an entire stranger, and just as soon as he could, he put his wife into a little house, mounted his horse, and with his pack of hounds started for the woods, where he lived most of the time, sleeping on the ground and living on wild game. He was a great foxhunter; that was all he lived for. One night he captured a grey fox, which was brought into camp and placed in a wagon screened with wire. One of the boys turned the fox loose, and the doctor was wild with rage and wanted to fight the whole camp. The boys protested their innocence but called the doctor's bluff, which seemed to smooth down his ruffled front, and peace was restored. From the time he left his bed until he retired, his whole talk was "fox." Just before we broke camp, he and his pack of hounds left.

It was a hound that caused his tragic end. He stole a hound, and the owner got out papers for his arrest. The constable of the precinct went to execute the mandate of the law but was obliged to kill the doctor, who resisted and attempted to shoot the officer.

You never hear of a foxhunt around Denison anymore, while in early days it was one of our most popular pastimes.

No. 34

Opening of the Alamo Hotel

Sunday Gazetteer, September 11, 1910
[Original newspaper labels this No. 32]

The most notable social event in the pioneer history of Denison was the opening of the Alamo Hotel, on Tuesday, March 18, 1873.

It was given in honor of the completion of the MK&T and the H&TC railways.

There were present distinguished personages from all portions of Texas, and an excursion car from Sedalia, Missouri, for the accommodation of guests arrived, being attached to the regular train. The MK&T officials were here in force, and a number of prominent people were picked up at Parsons, Kansas. The MK&T extended the courtesy of half fare. There were at least 500 guests present, and Denison has never seen, even up to this late period, such a gathering of "fair women and brave men." Swallowtail coats and plug hats were much in evidence, and many of the ladies' costumes were perfectly stunning.

The hall opened at 9 o'clock, and it was a very brilliant affair. The large dining room was set aside for the dance. The music was entrancing, and the gathering did not break up until the crowing of the cock. A Dallas correspondent was present and paid a very pretty compliment to the lady guests. At midnight, "The Fete Champetre" was given. The table d'hôte was never surpassed. There were delicacies from St. Louis and many other points, and there was genuine champagne served. The tickets for the supper and ball were $5.00 each, and it is said that 500 were disposed of.

Looking at the names of the floor managers, the committees of invitation and of reception, we are obliged to heave a sigh. Seventy-five per cent are dead, and the rest are scattered in all parts of the Union. Forty names appear in the lists of the committees, and of that number only one person is at present a resident of Denison. The invitations were gotten up in a beautiful manner, in three different colors, with a gilded lone star in the center.

The ball will never be forgotten by those present. It is a memory that will last as long as life lasts. It was the opening of social life in Denison. People were brought together and acquaintances made that were prolonged for years.

No. 35

The Circus

Sunday Gazetteer, September 18, 1910
[Original newspaper labels this No. 33]

The presence of the Wild West Show in the city last Friday, reminds the *Gazetteer* of old circus days. If we recollect rightly, the first circus to spread canvas here was the Barnum-Bailey combination; this was in the seventies, and the big show was on the lots of Main Street that were purchased recently by a syndicate. The admission was 50 cents and $1.00. As small as Denison was, the circus had big crowds. What helped out was the Indian Territory, people coming from as far north as Atoka and as far west as Paul's Valley. The three-ring feature was not then in vogue, and like everything else in this age of push and progress, the circus has kept up with the procession of events.

The circus people of that period were rougher than those of the present era. A number of fights took place between circus attachés and people who drifted in from the Territory and the country around Denison. On one or two occasions there were stabbing affrays.

The circus tax was not as heavy as at present, and the restrictions were not so tight-laced.

The Robinson Bros. was really the first great show that pitched canvas here. This was in the latter part of the eighties. The Robinson Bros. showed what great progress had been made in circus appurtenances. It was the first show that introduced electric lights for illumination. They had the three rings and the most extensive collection of wild animals ever seen.

Buffalo Bill and his rough riders put in an appearance in the nineties. This show had the biggest crowds of any. The performance was of a character that appealed to the general run of people.

We have had in the past thirty-six years many circuses, but it is a mistake to say they are all alike. They are a great deal better than in the pioneer period. There have been some very poor shows here, when the wagons were dilapidated and the stock run down.

The big shows finally moved over to the racetrack grounds, where the Katy tie-treating plant [W.J. Smith Wood Preserving Company] now is. Buffalo Bill showed over there, and several other large shows also. For the past three years, the shows have pitched their tents in the park, and we don't see that it has hurt the grounds, and it is so convenient to reach the grounds.

The circus is all right and should be encouraged. It is a character of amusement that pleases all. If they are cut out from the park, it is hard to tell where they will go, as we have no convenient grounds in the city limits.

The circus is the legitimate prey of the state, county, and city, and the present tax is high. The circus has devised ways and means to dodge the issue, but since Bill McDonald, the noted ex-captain of the Texas Rangers, has been appointed state tax collector, the shows have had a hard row to travel, and some of them are cutting Texas out of their circuit.

No. 36

Marriages

Successful and Unsuccessful

Sunday Gazetteer, September 25, 1910
[Original newspaper labels this No. 34]

Some of the most prominent nuptial events in Denison have turned out badly, resulting in divorce and a bitter fight for the possession of the child or children.

There was a sensational marriage in Denison along in the seventies. The parties were very prominent in business and social circles, such as it was at that early period. The church bloomed like an oriental flower garden, and the dainty feet of the bride walked on a velvet carpet laid from the entrance of the church to the carriage in waiting. Her wedding trousseau, with a trail several feet in length, was carried by two beautiful children. The presents were many and of a costly character. The wedding banquet is said to have cost much money. In two years this couple separated.

There was another wedding at this same church that turned out badly. The marriage event was a very elaborate affair, and the papers contained glowing accounts of the event and predicted much happiness and prosperity for the bride and groom, who were a young couple just starting out in life. This couple did not go it two years, but separated in about eighteen months, it is said, by the machinations of the bride's parents, who were purse proud, while the son-in-law was a poor young man and had borrowed money to marry. This fact got to the young wife's parents, and a separation soon ensued.

It is singular that another marriage took place at the same church that turned out unhappily, and in recent years there was another swell wedding at the same church, which bore bitter fruit. Then, right around the corner, at another church there have been several weddings where the parties got tired of the marriage ties and went to the divorce court for relief. Striving to keep up appearances, the husband, not being able to keep up with his wife's ambition to dress well and entertain, has separated a number of people in Denison. Some people who married abroad but were residents of Denison have separated. There are, living in Denison at the present, three grass widows who cut up capers in society circles, and whose husbands left them; one in Denver, Colorado, one in Dallas, and one in Houston. The swellest weddings in the history of Denison have, in some instances, turned out badly.

There was a well-known couple that married here and only lived together several months. The husband did not support his wife, so she told the writer, and she was disgusted with the situation and separated from him.

There was another, a Gandy Street marriage, that was short and sweet. They lived together for a brief period. What was the cause of the separation is a mystery—a case of natural disgust, we heard.

The runaway marriages have, on a general thing, turned out unhappily; and young people who have married at a very tender age, not realizing the responsibilities of the married state, have been cut asunder by the divorce courts. There is one woman, at present a resident of North Denison, who has had four husbands and is still in her prime and good looking. Two of her husbands are dead, and two are living.

Some people have been divorced and gone together again, and seem to be living happily. There are several couples of that character here. About two years ago, a well-known resident of Denison slipped off to a neighboring state and was married to a woman from whom he had been divorced for thirty years. He had buried a wife, and she, a husband. They were brought together by their children and are now living happily together in South Denison.

Some people are living together just for the sake of their children. They wish to avoid the scandal of a separation. There are a great many wives and husbands that hate each other but continue to hoodwink the world. They have no respect for the connubial ties and take a fancy to another man or another woman, and go all the gaits. What has happened in Denison has its counterparts in other towns and cities. There are some husbands who wink at the frailties of their wives. There is a commercial understanding between them.

In the seventies there was a marriage at the M.E. Church here that created some gossip. The bride, after living with her husband one week, returned to her parents. She said he was a monster, a brute; and the father of the girl whipped the groom in the Ed Norris livery establishment, in the 300 block West Main Street.

There have been many matrimonial entanglements in Denison which out of courtesy we cannot refer to, as the parties have settled down and are now living happily. Domestic skeletons in the closet are very plentiful. Railway towns seem to have more of them than is common.

Several old men have married young girls, and in almost every instance, the union has turned out very unhappily.

No. 37

Hunting Coon and O'possum

Sunday Gazetteer, October 2, 1910
[Original newspaper labels this No. 35]

A popular innovation in the seventies was coon and o'possum hunting. The country around Denison was then densely wooded, and the furried faces of these nocturnal animals looked out from many forest trees.

Coon and o'possum dogs were plentiful in those early days and were usually the property of Negroes who trained them for the quarry.

There used to be a great many o'possums on the Pawpaw [Creek], east of Denison. Persimmon trees were plentiful, the Pawpaw woods in those days had not as yet been disturbed by the woodsman's axe, and occasionally deer and wild turkey were seen. Deer and wild turkeys used to cross Red River and seek the cool shade of the great trees in the bottoms.

An o'possum hunt is the greatest of all sports; that is, if you have good dogs and congenial companions, and a real old-fashioned Negro along—the kind of colored brother who used to play the banjo at a shake-down before the cluster of cabins.

The o'possum is a wise animal, and the hunting is rather passive, as he will put up no fight against the dogs. A coon will fight to the death, and on Red River we saw a coon whip a dog so badly that he tucked his tail between his legs, and the coon escaped to the brush, the hunting party permitting it to escape.

We have seen an o'possum mauled by dogs and kicked around like a football, with eyes set and glassed. Take your dogs away and go a short distance from him, and the gray ball on the ground will begin to move, open his eyes, and look around. If he thinks the coast is clear, he will get a move on and disappear in the woods.

We once saw in the Pawpaw woods an o'possum hanging by his tail at least thirty feet in the air. A darkey with the party "cooned" the tree and tried in vain to shake the animal loose. As a last resort he shot and killed it, and the o'possum fell into the jaws of the pack of dogs at the foot of the tree.

A coon is a hard problem to dislodge from a tree. He will go out to the end of a tree sometimes, and it takes a gun to bring him.

One beautiful night in the latter part of October, a party of ladies and gentlemen left Denison to go to the Pawpaw woods. It was a merry party—all young people, bubbling over with life and enthusiasm. An old southern darkey was hired as a guide, with his pack of trained dogs that never made a false demonstration. When they stopped at the foot of a tree and gave voice to the night, there was sure to be something up there.

Two large, fat o'possums were killed, and a big campfire was made, and the old darkey and his son commenced to show their learning in preparing the o'possum for the feast. He was slowly barbecued before a fire of live coals. He was basted with bacon, the rich juice permeating the flesh. A lot of sweet potatoes were thrown into the ashes and roasted. In about three hours, the o'possum was announced ready. When knife and fork were thrust into the breast, the skin cracked and white flakes rolled up, and there was a delicious fragrance of roasted young pig. Bread and other fixings had been brought along, and beneath the great trees the banquet was commenced, and we cannot recollect that a party ever enjoyed a meal more. The moon was at its full, and the brilliant light flooded the forest. Thirty-two years have passed, but we cannot remember an occasion where there was so much genuine fun and frolic. We danced, sang, and shouted, and it was the hour when the cocks begin to salute morn before we turned homeward. We killed two o'possums and treed a coon "that would not come down," like the coon of Captain Scott. The men wanted to shoot him out of a crotch in the tree, but the girls of the party pleaded so hard for his life that he was not disturbed.

We had a memorable o'possum hunt with Captain Tom Wright one night in the Pawpaw woods. We got separated from the party and crawled into a dense thicket and went to sleep—too much red liquor. We also passed several nights hunting in the Hudson

Quarters woods and bagged three o'possums in one large persimmon tree.

At the old Fox marble yard on West Main Street, the greatest feast in the history of Denison was given. Col. J.D. Yocom was a guest on that occasion. Of the number who sat down to that table, four are dead. Two o'possums were served, being prepared in the old southern style by a darkey and his wife who had been there before. It was a great feast and lasted until midnight.

In the seventies and eighties, coon and o'possum hunting was much in vogue, and some of the happiest days of pioneer life were passed in the woods at the sport. But the good old days are gone, and it is a very rare occurrence that an o'possum and coon hunt takes place. The sport is confined almost entirely to the rural population. Before the Civil War, in the southern states it was a national pastime, indulged in by ladies and gentlemen, and every plantation had its pack of trained dogs and darkeys and old mammas who could prepare an o'possum in a manner never to be forgotten.

No. 38

Gold in Indian Territory

Sunday Gazetteer, October 9, 1910
[Original newspaper labels this No. 36]

In the seventies and eighties there was considerable excitement in Denison and throughout the country over the reported discovery of gold in the Wichita Mountains in the western portion of the Chickasaw Nation. Gold was declared to be taken out in paying quantities, and two or three companies were organized for exploration. A number of people fitted themselves out and went from Denison, and after traveling over the country and suffering many hardships, returned to Denison disappointed; for the truth of it was that not a particle of gold in paying quantities was ever dug out of the red hills of that country.

The excitement had almost subsided when, in a short period, St. Louis papers published a story giving an account of gold discoveries in that section, and [stating] that a nugget worth $500 had been brought out. This was a lie, but the report was sufficient to start another exodus from Denison and this section. One party was gone a month, and in the party was a young woman. They went to the Fort Arbuckle country. One day the young woman wandered from the camp and was soon lost in the many trails that seamed the hill. She wandered for several miles and nearly perished with hunger and fright. At night she heard the wolves running in the hills and the dismal hooting of owls. A party of cowboys was organized, and on the morning of the third day after her disappearance from the camp, the young lady was found. She was almost delirious. She had wandered about twenty miles, going west from the camp all the time. She never recovered from the experience and was ever after an invalid, dying in Tennessee later.

Another party had a gruesome experience. They ran across an old cabin in the foothills and discovered an old man dead, seated in a chair before a fireplace. He was a hermit and had lived there a number of years. His only companion was a faithful hound, that after the death of his master disappeared and was never seen or heard of again.

A great deal of prospecting was carried on, and the many holes dug in the mountains can yet be seen. A company introduced machinery and went after the precious metal in a systematic manner but at last, in supreme disgust, moved away.

The government sent an expert to that country, who in his report declared that there might be gold in the mountains. That expression, "might be gold," was another dazzling allurement, and parties went to the mountains from all over the country, some going from Denison.

A Denison party, headed by George Bridges, were glad to escape with their lives, as a roving party of horse thieves fired into their camp one night and killed a horse. The wagon was abandoned but afterwards recovered by cowboys who lived at old Fort Washita.

This country had evidently been worked for gold either by the early Spanish settlers or Indian tribes. There were tangible evidences of that. Crude machinery was discovered, and a large hole dug in the side of the mountain was still visible.

John Grant, who was for many years a trader and stock raiser near old Fort Arbuckle, said that gold in the mountains was only a myth. No later than ten years ago, there was great excitement over the reported discovery of gold in the Wichita Mountains, not far from Lawton, and excavations were carried on extensively, without much success.

Parties who went from Denison told a great many strange stories of their adventures. One man saw a panther, another a bear.

At that period, the Arbuckle country was a lonely section, with no settlements. It was a great refuge for desperate characters, murderers, and especially horse thieves. It was a great game country, deer and wild turkeys being plentiful. The writer once saw about thirty deer filing out of the mountains going to the prairies, and many large droves of wild turkeys.

The railroads have penetrated that country, and where wolves once bayed the moon and struck terror to the camper, the toot, toot of the locomotive is now heard.

No. 39

Newspaper Editors

Sunday Gazetteer, October 16, 1910
[Original newspaper labels this No. 36]

It is a singular fact that the newspaper editors of Denison since the publication of the first paper are nearly all dead. Those remaining are B.C. Murray, Geo. B. Goodwin, and R.P. Burhans.

The first man in the field was named [George A.] Cutler, who conducted the *Red River Journal*. After Mr. Murray began the publication of the *Daily News*, James W. Burson soon afterwards began the publication of the *Evening Cresset*. Mr. Burson later bought the *Daily News*, and the name of the paper was changed to the *Herald*. Regs M. Thomas published the *Evening Tribune*, which was a weakling [*sic*]. Thomas had the fashion of making his reporters sign their names to everything they wrote.

Colonel Bogie, a Missourian, published a daily in the second story of the Nolan building on the corner of Main Street and Austin Avenue. The Chapman Bros. [Charles W. and William M.] published a daily at the same time, and the city editor was Mr. [Willard Arnold] Johnson, who at the last state election was elected state senator. [Later he was lieutenant governor.] He has for a number of years published a paper at Memphis, in the Panhandle.

Col. T. [Thomas] J. Crooks fell heir to the Bogie plant, and after a short career, the Crooks outfit was absorbed by the celebrated editor, Mose Harris, who lasted only a short time. Lee Linn, a brilliant newspaperman, was brought here from Indiana to help the great boom out. His paper was the foundation of the *Denison Daily Herald*. Dr. [Robert H.] Saunders, a resident of the Indian Territory, published a daily in the John Ourand building, opposite the *Gazetteer* office.

A young fellow by the name of [Ed] Lane published a daily in an office in the 400 block of Main Street. It was a vituperative sheet and soon played out. The editor had a gun duel with Charley Scholl. The Scholl Bros. [Charles H. and Mortimer Maughs "Mort"] published a daily which was soon merged into a weekly. There was a weekly publication that appeared for about two months and suspended for lack of funds, the editor's name being Caruthers, who has been dead a number of years.

The above is about the history of the Denison press since the town started. With the advent of George B. Goodwin and E. [Elwin] A. Thompson, the *Daily Herald* has occupied the field as no other daily ever has, and now the financial genius of that paper has gone to join the great majority.

No. 40
Henry Tackett, Desperado

Sunday Gazetteer, October 23, 1910
[Original newspaper labels this No. 37]

Denison in the seventies was the home of many desperate men. They had drifted in from the cow-towns of Texas, Kansas, and Missouri. At that period we had all of the vices of the frontier town, and law and order were scoffed at. Dance houses, gambling resorts, and houses of prostitution outnumbered the respectable business houses. You could not escape them; they flourished everywhere, under the noses of respectable people. At night the demimonde flaunted their finery on Main Street, inviting people to the dance halls and other questionable abodes. Thousands of cattle were coming in from the west, and with them came that picturesque character—the cowboy.

There was a young fellow by the name of Henry Tackett, who arrived with one of the droves. Tackett was not a cowboy, but he had got in with them, helping at the chuck wagon. It was said that Tackett was a product of the Pecos country, and that he had killed a Mexican down there over a game of monte, cutting the Mexican's throat.

Tackett was in a great deal of trouble in Denison. There was then down on Skiddy Street (now respectable Chestnut Street) a small colony of mongrels—half Negroes, half Chinese. They were a bad lot and were frequently arrested. One of them, called "Dunce," was a desperate character. Dunce said that Tackett was the only man that he was ever afraid of. One night Tackett, while drunk, went to the home of Dunce, which was in the second story of an old building just back of the Muller Block [204 West Main]. The room was full of Negroes and Chinamen. When Tackett entered, he carried in his hand a dirk. Dunce screamed and, seeing no way of escape, jumped out of the window to the alley below, a distance of about ten feet, and thus escaped.

Tackett was a tinhorn gambler, and sometimes he would do respectable work. He made two or three trips as brakeman with "Long John" on the Katy, and was caught stealing from a cowboy while asleep and was put off the caboose at Eufaula, in the Creek Nation. The cowboy went for his gun to kill Tackett.

In a few days Tackett worked his way down to Denison. He next appeared in a row with a tinhorn gambler, and it was agreed between them that the difficulty should be settled in a duel with Winchesters on Crawford Street, in the 200 block. The hour was set, and Tackett was promptly on the ground with his forty-five. The writer was a reporter for the *Daily News* and went over to see battle, but the tinhorn gambler had a streak of yellow in him and did not show up. Tackett waited for him nearly an hour.

The incident was reported in the *Daily News*, and Tackett did not like the manner in which it was written, and said that he would cut the d—n reporter's throat. The writer was standing in the same building in which this is written and at the entrance to a hallway which was at the foot of a stairway on the east side of the building. Tackett crossed over from the opposite side of the street, and when he had arrived at the sidewalk, pulled out a large knife with the remark: "D—n you; I have come over to cut your throat!" Charley Everitt, a famous Katy conductor, who was a bad man, too, happened along and said to Tackett, "What are you going to do with that knife?" and stepped in front of him to put it up, and all hands go over to the "Blue Goose" and take a drink. We have always said that only the timely arrival of Everitt saved our life, for Tackett was intent on murder.

One day Tackett went up to old Red River City (now Warner) and commenced to "whoop-up" things. A northbound freight stopped, and Tackett swore that it was either "a free ride or a free fight" and jumped onto the platform of the caboose. There happened to be in the caboose Lee Hall of the Texas Rangers. Tackett, it seems, did not know Hall. The conductor requested Tackett to pay his fare or get off at Colbert. "I will not pay any fare or get off either," answered Tackett. Hall waited until the train arrived at Colbert and told Tackett to "vamoose." Tackett went for his knife. Hall knocked him over the head with a six-shooter and then pitched him onto the depot platform.

I have selected Tackett as one of the very worst men that ever lived in Denison. He was about 25 years old, short in stature, and as dark as an Indian. He left here and drifted to Fort Worth, where he got into serious trouble. He was finally killed in a dance-house row in the Panhandle, when the Fort Worth and Denver Railroad was building.

Fig. 13. Alpheus Remember Collins, leading Denison "boomer."

No. 41

Denison "Boomers"

Sunday Gazetteer, October 30, 1910
[Original newspaper labels this No. 38]

The greatest and the most resourceful boomer that Denison ever had was A.R. Collins. He was irrepressible. He did more to attract attention to Denison than any man who has ever lived here. There was in his character an element of Rooseveltism. He was a fighter in the commercial sense, and liked to meet and conquer obstacles. It is a pity that death took A.R. Collins away in the prime of manhood. He never failed to stand with a firm and unalterable determination for those factors which he believed would make Denison the pride of North Texas. There have been imitators, but none who could size up with A.R. Collins. Collins loved money, but he was never afraid to turn it loose when it would benefit Denison. He was supposed to be a very rich man, but his wealth to a great extent was fictitious.

We have no boomers at the present time compared with the leading spirits of the seventies and eighties. The present class do not seem to know how to go about the thing. Their efforts miscarry. There used to be a businessman here by the name of D.W.C. Davis. On his tomb should have been engraved the epitaph, "Killed by hard work in the rustle after the almighty dollar." While Davis was not a town builder, he was a valuable citizen and did much for Denison. He died at an early age and left a fortune for some other person to enjoy.

There was another boomer here who acquired wealth and then died. The widow married, and another man enjoyed the thousands that he left. There should have been placed upon this man's tombstone the dollar mark, if success if to be measured by dollars; if the chase for money is the true aim of humanity and its highest destiny, then of all places it should be engraved deeply on that one shaft where it has never yet been placed—the tombstone.

Lee Linn, who was brought here as an instrument to push the boom and conducted a daily paper along those lines, was a great editor. He had as an assistant a man of kindred spirit, Tobe Holt. Every day Linn would walk into the office, and his first remark was, "What shall it be today, Tobe?" Then Holt, in startling headlines, would tell of some enterprise that Denison was about to land, and which was pure fiction. Hundreds of such articles appeared in Linn's paper. Linn's journalism did a great deal of good for Denison and brought to the town much enterprise and wealth. As a boom writer, Linn was the greatest editor that Denison ever had.

Then we had George B. Goodwin, who helped Denison along a great deal. He was built on the boom order and told in more forcible editorials what was good for Denison than perhaps did Linn.

John J. Fairbanks used to be one of the most notable of Denison boomers. He was mixed up very conspicuously with the great boom of twenty-one years ago [1889] that almost made paupers of some of our best citizens, and they never got on their feet afterwards.

The early times and conditions brought to the front many boomers. They are incidental to western life as it was in Denison thirty and thirty-five years ago. There is not living in Denison at the present time a single man who has the courage or the audacity of the men who pushed Denison along in the pioneer days.

Tom Larkin [head of the Board of Trade] proved a failure here, not for want of effort but for the reason that his labors were not appreciated, and there were too many "pull backs" working against him. It seems that Beaumont is appreciating Larkin.

We have had a class of town-builders who were never willing to put out a dollar unless they could see a return of two. They are with us yet. Still, this class of men have done a good work for Denison in their selfishness. If they have made money, they have also spent money for public enterprises that have benefitted the public good.

Denison was a live town in the boom period. There was plenty of money in circulation, and times were better than they have ever been since. It was the period that put money in circulation. [Wendell P.] Rice and his followers built the cotton mill and helped Denison to expand. It was in boom days the liveliest and most up-to-date town in North Texas. There were plenty of men on our streets in those days who could sign a check for $100,000. Everything was pictured in roseate colors, and the future of Denison has never looked so hopeful since. We have settled down to a slow, steady growth, and we are living in hope if we die in despair. It looks as if we were on the eve of great things, and that Denison will take a great step forward. Prosperity is knocking loudly at our door, and we will open and let her in.

No. 42
Tandy C. Walker

Sunday Gazetteer, November 13, 1910
[Original newspaper labels this No. 39]

The papers recently announced the death of Tandy C. Walker. Tandy will be recollected in Denison, as he was in the eighties and a portion of the nineties almost a weekly visitor to the city.

The trainmen of the Katy on the Choctaw Division thirty years ago [1880] will have a vivid recollection of Tandy, as he used to break the monotony frequently with his six-shooter. Tandy used to live at the Canadian River, south side, on a high hill, and it was reported that he had two wives. Every trainman on the Choctaw Division was afraid of him, and when he got into a caboose, he always protested against paying his fare at the mouth of a six-shooter. He was a free passenger and no questions asked.

In 1879 he killed John Morrison and pulled out from the Canadian, and settled close to Stonewall. He was one of the Governor Overton regime, being appointed captain of the Chickasaw militia. In his playful moods, Tandy used to make the conductors and trainmen dance while he shot around their feet. The writer was in a caboose at Reams Switch when he shot several holes in the cupola and then rode free to Eufaula.

There used to be a notorious Creek Indian who lived on a farm on the Katy near the Canadian River. One morning he was found dead in the railway cut, with a bullet hole through his head. On the morning of the killing, Tandy was at Canadian Station and enquired of the section men if they had seen a dead Indian along the line, and no one ever questioned after that, that Walker was the man who killed him. The Indian was a notorious horse thief, and his riddance was a great relief.

In 1877, he [Tandy] was elected to the Choctaw council. He was also sheriff in the Canadian district in 1874. He was a Confederate soldier and was in a number of engagements, the most notable being Wilson Creek. He was a scout for Col. [Douglas H.] Cooper. In 1868 he was elected captain and provost marshal for Gen. [T.C.] Hindman. He was for a long period with the Dawes Commission.

At the Grand Southern saloon in this city one night, Tandy had a difficulty with Joe Bryan, a prominent official of the Choctaw Nation. Walker struck Bryan on the head with a six-shooter and then, grabbing him, threw him over the bar among the fixtures.

Tandy Walker was a remarkable Indian. He was a fine talker, and many a night in Dr. Yeidel's saloon have we listened to his reminiscences. He was for many years a subscriber to the *Gazetteer* and was a great reader of our hunting narratives, and it was at his instance that we described old Fort Washita. Walker was an educated Indian. He was educated at Scullyville [Oklahoma].

In early days, Walker was one of the best known of our Indian visitors. He was here about one year ago and was lamenting the great changes that had come to his country, and was not feeling very kindly toward the white people. He was married and leaves a large family of boys and girls. His mother was a Chickasaw and his father a Choctaw.

No. 43

Importance of the Indian Trade

Sunday Gazetteer, November 20, 1910
[Original newspaper labels this No. 40]

In the seventies and eighties, more Indians visited Denison than any city on the border. The majority were prominent in the national affairs of the Five Nations. They had plenty of money and spent it. Everything was wide open. The Indian was a high stepper and a prodigal spender. They gambled, drank, and went to see girls. Thousands of dollars were put into circulation by this class. They were liberal patrons of all classes of business; in fact, in those days at least 50 per cent of our revenue came from the Indian Territory. There were no towns of any commercial importance across the river. The trade area of Denison embraced 100 miles north and south and east and west, and sometimes it reached as far north as the Creek Nation. There were no land restrictions in the Five Nations. Many of the prominent Indians owned from 50,000 to 75,000 and 100,000 acres of land, which was devoted largely to stock raising. The MK&T, the only railway line operating in the Territory, was unable to carry all of the cattle to the eastern markets. The congestion was not relieved until the Santa Fe and other lines were put into operation.

When the Indian disposed of his cattle, he used to come to Denison and spend his money, get his goods, and have a good time. In the seventies and eighties they spent millions of dollars here. We have lost all that trade, and the conditions have changed in the Territory; the big pastures have gone and are now cut up into small possessions. Big cities have sprung up, big stores have opened, and the people can get what they want at home. Another thing—an Indian will not patronize a town where the saloon is disbanded. When they leave home, they want to have a good time and are willing to pay for it. The very few Indians that visit us patronize the bootlegging joints, and as a class they have but little money to spend. You hardly ever see a wealthy Indian on the streets of Denison at the present time. If they want liquor, they can get it openly and above board in Oklahoma, a state that has prohibition laws but which are not enforced.

In the seventies and a portion of the eighties, the trade of the Indian Territory was worth more to us than the payroll of the MK&T. The Indian of the early period was a romantic character. With his cattle feeding on the vast pastures and increasing in numbers rapidly, his purse was always full. He had many retainers, cowboys, who looked after the stock. They never were an agricultural people and tilled but little land. No provision was made for cattle in the winter. When the cold biting winds swept down from the north, the cattle drifted into the bottoms and picked up their living as best they could; thousands perished, but the increase kept the quota full. The motto of the Indian was, "Let tomorrow take care of tomorrow, leave the things of the future to fate; what is the use to anticipate sorrow, life's troubles never come too late."

When he visited Denison, he was almost sure to get on a high lonesome. The keys of the city were handed over to him, and the officers took but little notice of his escapades. He was as free to do as he pleased here as at home on his verdant prairies. We have seen a prominent Chickasaw official hatless, coatless, staggering through the streets, and he was as tenderly cared for as a lost child; and it would have been considered a sacrilege to have put him (where his condition should have consigned him) in jail. We have seen hundreds of such instances. The jail doors never opened yet to receive as a guest a prominent and wealthy Indian. Not only he, but a host of his friends, would have resented the insult, and it would have cost Denison thousands of dollars in trade.

Many prominent and wealthy white men who had married Indian women visited Denison. As a usual thing, they were wealthy. Some of them acquired property here. The Fishers and Rennies, for instance. Some were storekeepers in the Territory and did all of their trading here.

In the nineties [1890s], new railways and large towns were springing up, and the disbanding of the Five Nations began to cut seriously into the trade of Denison, and then Prohibition went into effect, and the Indian would not come here; and our trade with the Territory has been beaten into a frazzle.

No. 44

Jews in Early Denison

Sunday Gazetteer, November 27, 1910
[Original newspaper labels this No. 42]

The Jews have been the backbone of Denison ever since the town was incorporated. They were among the very first to raise the flag of trade, and they are today among our most prosperous and enterprising citizens. No nationality has done more to advance the material interests of Denison than the Israelites. They have stuck to Denison through thick and thin.

About the first to engage in the mercantile business here was the famous Star Store. The firm was known as Waterman, Star & Co. Then we had the Casper Bros., and later on Joe Linz and Phil Slutzkey, jewelers; and the wholesale and retail liquor house of Eppstein & Bro. The latter firm afterward was merged into Eppstein & Son. A. Teah was another merchant of the pioneer period. Henry Watermann used to conduct a livery, feed and sale stable. M. Goldsoll was a prominent businessman here in pioneer days, and L. Bernstein was a prosperous merchant. A large number of restaurants and saloons have been conducted by Jews here. They were in pioneer days large buyers of cotton; in fact, in the seventies they monopolized the cotton market.

About twenty-five years ago, the U.S. Clothing House people [Henry and Elias Regensburger] located here, and they have built up a business that is the pride of the city. Two of the most brilliant writers that have ever been connected with the Denison press were Jews. There is no walk in life that the Jews of Denison have not honored.

Where is there a better citizen than Dr. [Isaac] Yeidel? The leading sporting man of Denison (Sam Berliner) was a Jew, and he still owns property here. We have Max Goldman in the insurance business, a very popular businessman. Max Grundstein of the old Star Store was one of the most popular businessmen that ever lived here. We have Simon Hirsch with us yet, conducting a bookstore. Simon was one of the pillars of the Star Store.

We must not forget our old friend Albert Lichtenstein, one of the best citizens who has ever lived here, and Louis Lebrecht who was mayor for two terms and did so much to advance the material interests of the city. His death was a public calamity.

The Jewish population of this city have, as a general thing, been prosperous. They are well behaved, and it is very rare that they become involved in escapades. They have frequently held religious services here. We believe that the first Jew that was buried with religious rites was Joe Beers of the Eppstein liquor house. Dr. Yeidel has officiated in several occasions. Jewish young ladies have been leaders in our public schools and were among the best of their profession.

The Jews of this city never were a clannish class, but free and easy and always intimate and sociable with our people. The prosperous ones never held back when money was wanted to give the city a push ahead. Jewish blood has circulated in the arteries of business in Denison ever since the town was laid out. They have always been liberal patrons of the press, spending thousands of dollars in advertising their wares.

The Jews have a beautiful and well-kept cemetery [part of Oakwood Cemetery], and many who were early residents of Denison rest there.

No. 45

Dr. Lightfoot, Street Faker

Sunday Gazetteer, December 4, 1910
[Original newspaper labels this No. 42,
like the previous issue]

Ever since Denison was a town, it has been the stamping ground of street fakers. We call them street fakers, for the majority were frauds of the rankest character.

The chief among them all was the celebrated Dr. Lightfoot, who sold medicine and pulled teeth. The doctor was the smoothest, smartest orator that ever appeared upon our streets. He was a man of commanding presence, and many ladies in Denison thought him so handsome and fascinating that they opened their doors to him. One well-known woman actually fell in love with him, and the escapade created no little talk, not to say scandal.

Dr. Lightfoot dressed in a picturesque garb. He wore a cowboy hat, and his long black hair fell in graceful curls down on his shoulders. Thousands flocked to hear his talk, and thousands had their teeth extracted. The doctor had a band of music and flaming lights. After devoting an hour to teeth pulling, he closed with a very interesting talk. He sold in Denison thousands of bottles of his medicine. The people were captivated with him.

Lightfoot was of Indian extraction. His mother was a Potawatomi, and his father a trader. He was very proud of his Indian lineage. He was in Denison about one month, and the last night his crowds were as large as when he was at the height of his popularity.

He visited a number of Texas cities and in all received an ovation.

He went to San Antonio for the purpose of spending the winter but was attacked with smallpox and died at that place. The doctor was a fatalist. When ill, he was isolated in a tent and refused all succor, the papers stating that he said that his time had come and he wished to die. But the fact is, he persisted in drinking ice water contrary to the order of his physician, and that killed him.

He gave away in Denison considerable money and was generous to a fault. He made money very fast but did not seem to appreciate its value.

Dr. Lightfoot had many followers, but they were pygmies compared to him. He was the king of them all. He stated to the writer that he cleaned up several thousand dollars during his stay in this city, and we do not believe the statement exaggerated. The town went wild over him. His medicine was a preparation that was warranted to cure many ills. It was put on sale principally at the Waldron drug store, and thousands of bottles were sold, and it seemed to give satisfaction.

It was said that the doctor worshipped invisible spirits and would talk to them the same as in the flesh. He had a guardian spirit. When he appeared upon the streets, he always attracted much attention, which seemed to please him. He had a magnificent turnout [horse-drawn vehicle], and everything was done in a manner of royalty. He left at San Antonio about $50,000 in the banks.

No. 46

Christmas and Little Mary

Sunday Gazetteer, December 25, 1910
[Original newspaper labels this No. 43]

Christmas and New Year's of the early times was not like it is at the present. There was more fun, earnest joy, and a good time generally than you see now. Several Christmases brought snow, which heightened the pleasures of the holidays. All night long you could hear the jingle of the bells and the merry laugher of the young people who were out to make a night of it.

Denison was more cosmopolitan, and all classes mixed more generally. The ladies used to keep open house, and people were welcomed who would not be tolerated at present. There are nice social distinctions (a sort of codfish aristocracy) existing among those who have a little money but no manners, and many assume manners who have neither manners nor money. All of the churches had their Christmas trees, and happy throngs of children were present. Christmas trees and decorations were more elaborate than at present. The people had just as much money, but there are thousands of things in the toy world that were not thought of then. Still the pleasure and spirit were there, if the toys were not. At many houses the callers were treated to wine punch.

There was an incident that happened on Gandy Street worthy of mention. It was a moonlight night and snow was on the ground, and the weather was very cold. At the mansion, the parlor was lighted, and sweet strains of music floated out to the street. An old man with a distaff was espied looking wistfully into the lighted parlor, and he seemed entranced with the music played on the piano. The young lady of the house went out to the front porch, and seeing the old man, asked him if he was cold. He replied,

"Very cold and hungry." She invited him into the dining room and spread before him a feast of cold turkey, boiled ham, and other delicacies, and a large bowl of punch was also brought to him. The old man was so overcome with emotion that he wept and left the house blessing the young lady matron. They don't do that way now.

The saloons did an enormous business in the early days, and thousand of people from the Territory were our best patrons. It is a little curious, but at that period there were more business houses in Denison than at present. Everybody was flush, and the stores were always crowded. During the holidays, the poor people were hunted up. The churches and the benevolent people gave liberally. Many of the poorest children were brought to the churches and made happy around the Christmas trees.

Frequently there were public occasions at the halls, where people without class or distinction used to meet and enjoy themselves. Fireworks were a prominent feature of Christmas. We have seen the entire police force stand on opposite sides of Main Street fighting a battle with Roman candles. During the holiday week, the keys of the city were turned over to strangers, and the police looked leniently upon lawbreakers. The principal transgressors were the citizens of the Territory, who filled the little city jail in the 200 block on old Skiddy Street. That is about the oldest landmark here, and a fragment of it still remains. Gift making was as liberal then as now.

Let us tell you a little story that happened over on Crawford Street.

It was Christmas Eve. The day previous, there had been a heavy fall of snow, and the weather had turned very cold. The moon was at its full, and there was a white world beneath the million stars that scintillated in the firmament. A man wrapped in a buffalo coat stepped out of a saloon onto the sidewalk, stopped a moment, and then started down Main Street to Austin Avenue, going south as far as Crawford Street.

The dance halls were in full blast. There were drunken men and women carousing on the floor. "Get your partners for the next set," yelled the floor manager. The three dance houses on Skiddy Street and Austin Avenue were like beehives. The city was full of drunken Indians and cowmen. On any other occasion, the man would have tarried and probably entered one of the dance halls.

The man was one of the leading gamblers of Denison, and he had plenty of money and a big heart. Some person had told him that a little girl had been deserted by a drunken father. That she was not only without food, but in bed sick. The gambler walked a few yards and stopped before a dilapidated two-story house. While he was looking at the house, a low cry arrested his steps. The man pushed the front door open and entered the hall. He then ascended the stairs, which creaked and groaned beneath his weight like a living thing in torture. He reached the hall above and paused to listen. A feeble moan penetrated the dividing wall, stole out into the cold air, and died away amid the roaring of the wind outside, which seemed to shake the whole house. It was a child's voice, and the sadness of it seemed to touch him deeply.

On the floor in the hall was an empty whisky bottle with a candle in it that was almost spent. He took a match from his pocket and lit the candle. Before him was a door that was battered and dented as if by the blows of a hatchet. He lifted the latch and stepped into the room.

Would that I had the power to sketch that room as described to me by the gambler. It was the house of desolation and cheerlessness, and discomfort reigned supreme. The fireplace was unlighted by even a spark. A heap of sodden ashes and a mound of snow lay on the sunken and cracked hearthstone. One of the two windows was roughly boarded up, and the sash of the other bulged out with rags coarsely stuffed in. There were no chairs. At the farther corner stood a bedstead, or what had once been one. The headboard had disappeared, probably having been used for fuel. A heap of wheat straw covered by an old blanket composed the bed. It was a bed hardly fit for a dog to lie on, and yet a girl lay on it—a girl, too, born in the mould of beauty.

The gambler stood with clasped hands and gazed upon her. In years, she might have been eight winters. Her face was pallid and as white as the snow upon the floor and almost as cold. Her little features were shrunken, hunger and neglect having eaten away their fullness; and, mothers, where your fond darlings have plump, round cheeks, centered with a dimple which you have so often kissed, this wan cheek showed only a depression. Yet, emaciated as it was, the face was lovely. Starvation and sickness had done their utmost and yet had left it beautiful. She turned in bed and lifted her eyes to the countenance of the visitor wonderingly.

The gambler sat upon the edge of the bed, took her thin hand in his, and said: "My little girl, what is your name?"

And she, in a low, weak voice, replied, "Mary." She looked at him for a moment with her large, bright eyes, and said, "I wonder where Father is on such a night as this? How cold it is."

Tears moistened the eyes of the gambler, and then he said, "Mary, I am going right to work to make you happy and comfortable and get you well."

"I never, never shall get well, sir; I am going to die," she replied.

"Oh, no, you ain't; you must get well," answered the gambler.

"But it is so cold here. I will be warmer in the ground."

The gambler arose. Could it be possible that the child was dying? He pulled off his great buffalo coat and placed it over her; then he knelt beside her and smoothed back the tangled strands of golden hair that swept her forehead, and soothed her with low murmurs as a mother soothes her babe at her breast.

The gambler smiled; his face brightened in hope, and he said to himself: "If she can only sleep." And then aloud: "I must leave you for a moment. I am going to get some wood and make a nice warm fire, and bring you medicine and something good to eat, and tomorrow I will take you to my home, and you shall be my little girl."

The gambler went out into the night and cold. An hour probably passed when he entered the room again with a man who now sleeps at Preston. He approached the bed, stepping softly. Mary was perfectly quiet under the great robe. He placed his hand upon the cover and folded it slowly back, until her face, pillowed amid its wealth of golden hair, was seen white and cold. Mary was dead!

And then, as if stricken with the sense of some great loss—the fading out of some great hope—the gambler knelt at the bedside.

The wind roared outside, and the firelight died away in ghostly glimmers along the wall. The gambler broke out and sobbed aloud.

Mary had a nice casket, and the gambler managed to get a few flowers, but the mourners were few. Rev. [M.A.] Daugherty spoke a few words at the last resting place, and the little girl has slept for over thirty years at Oakwood; and if there is a future life and a place called heaven, little Mary is surely on the right hand.

No. 47
Fay Templeton, Actress

Sunday Gazetteer, January 8, 1911
[Original newspaper labels this No. 45]

What is left of the old guard, the first residents of Denison, will recollect little Fay Templeton. John Templeton's troupe was about the first to visit this city, and Fay, then a little girl in short dresses, was a star and a great favorite with Denison theatergoers. She was a beautiful child with large liquid black eyes, very fair complexion, and raven black hair that was disposed to curl. Fay was received in a number of homes here. When she performed, the house was crowded, and when she made her first appearance she never failed to receive an ovation.

Alice Vann, her mother, who married John Templeton, had a romantic and somewhat painful career. She was arrested and lodged in jail in Missouri as a Confederate spy. She was placed in jail with a number of other women. After she was granted her liberty, the old building fell down, and a number of women were buried beneath the wreck and killed.

Alice Vann, the mother of Fay, was sent out of the country and warned to never again appear within the Federal lines. At that period she was a very beautiful and fascinating young woman. It is said her beauty helped her to freedom. She had been released only a day or so when the jail collapsed. Among those killed were two sisters of Bill Anderson, the noted guerrilla who drenched the Missouri and Kansas border in human blood. It is said the killing of the Anderson girls started their brother on his bloody career, and he was a noted member of the Quantrill band until near the end of the war.

After Alice Vann was set at liberty, she met and eventually married John Templeton. The fruit of the marriage was Fay Templeton, who in her day was one of the most famous actresses on the American stage and won applause in London, Paris, Vienna and St. Petersburg.

For a number of years Fay played to Denison audiences, and she never lost her hold on the hearts and affections of our people. There used to be a theater on Woodard in the 200 block, where the wood yard of George Carver stood. If you pass there and look at the rear of the two-story brick, you will see an old and very dilapidated wooden building which was thirty years ago the only play house in Denison.

One night an incident happened there that caused a big sensation and was the talk of the town and exploited in the newspapers in big headlines. During the performance of a southern war drama, Fay Templeton appeared upon the stage with a Confederate flag and sang "Down in Dixie," or "The Bonnie Blue Flag." Major [Edward J.] Strang, U.S. Quartermaster of this district, was present. He jumped up in his seat and, pointing his finger at Fay, ordered her to stop the song and put the flag out of sight. There was a great uproar all over the house and yells and hisses to put the major out. The major's wife grabbed his coat tails and pulled him down to his seat, and, muttering threats, he left the theater. At that time there were a number of ex-Confederates living in this city and among them a few of Quantrill's band. They wanted to make a personal matter of the incident, but the Templetons only had a one-night's engagement, and the request to play another night, bring out the stars and bars, and sing the song over could not be granted.

The Templetons appeared here all through the seventies and eighties. Fay was growing in fame and was one of the most beautiful and clever actresses on the American stage. So the Templetons essayed a larger and more profitable field of action. Fay was a star all over the East, and Chicago, New York, and other large cities went wild over her. She pursued the course of all leading stage beauties, married two or three times and got a divorce each time she took on a husband.

Fay performed in Galveston and passed through here in her special car recently. It is said that she was deeply affected when she arrived here, and the tears stole into her eyes, and with quivering lips, she said: "Dear old Denison. Alas, how things have changed! I would like to stop here for a day and see the old town which was the scene of my early career."

Fay Templeton has grown enormously rich at her profession and has provided her mother with a magnificent home on the Hudson River near New York City. Old John Templeton, her father, is dead and sleeps in a Missouri town.

It is youth, beauty, and talent that win in the theatrical race. The first two have departed from the little girl who first made her appearance in Denison and delighted us for so many years. She has bloomed and faded, and prettier figures and faces have supplanted her place on the stage. She must be looking into the face of fifty years. The last account of her we read several years ago. She was then in New York City and quite a noted actress. She was then mentioned as having had trouble with her husband. She always retained her maiden name. She first appeared here when she was about twelve years of age. John Templeton was an ugly man. Fay inherited her wonderful beauty from her mother, Alice Vann, who was very pretty. Fay was developed beyond her years, and many of the "chappies" in Denison were in love with her, and no doubt she received lots of love billet-doux from them. If you are keeping tab on theatrical events, you will notice that her name never appears among the stage celebrities, and she is probably living with her mother on the Hudson. She had sense enough to save her money.

Fig. 14.
Fay Templeton, actress.
Source: Wikipedia.

No. 48

Old Man Bozarth and the Gobbler

Sunday Gazetteer, January 15, 1911
[Original newspaper labels this No. 46]

Thirty-six years ago, in company with John Collett, we left Denison and made our first trip to the [Indian] Territory woods. In the Sassafras Creek country, there was a little two-room log cabin. It was primitive on the inside and outside, and the grounds were also primitive. There was an old cornfield that had been cultivated by a Choctaw full-blood, but he had long ago left for parts unknown. The cabin was occupied by Joseph Bozarth [1840–1892] and wife and a little waif called Fannie [Sarah Frances Bozarth].

Bozarth had drifted down through the Territory and had planted his stakes at the cabin. He was a hunter and lived more by the chase than farming. His wife [Julia Eveline "Eva" Mershon] was one of the most remarkable women we ever met, a diamond in the rough that only needed a little polishing. If she had been thrown into another sphere of life, she would have been called a strong-minded woman and made her mark in the world. She was ambitious, a good talker, and even at this late period in life, we can remember some of her conversation which left a lasting impression.

"Old Man Bozarth," as her husband was called, from a mental standpoint was not the equal of his wife. He seemed to have no ambition beyond his pack of hounds and the chase. Like Nimrod, he was a mighty hunter. The wisest wild turkey that ever roamed the virgin Choctaw woods country was no more cunning than he. There used to be an old veteran gobbler over on Sassafras that had been shot at so often and escaped that the hunters and cowboys declared it was a spirit and when shot at sometimes would disappear. The old man heard the stories, and said he would have that gobbler or burst. Time and time again he would leave his bed before daylight and arrive at the grounds where the old gobbler was in the habit of appearing. The old man hunted that gobbler all winter and finally gave it up as a bad job. He took the matter so seriously that it made him sick. Now and then a cowboy would ride into camp and tell the old man that he had seen the monarch of the woods.

Spring had come, the woods were white with dogwood blossoms, and the air was as sweet and fragrant as a hot-house bouquet. The wild turkey (glorious bird) was abroad. It was the love-making period, and, stately parading in the sunshine, he walked along in the woods, admiring his fine person as it reflected in the clear water of some creek and then, like some vain lover, tossed his head as if to say, "I am lord of the domain!" Like the slipper of Cinderella to the imagination of the young prince, or the glimpse of a waving ringlet or jeweled hand to the glowing passion of the young heart, is the remembrance of the answer to his gobble-gobble of a moment ago. He speculates that in the surrounding forest there must be a lover waiting for his royal embrace.

Cluck!

How well timed the call. The gobbler spreads his magnificent banner of gold and bronze, opens wide his mouth, and rolls forth a volume of sound for his answer. No scene in the American forest is more thrilling than a wild turkey gobbler in the early season of the year, and no sport equals the hunting of this noble quarry.

The old man took his "turkey call" and, shouldering his Yager, started for the woods. He went to a small clump of woods where there were several pecan trees. This was said to be a favorite tramping ground for the great bird. Seated under a tree, he commenced to call, and then listened. In the distance his acute ear heard a very faint answer. He waited patiently; for nearly all hunters spoil the fun by calling too often. It was the old gobbler that had become the talk of every cowboy on the range. He must be handled very delicately. The old man waited at least a quarter of an hour before he raised the call to his lips and gave another cluck.

It now was growing quite light. About 500 yards away, an object was discerned in a little valley. It stopped and looked, and then disappeared behind a mound and did not appear for a few moments. The old veteran was cautious and was looking, studying the situation, and why shouldn't he? He had been fired at so often, one gentle zephyr, one falling twig, might break the charm, and the lover would wing his way, full of life, to the woods.

Cluck!

A perfect imitation of the hen, and with hopeful expectancy in her call.

It was the big gobbler. Bozarth held his breath and shut his eyes for a moment. He could not believe that there was such a bird in the forest. It was immense, stately, grand.

The noble bird, now certain of success, fairly dances with delight. He moves forward, his feathers and neck amorously playing as he advances. Now he commences his strut, his great body commencing to swell, the gorgeous plumage of his breast unfolding itself, and his neck curves downward; the wattles grow scarlet, while the skin that covers his head changes like rainbow tints; the long feathers of the wings brush the ground, the tail opens in a semi-circle, and the beautifully covered head becomes beautifully relieved in the center.

Bozarth raised his gun and fired, and the bird took wing and disappeared. The old man was stunned, dazed. He, the greatest hunter in that whole country, had missed the gobbler at a distance of 100 yards.

"Well, missing that gobbler so often took hold of my vitals, and I wasted away. The thing had been carried too far, and it reduced me in flesh faster than ager [ague?]. I could see that old gobbler in everything I did. He haunted me, and that, too, like a devil, which I began to think he was," said Bozarth.

Two or three cowboys had in the meantime taken a shot at him and missed, and one of them swore that when he flew away he laughed like a man. Bozarth hung his head and listened, but said nothing.

The next morning he said to his wife, "Old woman, I want you to tie up the hounds and cook me enough grub to last a week. I am going to kill that turkey or pack up and move away."

What strange things happen. The old man walked to the woods where he had shot at the gobbler and sat down. In a few moments he saw a big shadow and heard a noise like that of a turkey dragging his wings on the ground. He turned, and there was the big gobbler, strutting behind the brush. He fired, and in a moment the bird took wing, flew against a tree, and fell to the ground dead. The ball had passed entirely through the bird's body, leaving a ghastly wound, "and pitch me naked into a brier bush if that old turkey devil didn't weigh 45 pounds, and where the ball went through, the steam began to come out, and we took fourteen gobs of fat out of him, and that's no lie," said the old man.

[Note from Jim Sears: Murray tells us that Old Man Bozarth's first name was Joseph and that he and his wife had "drifted down from Missouri." They lived in a cabin in the woods near Allen Bayou. "Allen Bayou" and "Allen's Bayou" were names used incorrectly for Island Bayou, a creek that flows in an easterly direction through Bryan County, Oklahoma, and empties into the Red River in Fannin County, Texas. "Old Man" could have been a private joke between Bozarth and his wife, Julia, who was nine years his senior. Murray says Joseph called her "Old Woman."]

No. 49
The Gambling Era

Sunday Gazetteer, January 22, 1911
[Original newspaper labels this No. 46,
like the previous issue]

With the prospector came the gambler. The gambler was the dominating power in Denison for many years. They flowed into Denison like the river to the sea; the current was irresistible. They mixed much in commercial life. They acquired property and built houses, some of them business houses. Their purse strings were never drawn against an enterprise that would push Denison ahead. In a matter of charity they were ever liberal. They buried a great many poor people. The hat was

*Fig. 15. Rev. M.A.
Daugherty of the M.E.
Church (North).*

always passed around to help a poor family, and about the first to go to was among the sporting fraternity. They even helped to build churches. When the Rev. Daugherty of the M.E. Church North was hard up for funds, they chipped in liberally. A gambler seldom listened to a tale of woe and want that he did not relieve. We are speaking of the class that lived here in the seventies and eighties. There are hundreds of instances that we might relate that would touch the heart and start the tears to the eyes, when the liberality of the sporting class saved many families from want, helped the poor in many ways, and sent many a poor devil on his way rejoicing.

The gambler of the seventies and eighties fully exemplified the philosophy of those figurative verses which are now recalled to memory: "It is easy enough to be happy when life goes along like a song, but the man worth while is the man who will smile when everything goes dead wrong; for the test of the heart is trouble, and it always comes with the years, and the smile that is worth the homage of earth is the smile that shines through tears." [From the poem "Worth While," by Ella Wheeler Wilcox.]

The gambler's goodness was not of the type that reached its highest manifestations in ceremonious piety. It found its expression in many good deeds that were not blazoned to the world. The gambler lived and ruled in the poetic period of our early history. We ask, what better times existed in Denison than in the seventies and eighties? Unique beyond any present experience were those good old days—hardly orthodox, it is true, still not so bad. If a gambler shot and killed, it was usually one of his own class. Class was forgotten, and all men were equal. There was no fret and worry as to the future; it was all in the present, and men who live in the present are always the happiest.

What a study the old White Elephant was, and what a study other places were. They never closed; games always went on. There was more money exchanging hands than at the banks. Life was free and easy then, and the world jogged on. The poor were few, and if they wanted a stake to a meal or bed to sleep in, all they had to do was to go to the gambling halls, tell a hard luck story, and they feasted and slept well that night. No gambler ever turned a deaf ear to the unfortunate.

In those days, money came easy and flowed out like water. It was the world of sport, hilarity, and sometimes worse. The sport left the impress of his character upon all Denison, and through the medium of his financial power, he was able with his money to do many things that helped the city. In the seventies, the gamblers had more money in the banks of Denison than many businessmen. He wasted his money, it is true; but did it ever occur to you that the men and women of such a class upon whom he wasted it are yet men and women? A little happiness brought into their lives meant as much to them as happiness carried into the lives of the straight and the good. If you can take one ray of sunshine into the nightlife and thereby give a single hour of happiness, you are a benefactor. The gamblers of the early days did this.

The world has changed; the frontier and the West are gone, forever gone; but when the pleasures of life are taken into calculation, they were the happiest days that Denison has ever seen. The great struggle of life at present is for money. So it was then, but the money flowed into every channel, and where one person is made happy now, there were many more then.

The old-time gambler has had his day, and his local prototype of the present is a pygmy. The gamblers that lived and ruled in the early period had more humanity (the milk of human kindness in their hearts) than any other class that has lived here since.

No. 50

Cholera Epidemic

Sunday Gazetteer, January 29, 1911
[Original newspaper labels this No. 46,
like the previous two issues]

The most depressing season that Denison ever passed through was during the prevalence of the cholera in the latter part of the seventies.

The epidemic appeared shortly after a Fourth of July barbecue celebration in Forest Park, conducted by Al Hall, now deceased. There were a great many country people present. The meat was prepared in a pit south of the park. Hall declared that some of the meat was tainted, which started the epidemic. There were physicians who denied that the park barbecue had anything to do with the matter, but the general belief even to this day is that the tainted meat was the prime cause. A Doctor [Charles B.] Berry said that the disease was introduced from abroad.

How many died will never be known, for many strangers were stricken down and left no record behind. It is very safe to say that at least 200 people died, but some old residents who are living at the present time say not more than 100. No mortuary report was then kept as at present. A number died in a very few hours. There were present all of the signs of cholera. Two or three physicians from abroad, who had had some experience with the disease, declared that it was the true type of Asiatic cholera, and that it had been introduced, and hooted at the idea that the barbecue was the responsible agent.

In a few days after the barbecue, the epidemic had made good headway. The writer was playing cards at a resort on Main Street kept by Weaver & Bill. About 3 o'clock P.M., a man by the name of Cameron, brother-in-law of P. [Patrick] H. Tobin, dropped in and took a hand at a game of poker. Cameron was a splendid specimen of the young man in buoyant health, and one of the most sociable men that we ever met. He went home early in the evening, was taken sick, and died the next day.

Many of the cholera victims were buried at night over at Oakwood Cemetery, or rather a little west of the cemetery proper. When the Frisco was building, north of the old graveyard where so many cholera victims slept was dug up, and a large number of human bones exposed to view.

The epidemic was confined almost entirely to Denison. The quickest death, however, was reported on Iron Ore [Creek]. A party of campers remained in a wagon yard in Denison and started the next morning for the West. Between Denison and Iron Ore, a woman was attacked and died while camp was being made. She was buried out there. Col. Tom Lipscomb, who was passing at the time, helped to bury the woman. The body was held until a very rude coffin was sent out from Denison.

Many people were buried without any religious ceremony, and it was stated that terror had seized on the whites to such an extent that Negroes carried the bodies from the houses, and they were dumped into a hole and covered up very quickly.

A number of people left the city. Many gruesome tales were told of incidents of the cholera. A Negro woman ran away and left the body of her husband in the house, and the stench was what first attracted attention to the body. The woman went to Caddo, and the fact leaking out that she was from Denison and that her husband had died with cholera, the officers ordered her out of the town; she went north then as far as Atoka on foot, where she found refuge for a few days, but her tongue having divulged the incidents of her husband's death, she was ordered to move on, and she finally found her way back to this city [Denison].

The epidemic lasted for several weeks. It took hold of white people more than Negroes. There used to be a boarding house on Crawford Street, almost opposite the old Cameron House [a hotel]. A mysterious stranger died there with cholera. He refused to divulge his identity. He was a most interesting personage, cultivated, handsome, and well dressed when he entered the boarding house. That he was a person of some note was quite evident. He was visited by a minister but refused to give any information that would clear up who he was, his past life, etc. Many believed that he was a criminal hiding from justice. He was dumped into the ground with the others, his pallbearers being Negroes.

As we said at the beginning of this story, no one will ever know how many died, but we believe our estimate is correct—200.

No. 51
Extremes of Weather

Sunday Gazetteer, February 5, 1911
[Original newspaper labels this No. 46,
like the previous three issues]

The two extremes of hot and cold weather have prevailed in January [1911]. At the opening of the month, we had the coldest

January weather in a great many years, the thermometer registering three degrees below zero. This past week of January, the weather was balmy and spring-like. Last Saturday the thermometer was at 75.

There have been some remarkable weather episodes in the history of Denison. In February 1873, when the writer arrived here, phenomenal weather prevailed. Every afternoon spring showers prevailed, the grass was green, and the elm trees were in bud. Birds that migrate late in the spring appeared, among the rest Robin Red Breast. This state of weather continued until spring set in in earnest. The summer was delightful, the thermometer seldom going above 100, and the heat seemed to be tempered with a cool south wind, and the weather was not at all oppressive. The climate seems to have changed. There was very severe weather in the latter part of the seventies and throughout the eighties. There were several very heavy falls of snow, and in the seventies we had sleighing for a period of two weeks. All of the ponds were frozen hard, and hundreds of people received skates from St. Louis. The hardware house of D.W.C. Davis & Co. sold many pairs.

In the eighties, there were a number of snowfalls and some sleighing. Sixteen years ago we had the coldest weather ever known. One Sunday morning the thermometer showed 16 below zero. This cold snap was the severest ever known in North Texas. In the Indian Territory several people froze to death; that was the fate of two Indians who left Denison drunk and were picked up on Blue Prairie dead.

Old-timers who have lived here a great many years state that the winters are warmer.

There was a great deal of enjoyment in the winters when the snow was on the ground. The young people were always out in full force. The police did not restrain the boys who stood on the street corners from pelting persons who were in vehicles, and in many instances those on the sidewalk fared no better.

An old-timer who was here before the war cites many instances as an argument that a radical change has taken place and that the winters as a general thing are milder. It is only until recent years that weather conditions have been kept track of here. The rainfall is also known and is reported officially by Prof. T.V. Munson. Mr. Kingston also keeps a daily record by a thermometer that was graduated at Washington. The *Daily Herald* also has a Washington report, and conditions of the weather for a number of years past can now be referred to and accurately known.

The first weather station in Texas was established here in the seventies, and this office had a code of signals which were displayed from the second story daily, and were looked for with much interest by the people. Lieutenant Greeley, of Arctic fame, had a weather station at the corner of Main Street and Austin Avenue. It was continued here for several years.

No. 52

Horse Thieves

Sunday Gazetteer, February 12, 1911
[Original newspaper labels this No. 47]

When Denison was first incorporated, this section and the Indian Territory were a paradise for horse thieves. There was a regular traffic in stolen horses which embraced all the country as far north as the Kansas line and west to the Panhandle. The officers had their hands full chasing the horse thieves, and it was the most dangerous part of their official duties.

Horse thieves were so numerous that they carried the depredations into Denison, Sherman, and neighboring towns.

Dan Webster, a former postmaster of Denison, was a victim. He used to ride a white horse for years to whom he and his family were greatly attached. One night Mr. Webster left home and secured his horse on Main Street. The horse was stolen at an early hour of the night. In a few days the horse was heard from. A man was seen riding the horse in the Arbuckle Mountains. The description given of the animal was perfect, and Uncle Dan never doubted that it was his horse.

One morning Jim Massey, who resided in the 300 block of

Gandy Street, saw a man with a horse pass along. Massey was deputy sheriff of this county and U.S. deputy marshal also. The early hour and the appearance of the man excited Massey's suspicion, and he hailed the man, who paid no attention to his summons to stop. Massey got out his pistol and took after the man. Several shots were exchanged, but the horse thief escaped.

Many people had a perfect passion for stealing horses and would face any danger to engage in the enterprise. Many horses were stolen in Denison. A man named John Harper had an exciting adventure. Harper missed a valuable horse, a blooded animal. He went in pursuit of the horse, crossing Red River into the Territory. At the old Colbert farm, just across the river, a Negro told him that a man riding a horse answering the description of his had passed at daylight. The thief had several hours start, but Harper was well mounted and armed, and determined to follow him day and night.

At Carriage Point, Harper met a man who said the thief was on the Tishomingo road and had passed him about two hours previous. He was heavily armed and volunteered to accompany Harper. The day was well advanced, and at dusk the man suggested to Harper that they avoid the public highway and camp for the night in the woods. They had ridden about one mile when a light was seen. Harper then began to grow suspicious of his companion and said that he had ridden into the woods far enough. Both alighted, and quicker than a flash Harper was looking into the muzzle of a .45 pistol. Harper was a brave man and attempted to reach for his six-shooter. He was then felled, and when he regained consciousness found himself in the camp of several horse thieves. He was deprived of his horse and told to walk out of the country as fast as his legs would carry him. He was thankful to escape with his life. He afterwards learned that he was near Thief Neck, a place which travelers feared and avoided. Many people had been put out of the way there and never heard of again. It was the regular stopping place for horse thieves passing through the country.

It was a frequent occurrence for immigrants to reach Denison who had had their stock stolen in the Indian Territory.

While a guest of Chas. LeFlore, captain of the Indian police at Limestone Gap, the writer saw Marshal [James H.] Mershon, the famous criminal catcher, drive up in a wagon with his posse, having in custody nine men, seven of whom were wanted for horse stealing. Among the lot was a boy probably eighteen years of age that attracted our attention. At the breakfast table, the marshal was asked what the boy was arrested for. Mershon said that he was the worst in the whole outfit; that he was wanted for murder and horse stealing. He was a Texas boy, and his father was a prominent stock owner in San Saba County. The boy commenced stealing first from his father. He was arrested but turned loose later. He then allied himself with a gang of horse thieves, and all the officers in the Territory had papers for him. He was a handsome and manly young fellow, dressed in cowboy style. While at LeFlore's he was joking and laughing all the time. He killed an officer in the Panhandle who was pursuing him. He was captured in the Comanche country, Mershon and his party rushing the camp. The young man had married an Indian woman, and the marshal, fearing the Indians would attempt to rescue him (in fact they had become boisterous and indignant), he raised the American flag and gave them to understand that, if molested, the troops at Fort Sill would be down on them. He got out of that country as soon as possible, driving all night. He considered that the most critical of all his thrilling adventures among the bad men of the Indian Territory.

One day a Comanche chief appeared upon the streets of Denison. He was a man of enormous bulk and rode a little horse. Horses had been stolen from the Indian reservation, and the chief was here to consult with Captain Tom Wright, who was then the most famous of the U.S. marshals. The old chief made two visits to Denison, and we believe that Captain Wright recovered some of the horses.

There was regular relay of horse thieves that pushed their operations from the Kansas border to all portions of Texas. Marshal Mershon once said that he believed that there were at least 2,000 horse thieves in the Indian country and Texas. They were thoroughly organized and the most fearless of riders, riding the best horses in the world. Their mounts were equal perhaps to the Don Cossacks, and it was always impossible to capture them. As soon as the presence of the officers was known, word was passed, and the thieves would go into hiding in the many places that offered a safe retreat.

There sleeps over in Oakwood Cemetery a young man who

was shot and killed by the officers at a point now within the city limits. He belonged to one of the best of Denison families. The young man had a running fight with the officers from Jacksboro, having escaped from the jail at that place. He was charged with horse stealing. He arrived within the city limits and sat down on a log to sleep after his long ride of over 100 miles. He sent a young fellow to the city after something to eat, and the country boy told his suspicions to the officers, and a posse was organized and, guided by the boy, was conducted to the spot in the brush where the young man had fallen asleep. He was fired on and wounded, and brought to this city, where he died. It was a cold-blooded transaction, little better than a murder.

The bloodiest pages in the early history of Texas are the combats with horse thieves. This article conveys but a faint outline of their doings around Denison. Hundreds perished. They used to run stock across Red River west of here. It was almost a daily occurrence for the press to publish the theft of horses, the pursuit of thieves by sheriff's posse, and combats encountered. Thousands of horses were stolen, and but few of the immigrant outfits that passed through the Indian country escaped such an experience. The condition of some of these people was pitiful, as their horses were stolen and they could not travel.

While in the Kiamitia country, in Oklahoma, a number of years ago with a party of hunters, the writer went into camp at the most dismal spot that he had ever visited. No one lived near there, and but a few yards from our camp a whole family had been murdered. It was a land of desolation and silence. About midnight, Captain Butler, who was then postmaster at Durant, awakened the camp, stating that horse thieves were around, that he had seen one in the glare of the campfire. The horses gave the alarm, which had awakened Butler. The horses were brought in and secured to the wagons and a guard posted. At daybreak we broke camp and left hastily.

The seventies and eighties were the golden periods of the horse thief. It was almost a daily occurrence for country people to visit Denison and bring the story of their horses or mules having been stolen. Sometimes several head were stolen. The father-in-law of the writer, who then lived three miles east of Denison, had a mare stolen that had been in the family many years. A man called there and asked for some work. He was well dressed and very intelligent. He had the most peculiar eyes; the eyeballs were white, and there was a red circle around them. His presence was startling, and the neighbors all declared he was a dangerous man. One morning the mare was missing and the man ditto. Colonel Davis was very much affected over the loss.

The tide of civilization, the rapid settlement of the country, the railways, the telegraph lines, and the telephone service have made horse stealing a dangerous practice, but still it is going on. Some are born with the passion, and it will never cease.

No. 53
Farming Has Changed

Sunday Gazetteer, February 19, 1911
[Original not numbered]

How farming has changed in this section. To a great extent the old methods have been relegated to the past, and we are now adopting the modern methods which bring so much better results. Diversification has wrought wonders. The old style was corn and cotton, and ever since the first white settlement of this county, no attempt was ever made at diversification. The farmers around Denison were awakened from their Rip Van Winkle dreams, and now the rotation of crops is in full blast.

Corn and cotton are good money crops, but the farmers have learned that there are others that bring just as much. The farmers have had their eyes opened by government experts who have been sent down here and in speeches and practical examples in the field of experiment, have done much for intelligent farming. And the railways have taken up the matter. They have sent cars down here loaded with products, and a man accompanied the car who addressed the farmers, and very often distributed seeds. Cars loaded with thoroughbred cattle, hogs, etc., have often been exhibited on the railways. If the farmer has not learned, it is because he has not taken advantage of the advice and assistance rendered by the government and railways.

If you will travel over the country near Denison, you will be surprised at the agricultural machinery used on the farms, and you will notice another fact, that it is protected from the weather. The crops are harvested by machinery instead of by the hand. There is no feature of farming that cannot use improved agricultural implements. In many places cotton is being picked by machinery. This new invention has not as yet reached this section, but it is not far off.

Another incentive which has helped the farmer is in going into the organization, holding meetings at the schoolhouses, discussing farming or listening to addresses by speakers who know what they are talking about. The government has done for the farmer more than he can ever repay. Thousands of books and pamphlets have been published and distributed free to farmers. Every known feature of farming is treated intelligently, and letters to the government asking for information will always receive a prompt reply. The members of Congress who depend so much on the vote of the rural constituency always stand ready to help the farmer. The farms are paying better than ever around Denison. The government station two miles east (the inspiration of Tom Larkin) has helped out the situation. The corn clubs are all the rage. Valuable premiums are being offered for the best corn raised, and the farmer boys have worked up an enthusiasm that has never been surpassed. Every county in the most thickly [settled] portions of the state now has its corn clubs. There are several clubs in this county, and the membership is very large. These clubs work up an interest in farming which will bear fruit in the future.

Look at the past, when Denison was first known on the map—the period of the razorback hog and longhorn cattle, when the farmers lived mostly in log cabins. If you stopped at the house, scores of lean, hungry curs poured in a canine cataract over the worm-eaten fence, and the man at home with a cob pipe in his mouth greeted you with the poor man's vernacular. His perennial diet was hog; he delighted in cracklins and corn dodgers made of water. His cattle and horses were lean and hungry. When he plowed, he used a line made out of rope. He would neglect crops to come to town to get drunk. That was the way farming to a great extent was conducted in this vicinity forty years ago.

The evolution in the use of improved machinery on farms has worked a wonderful change. The interest manifested in the farmer by the government has been another great factor. The farming of forty years ago and the farming of the present are so radically different that the old way of tilling the soil has almost entirely disappeared. The farmers are living in better houses and have better barns and better road facilities for bringing their products to market. The automobile will soon be a commodity of the farm. There are several in Grayson County that are used to carry truck to the city. If the cities are coming into better things, so are the farmers.

No. 54

The Dick Lock War

Sunday Gazetteer, February 26, 1911
[Original not numbered]

Late dispatches announce that Dick Lock [Victor M. Locke Sr.] has been appointed principal chief of the Choctaw Nation. This dispatch recalls to mind one of the most thrilling episodes in the history of the Choctaw Nation since the Indians crossed west of the Mississippi and located in the Indian Territory which has been dropped from the map.

Dick Lock is a squaw man, his wife being a Choctaw—nearly a full-blood. Lock has for many years resided at Antlers, a small town on the Frisco [Railroad] near Paris, Texas. He conducted a large mercantile establishment.

About twenty years ago, civil war broke out in the eastern part of the Choctaw Nation. It was known to the outside world as the Antlers War, and a few called it the Dick Lock War. It was a political strife which involved the governorship. Armed bands of partisans roamed through the country, and a number were killed.

Dick Lock was the recognized leader of a powerful faction. He speaks the Indian dialect as well as any full-blood and is a natural born leader of men. With a hunting party bound for the Kiamitia Mountains, the writer happened to camp one night and part of the day at Antlers. The dogs of war had been let loose, and there had been considerable fighting.

Two days previous to the arrival of our party, the Lock mansion had been attacked by 500 Indians. Lock's mansion was two stories and would have been an ornament to most any city, costing several thousand dollars. It was a short distance west of the railroad track. The attacking party fought principally from behind a large barn and (Indian fashion) from behind trees. In the house were Dick Lock, his family, and a few followers. No less than 10,000 shots were fired into the Lock home. The writer went through the house and never saw such a sight. The rooms in the house and the furniture looked like a pepper box. The furniture had been purchased in St. Louis and cost many thousands of dollars. There were hundreds of articles in the house, and yet not a single one had escaped the storm of bullets. The attacking party were armed with Winchesters principally, and for two hours the Lock mansion was made a target of.

The escape of the party in the house was a miracle. They lay on the floor, not daring to expose their persons.

Lock picked out the spot where he fired from and repulsed the storming party, who twice attempted to enter the house, which had been barricaded.

When the attack was begun, the little daughter of Mrs. Lock was in the back yard. The mother never hesitated but rushed out after her, and when she had reached her child, she was immediately fired on but escaped a hundred bullets which splattered around her person. The U.S. troops were hurried from Fort Gibson to the scene, and the anti-Lock partisans retreated and disappeared in the surrounding woods.

When we made camp, Dick Lock came over from his house and sat down at the campfire. He advised us to move our camp, as he expected an attack that night.

Bredette C. Murray

We have never met a man who has impressed us more than Dick Lock. The *St. Louis Republic* contained an article written by the *Gazetteer* reporter, in which the Antler War was described and a pen picture [painted] of Dick Lock, whom we called "the Partisan Chief of the Kiamitia." He was a man of superb courage. Perhaps bravery is something that always has been and always will be admired. Lock was recklessly brave. He was a magnetic man who attracted and impressed all who came within the sphere of his influence. There was nothing of the bravado about him. The whole county was filled with strolling bands bent on murder, but Lock managed to keep them within the bounds of legitimate war. He was an imposing figure with a bulk like an ox, possessing the strength of three ordinary men.

When he entered our camp, he had two pistols strapped to his person. He was accompanied by two other persons who were heavily armed. The Lock home, or rather the hallway, was filled with boxes containing Winchesters and ammunition. The Lock partisans were pouring into Antlers, which looked like an armed camp. After leaving Antlers and going to the mountains, we noticed a large number of armed Indians proceeding to Antlers. They were nearly all full-bloods, a wild and fierce-looking set of men. There was at Antlers and close at hand several hundred of the Dick Lock followers. A battle was expected at any moment. The U.S. troops, which consisted of one company, were watching the situation very carefully and had scouts thrown out.

When our hunting party returned from the mountains, it was learned that the trouble was over, and that Dick Lock was master of the situation. The elevation of Dick Lock to the governorship was a well-merited compliment, and in whatever position he occupies he always makes good.

Section Two

Little Stories of the Past

[Originals were not numbered]

No. 55

A Visit with Quanah Parker

Sunday Gazetteer, March 5, 1911

The death of the famous Comanche chief, Quanah Parker, near Lawton, Oklahoma, recalls a visit to his home when his country was opened for settlement several years ago. The chief was residing with his family of several wives and a number of children at the foothills of the Wichita Mountains. It was a modern two-story house painted white. The public road ran a short distance of Quanah's ranch. We called it a ranch, for when the government opened the country and segregated the land, the chief was given several sections in about the prettiest spot in the Comanche Nation. Thousand of acres spread out into a beautiful landscape of rich prairie lands, beautiful groves, and streams of pure water. For hundreds of years this warlike nation had made this spot their home. This was the starting point of the Comanches when they made their raids into Texas and Mexico. For the Comanches got their richest spoils in the latter nation and sometimes appeared almost at the gates of the ancient city of Montezuma.

The chief lived like an old feudal baron on the banks of the River Rhine. He had his retinue, and among the number we noticed several white cowboys and swarthy Mexicans, and lounging around were a number of Indians, who were sunning themselves in the warm autumn sun. In the corral we noticed many horses and mules, and there was a double-seated carriage in which Quanah and his wives rode to Lawton or Fort Sill in state.

The arrival of our party seemed to create no unusual stir. The Indians, who were asleep or awake, and the cowboys did not approach and ask our business. We learned that the object of our visit was in the house. We pushed ahead through two gates and were greeted by a Mexican, who spoke indifferent English, saying that he would go and apprise the chief of our presence. While conversing, we spied several faces (women) peeping at our party through the closed windows.

The Mexican was gone several moments and on his return stated that he would conduct us into the presence of the chief, who was a little under the weather. Ascending the steps, a door was opened, and we noticed a large Indian reclining on a couch. It seemed a great effort for him to arise. The only greeting was, "How!" There were several chairs in the room, but our attention was attracted to a magnificent saddle that hung on the wall. The leather was covered with many buttons, which we learned afterwards were of pure silver. The saddle, with its gold and silver ornaments, was said to be worth $1,500.

We looked at Quanah, and he looked at us. "Where from?" he grunted out, and we replied, "Lawton."

"After land, home; many white people want Comanche lands." And a strange wild look animated the chief's face.

A couple of doors were slightly ajar, and we saw the faces of several Indian girls with laughing expressions. The chief said something in the native language, and the doors closed softly, and we saw no more of them.

The old chief seemed to be bored by our presence and not inclined to talk, and we suggested to the party to "vamoose the ranch." We asked after his health and his family's, and he merely grunted. He finally got on his feet, shook hands with us, and seemed to thaw out all of a sudden. He remarked, "Sore throat; bones feel bad; can't talk much; glad to see you. Where you go? Are you government men?" He then returned to his couch and laid down with a grunt.

We told him that we had come a long distance, from Texas, not so much to take up land as to visit him: "Quanah, I have seen the graves of your mother and sister near Palestine."

At this the chief arose to his feet, pulled a chair up, and sat at our side. The weariness and the languid expression was gone, and the chief said, "My mother good woman; heap good little Prairie Flower. Tell me about my mother."

We replied that we had only seen the grave, but that we knew all about his mother in the books, and about his father, Nocona, who was shot and killed by General Sul Ross. From that moment the chief seemed to be a new man. He yelled out something, and the doors were opened, and three or four squaws marched into the room and were introduced by the chief.

"You very tired; stay with me tonight. Plenty of room; plenty to eat." When we told Quanah that we must be at Lawton the next day and would have to travel by night, he said, "How! How!" several times. It was growing dark. "You must eat; long travel," said the chief.

"No, Quanah, we must travel; heap of business at Lawton. Will try and come again."

The night was growing pale, and the stars were sparkling in the firmament when we left. The old chief followed us to the carriage, and his wives came to the porch to look at us. "Come again; I want to talk about my mother and sister. I visit you when the grass comes up. Come again, you must not forget."

The Mexican opened the gate and, waving adieu to the Comanche chief (who was one of the most noted figures of southwestern history), we drove away.

And now Quanah is dead and gone to the land of spirits, and, if we believe in the cult of a future life, is with his mother, father, and sister, who in their day shook the fabric of Texas and Mexico.

Fig. 16. Chief Quanah Parker.
Photo from National Archive.

No. 56
Fourth of July Festivities

Sunday Gazetteer, March 12, 1911

In the matter of public celebrations, there has been a great change within the past few years. The Fourth of July was a great event and was never permitted to go by without a big time. Thousands of people from the surrounding country and the Indian Territory were present. The most popular feature was the old-fashioned barbecue. It was no trouble to go among the businessmen and raise several hundred dollars.

There were other celebrations. Denison's birthday was a great event. All of the business houses had appropriate floats in the procession, and many of them were quite expensive and elaborate affairs. The old Star Store used to make some wonderful displays, and the Katy shops turned out unique floats; and the various trade unions marched in line several blocks. Sometimes the Sherman people would come over and celebrate. There was a big procession marching through the streets when the news was received that [Charles Julius] Guiteau had shot President [James A.] Garfield [July 2, 1881].

The decorations of public and private buildings were very elaborate. There was in the eighties [1880s] a magnificent arch erected on Main Street, in the 200 block, which spanned the entire street, and thousands of footmen passed under it.

The visitors used to spend lots of money. The saloons were in a blaze of glory, and the gambling houses were wide open and a great deal of money changed hands. In those days you could get a square meal at the card tables.

The celebrations were usually held at Forest Park and sometimes at the old Boulevard grounds. The gun clubs held their tournaments out there and at the old fairgrounds [West Morton Street].

A frightful tragedy took place at a Fourth of July celebration. The night previous to the celebration, the body of a Chickasaw Indian (who had been murdered) was found in the rear of a saloon on Main Street. The next day two men were killed, and a third one died in a few days from the effects of a wound. At that period Denison was wild and woolly, and 50 per cent of the population "toted" a gun.

From 1874 until 1890, there was a big public celebration held every year. The labor unions have kept up the practice but not on a scale to compare with the big old-time blowouts.

After the day's sport was over, there were many dinners. A platform was erected in Forest Park for the general public. Sometimes two or three dances were in full blast, to which a small admission was charged.

One of the most amusing sights at the dances at Forest Park was old Simon Overturf "tripping the light fantastic." Many people used to go on purpose to see the old man dance the Virginia Reel.

With many other of the old-time customs, public celebrations are a thing of the past. The crowds do not come here any more and turn their money loose. The truth is that the public doesn't go to a straight-laced town to have a good time. The people were closer together than at present, and while they were striving for the almighty dollar, they were more generous; and when a contribution was wanted for a celebration, there was no trouble in getting it. There was a spirit of hospitality, the old kind welcome, which has disappeared and will probably never be revived. The times have changed so much.

Fig. 17. Spoon race in Forest Park on July 4. Photo by Jack Hendricks.

No. 57
Denison Gun Club

Sunday Gazetteer, March 19, 1911

In the seventies and eighties, Denison was the leading city in Texas for sportsmen, fine dogs, and fine guns. The spirit of emulation never was so high since. We have the Denison Rod and Gun Club [later Denison Country Club], but they are a different personality. Of course the conditions have changed, the game has been killed out, and the country north of the [Red] river is at present hedged in by such stringent game laws that hunting is a forbidden pleasure.

The old Denison Gun Club that went out of existence in the eighties was the most famous club of sportsmen that have ever had an organization of the kind in the Southwest. Many crack clubs were pitted against them, but they all went down in defeat.

Twenty-eight years ago, the Denison Gun Club, like Hannibal, had no more worlds to conquer. The most noted members are still alive and residents of Denison—T.W. Dollarhide and Col. J.D. Yocom, the latter our present efficient city secretary. Dollarhide and Yocom were almost invincible, and their reputation as crack shots of the traps extended all over Texas.

Many famous clubs came here to try conclusions with our club, but always met their Waterloo. There was no feature of public amusement that drew such crowds as the gun club tournaments. The writer has seen as many ladies at the grounds as men. The newspapers had more to say of the gun clubs' shoots than any other public event. A full account was given of the tournaments, and written in a style that attracted attention all over the state. At every public celebration, the Denison Gun Club was one of the leading attractions. Clubs all over Texas sent in challenges to our home club.

Many of the most famous shots are dead—Ellis, Leaverton,

Maughs—good fellows, crack shots. The Denison Gun Club, after defeating every club that came here, went abroad looking for more worlds to conquer. Colonel Yocom has at his home a magnificent silver trophy that was presented to him by a foreign gun club.

At the beginning of the gun club era, live pigeons were used at the traps. The birds were brought here from the immense roosts in the Indian Territory. When the wild pigeons left, tame pigeons were sometimes used; then later came the clay pigeon, a saucer-like contrivance that is sprung from a trap and is shot at while sailing through the air. It is a poor substitute for the live bird.

The members of the Denison club had the finest dogs and guns in the world. Some of the guns cost two, three, and four hundred dollars each, and their dogs were of the finest strains that the most famous kennels produced. Yocom and Dollarhide had each several dogs that represented hundreds of dollars.

The members of the Denison club were a jolly set of fellows. The old Grand Southern saloon, where Red Front [Clothing Store] now stands, was the rallying point, and the stories and adventures that have been told there would fill a volume; and even at this late day, it would be highly entertaining reading. The spirit of good cheer, good fellowship, was abroad, and a more congenial set of good fellows never gathered at the campfire or at the tournament grounds. At that period, hunting parties in the spring, fall, and winter were always in the fields, and nearly all of them were members of the Denison Gun Club.

Wild game was plentiful within a day's ride of Denison. All of the little prairie streams harbored thousands of quail, and there were jack snipe and duck shooting galore. The members of the club shot thousands of jack snipe at Warren Flats, which was then swampy grounds. The meadowlands around Denison were not under fence, and when the plover were going north, thousands were killed.

In the seventies and eighties, the sport around Denison was superb. Our businessmen were nearly all sportsmen and members of the Denison Gun Club. How many times have we, on entering a business house, asked for so-and-so, and the reply was, "He has gone hunting."

At that period, the meat markets were displaying game—deer, wild turkeys, ducks, snipe, quail, squirrels; and now and then antelope from the plains could be seen. During the holidays, we have seen bear and buffalo hanging at the markets trimmed with beautiful ribbons. Sometimes a live bear would be chained in front of a market.

The Denison Gun Club at the height of its efficiency—and we might say glory—embraced about fifty numbers. Where are they now? Nearly all are dead, and Dollarhide, Yocom, and J.T. Munson are all that live in Denison. Yocom and Dollarhide, the two greatest shots, are all that are left of the charter members.

Yocom cannot shoot anymore, owing to impaired eyesight. Jesse says, "I am getting old and stiff, and my hunting days are over forever." What a spirit of enthusiasm the name of Yocom evoked in the seventies and eighties. His name was on the lips of every sportsman in Texas. When Yocom and Dollarhide stepped forward to the traps, there was a great hush over the grounds, and then wild enthusiasm would break the great silence at their splendid pigeon shooting. The people always felt that when Jesse Yocom and Tom Dollarhide were on hand, the Denison Gun Club was sure of victory, and the boys never disappointed them.

Did you ever see Tom Dollarhide handle a gun at the traps? It is worth the seeing. He handles a gun like a great artist handling his brush. He has an elegant swing of getting his gun in position for deadly work. He is today the most unique and graceful man behind a shotgun in Texas.

Yocom was deliberate and deadly. It was good-bye, Mr. Bird, when Jess pointed his gun; it was a dead bird. Yocom had a delightful personality which made him very popular with the visiting clubs, and he was looked up to for advice.

We might cover many pages describing the victories of this incomparable club of sportsmen. They were never surpassed, never equaled. They were the nobility of dog and gun. Everything they did at the traps had spirit and éclat in it. They were a splendid lot of men, and the sorrow is that death has been so busy among them. From Wyoming to the Rio Grande they are sleeping—eternally "at rest."

Denison will never have another such set of men, for the times and circumstances do not produce them. Like so many features of the good old early days, the Denison Gun Club will only be associated with the pleasantest of memories.

No. 58

Hunting on the Sassafras Creek

Sunday Gazetteer, March 26, 1911

Recalling thirty-five years' experience in the woods, the most singular thing that we can remember happened on a small watercourse known as the Sassafras, that empties into Allen Bayou, in Chickasaw Nation. At that period, there was not a wire fence in all Panola County, in the eastern portion of the Nation and north of Denison—just across the river.

It was in the month of November. The section was settled up with a few white men (squaw men) and Indians. It was a hunter's paradise. Deer, wild turkey, squirrels, ducks—in fact, all kinds of game—were so plentiful that they were always in sight. We were then living in a cabin with old man Bozarth and wife, who had drifted down from Missouri, built a two-room cabin, and were leading a secluded life in the woods. The nearest neighbor was ten miles away. Hunting parties had not as yet visited that country. There was never a day in the fall and winter that deer, turkeys, and other wild game did not hang at the cabin. We wandered around that section off and on for many months and never saw a white visitor at the cabin.

One perfect fall morning, when the air was as exhilarating as a draught of champagne and the woods were painted in many colors by Jack Frost, we took our gun and crossed the Sassafras to Allen Bayou. At that early hour, all the wild game is generally astir, and it was so warm and pleasant that we heard in the hills the gobble of a wild turkey.

While seated on a log, yelping for the gobbler, our attention was attracted to a noise like some animal walking in the bed of the creek. Presently a deer came into sight, the largest animal of the kind that we had ever seen. The deer must have weighed over 200 pounds. When within twenty yards, it stopped and faced around, looking at us intently. We were probably the first white man that the animal had ever seen. On leaving the cabin, we had forgotten our buckshot shells and had in the gun No. 6, fine shot. The magnificent animal manifested no fear but just stood there and gazed, and we had no desire to fire and wound it. It is no exaggeration to say that the deer remained there at least fifteen minutes. The only movement was to now and then elevate its head, to get a better view of the strange object, and then it would settle down with the intent look. It was a beautiful creature of the woods.

We were so intent looking at the deer that we had not noticed the tawny thing creeping through the brush with hair erect and white fangs displayed in the mouth wide open. It was the biggest wild cat that we had ever seen. The deer paid no attention to the cat that was now crawling on its belly and getting ready to spring upon it. The cat saw us and stopped. We wounded the cat, and it disappeared in the woods.

The charm was broken, and the deer sprang up the hillside and was out of sight in a moment.

No. 59
The Opera Singer and Her Guardian

Sunday Gazetteer, April 2, 1911

About thirty years ago, a mother and her little daughter resided on Woodard Street, in the 300 block. The woman was a widow, and she received a small income from an estate in England. The little girl was precocious, bright, intelligent, loveable, and pretty. To help her mother, she used to go on the streets and sell articles that were useful in the household. She had a sweet voice and such a captivating manner that many people purchased who did not need the articles. In the fall and winter she attended school; in summer she was on the streets with her commodities. She would sometimes go home at night with as much as five dollars. The street associations did not take the edge off of her maiden modesty. She was pure as the beautiful snow.

In the evening, the mother with her sewing would appear upon the porch, and the little girl, seated at her feet, would read aloud. The neighborhood was not the best, the children were bad and rude, and when they passed the little girl, they would call her "stuck up" and sometimes strike her. Even the boys would torment her. She had beautiful hair, the color of old gold, that streamed down her back and was tied at the end with a ribbon. As she grew older, her beauty increased, and many called her the most beautiful girl in Denison.

A railroad contractor took a fancy to the little girl and used to contribute to the support of the family. He left here and went to Kansas City, where he secured a contract on the Missouri Pacific. He sent for the woman and child and provided them with a comfortable home. The girl was sent to Boston and placed under the care of the Conservatory of Music. Of the thousand pupils there, she soon surpassed them all. She could not only sing divinely, but was a master of the piano.

A golden future opened up before her. People were captivated with her grand figure and beautiful face, and she had many flattering offers to go on the stage, but her guardian turned them all down. To round out her musical education, she was sent to the Austrian capital where she remained two years. She attached herself to an opera troupe. Her first appearance was at the capital of Hungary, and she scored a grand success. The manager closed a contract with her guardian at a salary of $300 per week. The aristocracy and nobility were at her feet. She was called the most beautiful woman in Europe, and she spurned many offers of marriage. Her whole life was wrapped up in her guardian.

It is said that in the third year of her career on the stage, she received $500 per night. As is customary, she changed her name to one which had a foreign accent to it, this being a fad with many people. She went to Paris and London, and the two cities were at her feet. In her greatest trials, the child who had lived on Woodard Street never lost her head.

And now this little story of romance must end. The actress left the stage and married her guardian. She had acquired by her profession something like $500,000, and her husband was a very rich man. The guardian was about forty years her senior, but she was grateful and loved him. They divide their time between Europe and the United States.

When the mother and daughter lived in Denison, they were known by the name of Dixon, and the name appears in the first city directory.

This is the story told us the past week by a lady who has lived here many years and knows the circumstances, partly by correspondence.

No. 60

The Old-Time Preacher

Sunday Gazetteer, April 9, 1911

One of the most vivid recollections of childhood days was the old-time preacher that used to travel around the country on horseback with his saddlebags, visiting the sick and consoling those who were about to go to that land from which no traveler ever returns. The old-time preacher believed in hellfire and brimstone. To doubt the literal bonfire for the unredeemed was treason. In those days he seldom preached a sermon that was not illuminated by hellfire, that being his strongest card. The old-time preacher, although a fanatic, was better and more earnest than the modern prototype. He accepted the gospel as the divine message from the heavenly father.

We can recollect a man named McLaurin, who questioned some of the teachings of the gospel. The feeling was so strong against him that he sold his little store and moved to Troy. He had, while on a visit to New York City, purchased an old book (Thomas Paine's *Age of Reason*) and was so impressed with it that he was bold enough to go out in front of his store, whittle on sticks, and discuss the contents of the book. Many threatening letters were dropped at his door, and the preacher took the matter up and denounced him from the pulpit; and what little trade he had left him.

A traveling Catholic priest came on the stage and stopped overnight at the tavern kept by the writer's parents. People looked in at the dining rooms, and one would have supposed that a wild animal was caged there. There was not a Catholic in the whole community; in fact, a Catholic then was considered worse than an infidel. The town is at least 100 years old, and there is not a Catholic church there yet.

We have heard the old-time preacher stand up in his rude pulpit and condemn to literal torment a babe that died almost before it commenced to live. There was the heartbroken mother listening to the preacher's rantings of "the elect"; [saying] that people were condemned to go to hell because it was so ordained and that only the elect would be saved. This horrible doctrine was believed by all; for everybody went to church and believed the old orthodox creed that has at present but few sincere believers. The church has felt the spirit of progress; and creeds, like the times, have changed.

Every fall there was a big revival held in the woods. People attended from all over the country. The revivals were big affairs and lasted sometimes for several weeks. Families lived there. The spirit of hospitality prevailed, and we never shall forget the old-fashioned meals that we sat down to. The housewives of the present day are not as good cooks as our ancestors. People who attended the camp meetings put up rude wooden structures or arbors made of brush. When it rained, they would seek the protection of the wooden shacks. Rude benches that sometimes tore the seat of a man's breeches were placed over the ground, the pulpit being in the center. The preachers from all over the country were present.

There was always an organ and choir composed of pretty rosy-cheeked girls and young men, dressed in homespun. The church music was started by a tuning fork made of steel which, when struck on an object and placed to the ear, vibrated a sound which the leader of the choir would suit his voice to, and the sacred singing would begin. After the singing, the home preacher would kneel for prayer, which we have frequently seen last for half an hour. The preachers of the primitive period were strong of voice and robust in health and, when worked up to a pitch of religious enthusiasm, could be heard several hundred yards. It seemed to be a contest between the preachers as to who could put the most hell-fire into their sermons and yell the loudest and pound the pulpit the hardest.

When a convert came forward and knelt at the mourner's bench, there were great cries of "Hallelujah! Another soul saved from the burning. Hold fast, dear brother and sister."

We have seen persons (largely women) go into a comatose state, attempt to tear the clothing from their person, and cut up capers that were obscene—hug and kiss each other and yell like a lot of Comanches on the warpath. We have seen girls go among the young men and drag them from their seats, shouting, "Come to Jesus and be saved"; the preachers all the time shouting "Hallelujah!" from all points of the grounds. The camp meetings would start at an early hour and often last until midnight. The lights furnished were from tallow candles that flickered a ghostly light.

The camp meetings were not always productive of good. Hundreds professed religion, but as a general thing the conversions were only temporary, and they would soon fall from grace. The Methodists were the only denominations that held camp meetings.

The old-time preacher was poorly paid; his salary in the back-woods district never exceeded $500 per annum, and it was a very rare thing that he received that much. This low salary was offset by an appointed day and night when the members used to bring donations, consisting of groceries and clothing for the pastor, his wife, and family. Sometimes a little money was contributed, but this was rare. Such a thing as giving money for the performance of the marriage ceremony was unknown. With his low salary, living from hand to mouth, the old-time preacher was a good old soul. He always appeared happy and contented, with his patient devotion to his work. He lived in humble quarters, and his rent was paid by the church. I can recollect but one disagreeable instance. A young man was sent to take charge of the Methodist flock. His first appearance in the pulpit excited much comment. He dressed too well to suit the congregation. He wore a silk tie and a modern suit of clothes, and he had a wife who affected the city style. The congregation said they were "stuck up" and were too fashionable to have much religion. His connection with the church did not change the drift of sentiment. His wife, an educated and refined woman, resented the gossip, and the young preacher decided to resign or be changed to another district. So he went away, and the pulpit was filled with a genuine type of the old-time preacher, who said a good deal about hell and little about the other place.

The old-time preacher has passed away. He is now and then found in the remote backwoods settlements and still preserves the characteristics of those gone before. Take him all in all, the old-time preacher is a pleasant memory of that period in life when we went barefooted, wore stone-bruises on our feet, and occasionally had the itch.

No. 61

"Rowdy Kate"

Sunday Gazetteer, April 16, 1911

There appeared upon the streets of Denison about twenty-five years ago a bad woman. She was a product of the Indian Territory. You have heard of the bad man—she was the bad woman. She was here several times and was placed in jail twice on a charge of drunkenness. She wore a man's hat and toted a gun. Her sobriquet was "Rowdy Kate," and rowdy she was.

The woman was born in the Cherokee Nation. Her father was a white man, her mother being a half-breed Cherokee. The parental stock was bad. Her father had been killed because of a fondness for other people's horses; and her mother, while seated in the front yard of her cabin on the Canadian River, was shot and killed from ambush. Her brother was killed in the Cherokee Strip while fleeing from the officers.

Rowdy Kate was a whisky peddler and used to, in the seventies, purchase the product in Denison. She sometimes hung up with the Star gang in the Cherokee Nation. The Stars, although a bad lot with a notorious criminal record, were high-toned, with cattle on a thousand hills, and there was some good blood in the family; and they are today among the most respected people of Oklahoma. In the bloody feuds of many years ago that were always on hand in the Indian Territory, this family was almost wiped out.

Rowdy Kate was told to vamoose and, it is said by a man who knew her history well, she never appeared in that section again.

A cattleman by the name of Buck Higgins was killed on the Canadian, and among the persons mixed up in the affair was Rowdy Kate. She was taken to Fort Smith and laid in the federal jail for several months, but at the trial the evidence was so conflicting that she was discharged.

The woman was so coarse, brutal, and ornery that we don't suppose she ever had a love affair in her life. Every once in a while the papers noted her escapades in the towns of the Indian Territory. U.S. Marshal Mershon had papers for her arrest. He told the writer the following: "I heard that Kate and two men were in the Arbuckle Mountains. I was riding, intending to pass the night with John Grant, who had a ranch at the old fort. Just before I arrived (it was almost dark), I saw in the open woods a woman and three men. Then a shot was fired, and a bullet whizzed by my head. The men and woman disappeared. Grant told me that the men and woman had camped in the woods the night previous, and, suspecting they wanted to appropriate some of his stock, he directed his men to keep a close watch. Grant did not know the woman, but he instantly recognized her from my description."

The woman followed the railway towns and always managed to get drunk at each one. The officers had a great deal of trouble with her. She was always in the public eye when she turned up here.

On one occasion City Marshal Bill Hardwick arrested her on Austin Avenue, near what is now Chestnut Street. The woman resisted, pulled a pistol, and stuck the muzzle against the officer's stomach. The officer dropped her like a hotcake. She was then grabbed by a big Negro, who held her until the officer put the irons on her wrists.

Her last appearance in Denison led to a terrible tragedy in the old depot at Caddo [Oklahoma]. Kate had been here and got in with a very prominent Indian who was a member of the Light Horse and also a member of the U.S. marshal force. The two left Denison very drunk. At Caddo, the officer and woman turned themselves loose. They stampeded the Katy depot agent and operator at that place. It was about midnight when Tandy Fulsom, one of the most desperate and fearless outlaws of the Indian Territory, came in on the freight train. To make a good man of Fulsom, who had been outlawed for years, the government had granted him an unconditional pardon and made him a U.S. officer. Tandy walked in on the man and woman and demanded that they keep quiet. The man commenced to curse, ordering Tandy to leave the depot. The lamp in the depot had gone out, and it was quite dark. There was a slash in the darkness—the Indian had fired at Fulsom. The woman was yelling, "Don't give up! Kill him!" Fulsom's gun responded to the flash, and two or three more shots were fired. The Indian rolled from his seat to the floor dead. Fulsom's shots had all taken deadly effect. He told the writer that his first impulse was to then kill the woman and had actually trained his gun on her.

Fulsom was acquitted and the woman ordered to leave the country. She afterwards got into a shooting scrape at old Fishertown, on the line of the Katy. A Creek Negro Indian was killed. He jumped in front of Kate and received a bullet in his heart. She escaped out of the back door. She wandered over the Choctaw and Chickasaw nations, drunk and desperate to the last. If our memory is not at fault, she died in jail at Ardmore.

No. 62
Paving the Streets

Sunday Gazetteer, April 23, 1911

People who live here at present in comfortable homes and can go almost all over the entire city dry shod on brick or cement pavements, have no idea how things have changed for the better. We can recollect when there was not a decent crossing in the entire city, and in many places in muddy or rainy weather there was a long walk to avoid the mud and slush which was shoe-mouth deep. The present population can well recollect what Main Street was until the brick pavement was put down. The best and most frequented street in the city was a loblolly hole, and we have seen wagons mired down in the mud almost to the hub.

The old order of running the city government never accomplished much for street improvement, although a street force was maintained and thousands of dollars spent in that direction. The work done had been in the hands of incompetent men in many instances. The streets worked were as bad in a few weeks as ever. Politics had a great deal to do with the street work. You had to have pull to get on the street force, and if the inside facts had been brought out, they sometimes had to pay to get the position.

The commission form of government has changed things for the better. The streets were about the first proposition tackled. Cement crossings were put down all over the city, and cement sidewalks kept in touch with street improvements; and a great change has been made. Civic pride was appealed to. Meetings were held, largely inspired by Tom Larkin, who never got credit for the work he did in arousing public sentiment in regard to street and sidewalk improvements. The reader can start at present from almost any section and find good sidewalks. You can start from the suburban home of Mayor Acheson [1419 West Woodard Street] and walk to the Union Depot on brick or cement sidewalks.

Several years ago, it was in this distance, at many points, a wade in the mud. The most marked improvements in streets and sidewalks have been made north of Main Street. The residents over there have more money. The southeast and southwest sections have not done as well, but a marked improvement has taken place from the old order of things.

The man in charge of the street work would be greatly benefited if he would spend a dollar for Warner's book on the manner in which street work should be done. Warner says that street work should be directed by an intelligent man who has some knowledge of civil engineering.

Nothing creates a more favorable impression on the visitor than well-ordered streets and sidewalks. That is one of the principal factors by which a town is judged; and it is right that it should be so. A slothful town shows a slothful people.

There is no city in Texas where the conditions are so favorable for good streets. The natural drainage is perfect, and the soil conditions unsurpassed.

In the seventies, Main Street was about the worst in the city because it was the most traveled. We can recollect that, in front of this office [112 West Main], there was a trench full of water, and as far west as the high school building [700 block of West Main] there was mud galore. All over town there were many eyesores, and the press pleaded, but little was done to better conditions. The street force was out, but little permanent work was done. There were pools of stagnant water festering in the summer sun, and much sickness was the consequence. Good streets and sidewalks are conducive to health.

The *Herald,* in the late city campaign, slurred the cement sidewalks and crossings because they lacked regularity. That argument was on a par with some other arguments that the *Herald* put up. Thousands of people who crossed over them were satisfied. They may not in some instances conform to geometrical lines, but they are permanent and all right.

We look forward to a great era in street improvement, [when] the city is conducted by men who are inspired with civic pride. When their work is done, Denison will be a long way ahead of the present in street improvements.

No. 63

Wild Rose of the Brazos Bottom

Sunday Gazetteer, April 30, 1911

The city editor was a member of the first surveying party that left Hearne to run a line west as far as San Antonio in the interest of the International and Great Northern Railway. The surveying party was in charge of Major [D.W.] Washburn, who was afterwards chief engineer of the Texas & Pacific and was killed [February 7, 1882] on a flat car near Fort Worth. Hearne is about six miles east of the Brazos River. At that time, the general offices of the I. & G.N. were located at Hearne and afterwards moved to Palestine, when the line was built beyond Hearne.

We left Hearne in three covered Studebaker wagons and crossed the river on an old ferry boat, going into camp at the ferryman's house, which was built of logs with a wooden addition on the south side. The ferryman had resided on the Brazos River many years. A few years previous, the Comanches had raided almost up to his door and killed his son, who was rounding up cattle for the night. He had three pretty girls—strong, robust of limbs, and the picture of exuberant health. They could ride a horse bareback and were experts with the rifle. One of the girls, Linda Ann, we named the "Wild Rose of the Brazos Bottom." She was magnificent, and, thinking the matter over, she was one of the most remarkable girls we ever met in our life, and only needed to rub up against civilized life to become a queen of society. She is a bright spot in memory and will never be forgotten.

At Austin we received a letter from her on the eve of her departure for far-off West Texas, stating that she was getting ready to leave on a fortnight's journey to visit a sister, with a relative and dog for companions. Mounted on horseback with a rifle at her saddle, she started on the long journey of 300 miles. When almost in sight of her sister's home, she was waylaid by a war party of Comanches, scalped, and the body horribly mutilated.

The rainy season set in, and our party was detained at the ferryman's place for about four days. The girls got together and sent word into the settlement that they intended to give a dance in honor of the boys of the surveying party. We can recollect a young man and girl who came a distance of thirty miles. A one-eyed colored fiddler furnished the music, and tallow candles stuck in wooden handles furnished the light. We danced until daylight; and, looking back over forty years, we can truthfully say that never before or since did we pass such an enjoyable night. Linda Ann and the writer found time to stray away from the party and say sweet things to one another. And we vowed that when the survey was over, we would make it convenient to renew the acquaintance. It was a case of love, and true love, at first sight. In a few months, she lay dead in a creek bottom beneath the Comanche's war knife. In general intelligence, beautiful face, and magnificent figure, she was the most remarkable girl we ever met.

When Captain Washburn arrived from Hearne and told the party they must break camp and make an early start in the morning, everybody felt sad. We had been treated so nicely we were loathe to leave. It was a sad farewell when we turned our faces to the far west and said, "Goodbye, girls; hope that we shall meet again."

It was the open prairie, and we made about nine miles that day. It was a delicious moonlight night. In the gloaming, we saw three persons dashing across the prairie, swinging their quirts over their heads, and heard the whoop-pa-la of female voices. They dashed into camp, almost riding over us. It was the girls of the Brazos bottom, wild and bareheaded, their hair streaming out in the wind. They jumped off and were soon stretched on the ground at the campfire. It was nearly midnight when they left camp. We asked them if they were afraid. They laughed and said, "We can ride so fast that even an Indian can't catch us, and we can fight, too"; and they caressed their Winchesters that hung to their saddles. With a yell, they streamed across the prairie and disappeared in the night. We never saw them afterwards, but learned that the two girls had married city fellows and were doing well. They were living at Hearne. The old ferryman had left the river and was residing near Hempstead.

We were so impressed with the Wild Rose of the Brazos Bottom that we intended to correspond with her and on our return make her our wife; and, in concluding this, we will say again she was the most lovable woman that has ever crossed our path, and we have often thought if we had the money and time, that we would visit her grave, which is in Lubbock County.

No. 64
Arbuckle Mountain Murders

Sunday Gazetteer, May 7, 1911

In the early seventies, an article appeared in the newspapers of the discovery of the bodies of a man and woman in the Arbuckle Mountains. The discovery was made by a party of hunters in the extreme cold of mid-winter. The cabin contained two beds, and the walls were adorned with a number of pictures and portraits. The floor was laid with puncheon, which was covered with the skins of wild animals that had been sewed together.

The man and woman arrived in the country in a wagon drawn by a pair of mules. With the assistance of cowmen who worked for old John Grant at Fort Arbuckle (an abandoned military post), they made a road through the woods to the highest peak of the mountains, where they erected a one-room log cabin. They had plenty of provisions and everything else to make the little cabin comfortable in the coldest weather. A shepherd dog accompanied them, and a cat that was inseparable from the dog, as the cowboys frequently saw them roaming the forest together.

The man claimed the young woman was his daughter. What attracted unusual attention was that the girl was pretty, refined, and intelligent, and the man had evidently seen better days. What brought this strange couple to the woods was a mystery.

Old John Grant told the writer that he sometimes visited them, and frequently sent them fresh beef. All effort to draw them out was a failure. They claimed to have come to the country from Massachusetts. At Parsons, Kansas, they purchased a good wagon and a mule team and drove through to the mountain country. Grant said that once in a great while they received a letter, the writing always being in the same hand, and the writer was evidently a woman. Grant could not recollect that they ever sent a letter. Cowmen stated the young woman was frequently seen seated outside the cabin writing. They brought with them a large number of books. The old man hunted and fished a great deal. The girl purchased a pony and was a hard rider.

The only remark that the man dropped that might clear up his presence was that he was tired of city life, its shams and shambles, and that he wanted to go to a country where he would see but little of his fellow man, and that at least he had found the place that suited him and was congenial to his daughter.

It was very rare that the old man visited the old fort, and then his stay was very brief. He did not loaf, spit tobacco juice, whittle a stick, or tell any stories. He never asked the news of the day or borrowed a newspaper. The cowboys were graciously received at the cabin, but when they attempted to spark the girl, they received a chilling reception.

The man and woman were in the mountains about one and a half years, but in that period the young woman never paid a visit to the old fort, although old John Grant was one of the most jolly and hospitable entertainers in the Indian country. Grant was a gentleman, a white man, and wealthy.

The mountain people had brought along a stove, and in the coldest weather the little cabin was warm and cheery. Belated cowmen used to stop and listen to the wonderful sweet voice that proceeded from the cabin. The girl had a guitar, but it seldom accompanied her voice.

One cold winter day, a party of hunters, bewildered by a storm that was raging in the mountains, espied the cabin. It was a lucky find, as they had lost their bearing and bid fair to pass the night in the forest. They approached the cabin and knocked, but there was no response. After repeated knocks, they looked into the only window in the cabin. They saw a ghastly face staring at them. The door was strong and had been secured on the inside with a heavy chain. A consultation was held, and it was agreed to break in the window and effect an entrance to the room. When the man entered, a cat flew at him, attempting to reach his throat or face. The door was forced open and the hunters entered.

The man and young woman were both dead. The pictures had been taken from the wall; the big trunk was missing and evidently been taken outside and burned. There was no evidence of foul play, but it was certain that both had died in the same way, by poison. The matter was reported to the authorities and the bodies buried near their lonely home on the top of the mountains. The mystery has never been cleared. Cowmen with long visage solemnly averred that the place was haunted and that on wild winter nights they heard the voice of the girl and the sound of the guitar.

The cat and the dog went wild and were seen in the mountains, catching birds on which they lived.

"It was singular," said Mr. Grant, "that no letter ever came after the people were dead."

No. 65

The Runaway Bride

Sunday Gazetteer, May 14, 1911

There is scarcely anything in the world that a woman will not do or undertake for the man she loves. She will brave any sort of danger and death itself, if necessary. It does not matter that the object of her affection is unworthy; she will follow him to the ends of the earth, through poverty, social ostracism, disgrace, everything. There is no price possible for a human that she will not pay. Her constancy is one of the marvels of men, and who does not appreciate her sacrifices?

This little introductory is illustrated in an incident when Denison was young.

There appeared in this city in 1874 a man and woman who registered at Ike Furber's hotel, at the [southwest] corner of Main Street and Houston Avenue, where Brucker Brothers are at present. The woman was beautiful, and her conversation showed that she was educated and refined. The husband was considerably older. They kept to their rooms, going out only at night. They seemed to have plenty of money and were liberal buyers at the dry goods houses.

After a stay of two weeks or so, the man called at the office and settled his bill, requesting the clerk to call him for the early morning train which went south. That night a man arrived at the same hotel and registered from a distant state. He looked over the register book and then pulled up a chair to the desk, prepared a telegram, and left the hotel. In about an hour he returned.

When the man and woman were passing into the hotel dining room, he pulled a pistol and ordered the man who was with the woman to hold up his hands, but as quick as lightning the man knocked down the party with the pistol and wrested it from his grasp and fled. The woman rushed from the dining room and grabbed the officer to prevent him from pursuing her husband. The man was never seen afterwards.

The officer, who had followed the couple from Chicago, stated that they had eloped about one year previous. The man was a thief and, when he left with the girl, had taken considerable money. The parents of the girl were rich, her father being one of the leading merchants of Chicago. She made the acquaintance of the confidence man while she was attending school. He was very smooth, fashionably dressed, good looking, and a sweet talker. The young girl fell in love with him, and they ran away. The man was an exception to the general rule. He married her, loved her, and was very devoted. The parents were outraged and, determined to bring their daughter home, put a detective on their trail. After they left Chicago, they went to Montana, and he opened a gambling house at Butte; from there the couple drifted to California. The purpose of his visit to Texas was to purchase a ranch and settle down to a respectable life.

After the escape of her husband, the woman remained at the hotel for a day or so. The detective endeavored to have her return to her home, but she flaunted the marriage certificate in his face and declared that she was a free agent.

Chief of Police McDowell threw a little light on the sequel. The man and woman got together again, threw themselves on the mercy of the parents, and were forgiven. The old man started the couple on a ranch in southwest Texas, where they settled, raised a family, and lived happily. That was a very happy ending.

Most of these cases, or at least nine out of ten, turn out badly. After a few months of pleasure, the woman is deserted and left on her own resources. She goes to the bad very rapidly and closes her career in the potter's field. But this case was one of true love; the woman took an awful chance—and won out.

Fig. 18. Grand Southern Hotel, 200 West Main Street.

No. 66

At the Grand Southern Saloon

Sunday Gazetteer, May 21, 1911

Where the Red Front Store now is, there used to be the Grand Southern Saloon [200 West Main]. The place was destroyed by fire a number of years ago. The Grand Southern was in pioneer history a noted resort, for several of the leading citizens of the business world made their start there. Mr. Justin Raynal, our public school benefactor, conducted business there and died in the second story. Mr. Chichet, who died [July 6, 1883] and left considerable property, sold out to Raynal.

It was very natural for the people going and coming to the notorious haunts of old Skiddy Street to stop at the Grand Southern. The place was very fortunate in having a proprietor and barkeepers who were the pink of politeness. Probably the most popular was Tony Stauffacher, father of Monk, at present with C.J. O'Maley. He was highly esteemed and respected. We never heard a vulgar or profane word fall from his lips.

The Grand Southern was the first place in Denison where free soup was served, and a lady (who evolved into a prominent church woman) handed out the soup. Her husband died and left considerable money. She married at the Presbyterian Church and afterwards raised a large family.

One of the first gambling houses was conducted in the second story. A keno room was run there by a man who afterwards became rich. He was also a city father and prominent in business circles. We can recollect one night at a late hour that the cards were worth one dollar each, and the "pot" at midnight ran up to nearly one hundred dollars, and was won by a Choctaw cattleman from the Indian Territory. When the play was over, everyone in the room was invited downstairs to take a drink at his expense, and in the bar-room were a number of old rounders, and they too were invited up to the bar. When the cattleman settled the bill, it was about twenty dollars.

The Grand Southern was the scene of one of the most noted tragedies in the history of Texas. A policeman named Patman was shot and killed by a notorious bad man named Doran. The trial dragged along for years. The murderer had the best legal talent in the Southwest. It was a cold-blooded murder, but Doran escaped hanging, which he richly deserved. There is only one man in Denison who was a witness to the murder—Barney Daniels—who was then a member of the police force.

The Grand Southern Saloon was a visiting place for the Indian full-bloods, who were numerous in those days and never failed to start a row before they left for their homes. One night Willie Jones, son of Ex-Governor Jones of the Choctaw Nation, came in there with a crowd. He called for drinks and, picking up the glasses on the counter, he hurled them against the bar mirrors. In those days the Indian visitors could do about as they pleased and escape arrest. Jones was not disturbed. The next morning he called around and settled the damage, which footed up about fifty dollars.

Jones' father was immensely rich in lands and cattle, and his son Willie was always flush when he came to town. He committed one of the most dastardly murders in the annals of the bloody Indian Territory. One night at Caddo, he shot and killed a white man named Bouton when he was coming from a show with his wife. Of course the murderer escaped. Bouton was a citizen, having married an Indian woman. The Indian courts winked at the murder.

Jones afterwards met his just deserts on the Blue Prairie west of Caddo. In a drunken row he was shot and killed, and the body remained there one day and night before the governor had it brought in.

The Grand Southern was the resort of the most noted Indian desperado that ever lived in the Choctaw and Chickasaw countries—Tandy Fulsom. He was a genuine "bad man," and the officers were all afraid of him. He was an outlaw for a number of years, and the U.S. marshals all carried papers for him. The government, to make a good Indian of him, sent him word by Judge Parker of the federal court at Fort Smith, that if he would come in and surrender, they would give him a commission as U.S. deputy marshal. Tandy accepted the olive branch and was for a number of years an efficient member of the force, one of his most notable deeds as a deputy U.S. marshal being the following.

At the meetings of the Choctaw council, the bootleggers always reaped a rich harvest. The members of the council were nearly all hard drinkers and when under the influence of tanglefoot were dangerous, and many desperate encounters took place. There were petty factions, and when they met at the Indian council, there was sure to be trouble. The U.S. government wanted this stopped and selected Officer Fulsom to do the work.

Fulsom went to Tuskahoma. It was one of the most dangerous missions that ever fell to the lot of an officer. In the council were a number of gunfighters, men who would fight at the drop of a hat and had notches on their guns of the men they had killed. But this made no difference to Tandy. He went down into the cellar of the capital building and found a lot of whisky, which was spilled. He met two or three of the members of the council who were drunk and took the bottles out of their pockets and smashed them. They threatened to kill him, but a second sober thought convinced them that, if they started in on the job, there would be a street full of dead men. They knew Fulsom was a fighter, a dead shot and quick as lightning with a gun. In a few hours, Fulsom had the situation in hand, and there was a sober council at Tuskahoma for the first time in many years.

Fulsom killed himself at his mother's home near Durant. He used to go to the second story of the Grand Southern and, when drunk, flop down on a bed with his boots on. This was not to the liking of Raynal, and he complained to the police, who attempted to arrest Fulsom. They finally gave it up as a bad job, as he was always armed when he came to town. They "rushed" him on several occasions, but it took the whole force to put him behind the bars. The officers got so many warrants out for him that he would not come here but turned out to be the most dangerous outlaw in the Five Nations. His name was a terror. There is no doubt but that he and his gang of rough riders killed many men.

While in company with C.P. Fox of Denison and Tack Harkins, an Indian, Fulsom and his gang stopped our carriage near

Robbers Roost. They wanted whisky, and we had it under the seat. They found it, and with a blood-curdling yell and firing their pistols into the air, they dashed away over the prairie. That night they went to a dance and shot and killed the fiddler, an inoffensive Negro. The old-time officers all agree that Tandy Fulsom was the worst man who figured in the early history of Denison.

The Grand Southern was the meeting place of the old Denison Gun Club, the most famous shots in the field and at the traps in the history of Texas. We have just skimmed over the history of that famous resort and may take the matter up in a future issue.

No. 67
The Bennetts

Sunday Gazetteer, May 28, 1911

Among the earliest businessmen in Denison were "the Bennetts." Will Bennett, who is at present down with paralysis at the home of his daughter, Mrs. Lewis, at Van Alstyne, was a prominent business factor. Thirty-five years ago he commanded the largest trade that came here from the Indian Territory. He was in business for himself a number of years and had his brother George associated with him. They were associated with A. Teah, who is a merchant at Palestine. The magnitude of their business relations extended all over the country.

Uncle George Bennett was a noted character. He was a businessman and also a sporting man. He was pre-eminently a man of the world, a philosopher, and took life as he found it and never said "Why?" Everybody was fond of Uncle George. He was a very entertaining man and could tell a good story with as much éclat as the famous Tom Ochiltree. Uncle George was a very dignified man, a true ideal of the old-time southerner "befo' de war." He was a gallant soldier of the Confederate cause and was with the Confeds east of the Mississippi.

When Uncle George had money, he used to patronize the faro bank and sometimes played poker. The people of the [Indian] Territory were fond of Uncle George, and he was a drawing card for any house. He was sometimes idle, but it was his own fault, as he liked to rest and take life easy. No man ever saw him without a cigar. He was a man of many noble qualities and would divide his last penny with an unfortunate. Always cordial and unselfish, everybody warmed toward him. We don't believe that Uncle George had an enemy in the world. At last death called him, and he passed away much regretted.

Will Bennett was intensely business and was always a hard worker. He never was a rich man but was prosperous until he was shipwrecked, like many Denison businessmen who are now dead and forgotten. His services were always in demand. He has a son who is at present division superintendent of the Illinois Central Railroad. He has several children living. Several years ago, physical decadence set in. He was stricken with paralysis but managed to keep his feet and struggle on, hopeful to the last.

There is another Bennett, "Baldy," who is looking 90 years in the face, and still hale and hearty. Next to Col. [J.B.] McDougall, he is the oldest active man in Denison. You can see him on the streets any day delivering milk to customers. He was for a number of years an active businessman of Denison. Like his brother, Uncle George, he is always good-natured, full of fun and frolic. He bears his years remarkably well. His wife is a wonderful woman, and by her tact, energy, and foresight has acquired considerable property. Mr. and Mrs. Bennett will rest and take life easy the balance of their days, but they will die in the harness. The older they grow, the more they like to work.

And there was another remarkable Bennett—W.M. He was a dreamer. He spent the greater portion of his life in mining speculations; for forty years or more, it was his hobby. His life was a romance. He spent thousands of dollars, a vast fortune, in his life chasing after what was only a shadow—a phantasmagoria. Just about the time that mountains of gold dawned before his vision, the view was dissolved, and he died poor. He was the most persistent gold seeker that ever lived; his spirit was dauntless; he never surrendered.

In the seventies and eighties, the Bennetts were always in the public eye. They came here from Fort Smith, Arkansas, where they were very prominent. They could tell many stories of old times before the Civil War. They were large slave owners and lived like the old feudal barons. They have many descendents, but the parent trees are dead and forgotten, as we soon will be.

No. 68
Warren Flats

Sunday Gazetteer, June 4, 1911

The death of Hugh Tumulty of Warren Flats recalls to memory many incidents of that section which may almost be called historic. Twenty or twenty-five years ago, that was the most famous and most frequented spot near Denison.

Warren Flats is about two miles east of the city. It is a low tract of land covering many acres and used to be covered with water and swamps. In season, thousands of wild ducks, geese, and jack snipe used to stop there in their migrations to feed. Hundreds of Denison sportsmen enjoyed fine sport down there. In the past few years, a great deal of the land in the flats has become arable for farming purposes, and the glorious sport of twenty or twenty-five years ago is a thing of the past. A great deal of the land has been ditched and drained, and the water that used to stand two or three feet over hundreds of acres, looking like an inland sea, has been superseded by dry land and growing crops. No one goes to the flats; it is deserted and silent.

There used to be snipe down there by the thousands, and snipe shooting is very difficult and exciting sport. The bird flies zigzag for a few yards and then suddenly darts down into the shallow water in the high grass. The members of the old Denison Gun Club were great snipe shooters and understood the erratic flight of the birds. They never failed to bring home large bags. The jack snipe is a delicious morsel when cooked properly—not fried, but toasted over a bed of hot coals.

Thousands of wild ducks used to settle in the swamps, and in season there were many wild geese. Now and then a canvasback, the best eating of the duck family, was killed. Major [L.L.] Maughs, a famous shot and member of the old gun club, once brought home two canvasback ducks. There used to be an old vacant house at the edge of the flats, and there the sportsmen spent the nights bunking down on the floor. There was a stove, and in the cold winter nights a roaring fire was kept going, and around this the boys used to sit, telling yarns. The bottle was passed around, and, inspired with good cheer, the old rafters echoed to songs and laughter. Many a good hunter's meal was prepared on that old rusty stove. In very rainy weather the old house was isolated, and to get to it one had to wade through water. Hugh Tumulty lived there, and the latchstring was always on the outside. His hospitality was not of the stinted kind, and he kept "open house" to the Denison boys.

Once upon a time George B. Goodwin, the first editor of the *Denison Herald*, and Col. I.M. Standifer went down to the flats to spend the night. The old house was full of boys who were hilarious and well tanked up. Goodwin and his party concluded that they would pass the night on a haymow near the house. Colonel Standifer had on an elegant silk hat which cost about $10. The hat was placed in a conspicuous place. At daylight, while Goodwin and Standifer were asleep, the hunters turned their shotguns loose and fired at least a thousand fine shot into Ike's plug hat. It was riddled. For a few moments the colonel was fighting mad, and he swore like a trooper, but he soon cooled off, and the presence of the bottle quieted matters. Goodwin and the colonel left after breakfast.

Duck shooting was the greatest sport down there, and thousands were killed. Ducks were so plentiful that even an indifferent shot could make a good bag. The cool, wet weather would bring them in by the thousands, and they would settle all around the hunters, and such cannonading was never since heard.

Many ducks were killed on moonlight nights when they would come in to roost.

One Saturday morning Mike Brown, Major Maughs, and one or two others left Denison for the flats. While on the Carpenter Bluff highway, a covey of quail got up. The dogs were turned loose from the wagon, and Mike Brown reached for his gun, pulling the muzzle toward him. In springing from the wagon, one of the dogs touched the trigger, and the whole load of shot was fired into the heart of Brown, killing him instantly. There was a hole in his breast so large that a hand could have been thrust into it.

For a number of years, Warren Flats was a favorite hunting resort. In season, every day sportsmen left for there, and jolly sport it was. From the early seventies, for a period of fifteen years, it was the Mecca for Denison sportsmen. But, alas! where are they now? Hugh Tumulty, now dead, was the last link that binds memory to the dear old spot. The old building that harbored so many Denison sportsmen has crumbled to pieces from old age and disappeared. The screech of the locomotive is now heard at the flats, and civilization usurps a section which will live in memory as long as life lasts.

No. 69

Pursuing a Horse Thief

Sunday Gazetteer, June 11, 1911

The longest ride after a horse thief in our recollection was in the fall of 1879. A thoroughbred horse was stolen from Fremont, Nebraska. The thief had about three days start, as the owner was absent at the time in Omaha. The horse was valued at $2,000 and had made a record on the turf.

One morning the thief presented himself at the home of the owner and claimed that he was an intimate friend; to confirm this, he related so many incidents that he disarmed all suspicion. He presented a letter that authorized him to bring the horse to North Platte, where he was to meet the owner. He left with the horse.

When the owner returned home, the whole plot was disclosed. He telegraphed along the line of the Union Pacific and then started in pursuit on horseback. The thief, having three days' start, cut loose from the railroads and telegraph wires. He crossed the line into Kansas, traveling by easy stretches. When arrested by Sheriff Everheart, he stated that he did not make over twenty-five miles per day, so as to save horseflesh and bring him in good condition to Texas, where he had a sale for him.

When the owner arrived in Kansas, he got the first clue of the stolen animal. When the man left Nebraska, he left an envelope that bore a Texas postmark, and the owner of the horse supposed that he would head for this state. He learned in Kansas that a man had passed through a certain section riding a horse answering the description of the one stolen. Hundreds of notices describing the horse and the man were sent to the officers of Kansas and Texas. A valuable reward was offered. Bill Everheart received one of the notices.

The thief left Kansas and went to the Osage Nation, where he had friends, and rested there for several days. The pursuer was baffled, having lost all trace of the thief. He did a great deal of telegraphing. The thief traveled at night, as he was well acquainted with the country. In daytime he would go to the deep woods, feed his horse, sleep, and rest; and when darkness set in, he proceeded on his journey. He took good care of the horse, and when captured the animal was in fair condition, notwithstanding his long journey of 1,500 miles.

The thief also had friends in the Choctaw Nation and passed several days in a full-blood settlement on the Canadian, where the horse was well fed and rested. It was there that the man received the first intimation that he was pursued. An Indian had been to the railway station and read the notice posted at the depot.

That night another horse thief rode into camp with a fine animal which had been stolen in Kansas. The two started together for Texas. When they reached the Chickasaw Nation, they met an officer who attempted to arrest them. They promptly shot and killed him. The new arrival (in the fight) was also shot, and when they reached Texas he went to a cabin near Coffee Bend, where he was cared for until he got well. Here another rest was made. By this time, the owner had arrived in Sherman, as he was confident the thief was heading for Texas and had probably entered the state. The reward offered was of such magnitude that he felt sure that the man would be captured.

After leaving Coffee Band, the horse thief started for the Preston district. Sheriff Everheart and deputy, while riding through a piece of woods, saw a man in the distance so faintly discernable that only keen eyes could have seen him. He was on the ground munching cheese and crackers. They rode up to him, and the sheriff immediately recognized the Nebraska animal. The horse thief had drawn his pistol and backed up against a tree. The sheriff asked him if he had seen any cattle, and dismounted. This remark caused the man to lower his gun. The sheriff asked what he meant by pulling his gun; that he was after cattle. The thief then went to his horse and mounted. He was leading the Nebraska horse. The sheriff and the deputy got in ahead of him and at the turn of the road held him up with their Winchesters. The thief at this point was obliged to keep to the highway, owing to the wire fences.

The man and the two horses were taken to Sherman and the owner communicated with. On a requisition from the governor of Nebraska, the horse thief was taken back, tried, convicted, and sent to the penitentiary for ten years.

This case was declared by the newspapers to be the longest pursuit after a horse thief ever known. The distance traveled by the man was over two thousand miles. In the Osage country, the man had purchased another horse and led the stolen animal. The horse was shipped back to Nebraska in a boxcar. The owner, in the pursuit, had ridden down two horses and arrived at Sherman on the cars. The thief hailed from San Saba County and was the son of a prominent cattle raiser. He was mixed up with a gang of horse thieves who used to steal animals in Kansas and Missouri and sell them in Texas. He was a young man, about thirty years of age.

No. 70

Old Cale, Indian Territory

Sunday Gazetteer, June 18, 1911

We used to call it "Old Cale," and when the town began to grow the name was changed to Sterrett [later Calera]. Sterrett is about fifteen miles from Denison on the MK&T. This sketch has nothing to do with the modern town, which at present has a population of about 2,500.

Sterrett is too near to Durant, but it is surrounded by a rich agricultural district and will always be a town of considerable commercial importance.

Old Cale, under the Indian regime, was merely a sidetrack, and about the only person who lived there was George T. Black. George lived northwest of the present townsite, close to the railway track. He married an Indian lady. When the Denison sportsmen went up there chicken shooting, they put up with George, as he had good water and an open hand and heart for Denison visitors. There were long hay sheds, under which we have passed many a night, making an early start for the prairie chicken grounds.

There was good shooting in every direction, but the hunters used to go east, as usually good water for the dogs could be found. Thousands of prairie chickens have been killed within a radius of a few miles of Old Cale. Cale, Durant, and Caddo were the favorite grounds for sportsmen from Denison. You could make a night start from here, reach the grounds sufficiently early to have a good morning's shoot and return in the evening. The sweetest sleep and the sweetest dreams of our early life were under the old hay sheds of George Black's at Cale.

We went there several times with Owen McCarthy. Owen was a royal good camp fellow, a capital storyteller, and a fair shot. At that period but very few people lived in the country. It was the open country, as the barbed wire fence had not yet come. You could travel on the open prairie all day and never be interrupted by a wire fence. Cattle fed on a thousand hills, and deer and wild turkey were killed within sight of the town. We can recollect seeing a band of at least twenty deer about five miles east of Cale, and quail, squirrels, and prairie chickens were always plentiful. We never saw Enoch Hughes make a potshot but one time, and that was east of Cale. A large covey of quail were bunched at the edge of some sumac brush. Enoch called our attention, but we were standing in a position where we could not see them. Hughes shot into the bunch and almost annihilated them. If we recollect, he killed twenty birds.

Thirty years ago, grouse were plentiful on the prairies just across the river.

We preferred Cale as a stopping place, because it was so pleasant to seek the shade of Black's hay sheds and rest, and then the water was cool and delicious. George would leave the house and come down and mix with the boys. He was, in his day and prime, a great hunter, one of the best known in the Indian country. He used to make up a party in the fall and go to the game country in the eastern portion of the Choctaw Nation, and some of his game records were the talk of the times. He used to bring deer and wild turkeys to the Denison market by the wagonload. At that period you could travel nearly a day and never meet a man or see a house. It was the ideal country for a man who loved the outdoor life. In those good old days, what a glorious country was the Five Nations. The cup of happiness was full to the brim, and the ominous shadow of civilization had not as yet darkened the land. Game was plentiful and the hunters few. We have seen wild turkeys displayed for sale here at 25 cents each, and venison hams were very cheap.

Many Denison sportsmen (if alive) will remember with emotions of pleasure Old Cale and the hospitable host, George Black. He is still a resident of Cale, hale and hearty, and engaged in the mercantile business. Cale, now called Sterrett, will never have the charm again of that period when only a single house was there and we used to bunk under the old hay sheds.

No. 71
Justice Slow But Sure

Sunday Gazetteer, June 25, 1911

Judge [A.W.] Mixson tells an incident of his official career—twenty years ago, when he was constable—that is quite thrilling.

A house had been robbed in the Indian Territory. A man who lived there crossed Red River into Texas, and seeing a party of campers near the river, alighted from his horse to warm [himself,] as the weather was very cold. He recognized a pair of boots on the feet of the camper, which belonged to him. The camp was composed of two wagons containing men, women, and children. The man mounted his horse and, arriving at Denison, notified the officers; and Tom Nelms, who was a deputy under Constable Mixson, and Bud East, then an officer, started in pursuit of the wagons.

The officers were dressed in uniform, and when they came in view of the wagons, the men handed the lines to the womenfolk, grabbed their Winchesters, and pulled them to full cock, and waited for developments. Nelms and East saw the chances were against them in a fight and rode on, but when out of sight cut around the cross country and returned to town. Constable Mixson, who was at home, was notified by Officer Nelms. He saddled up his horse and, gathering a posse of six men, started for the river. They went to Baer's ferry and traveled over the country for some time without seeing the wagons. Near where the Shawnee reservoir is at present was a spot known as the "Blue Hole." It is a good camping spot and has for many years been patronized by travelers.

Constable Mixson was in the lead of the party and espied the tops of the wagons through the woods. He halted and waved his hands to his companions to halt. When they charged on the wagons, they fired from behind cottonwood trees, and for a moment or so there was brisk cannonading. The men mounted their horses and escaped, however. Constable Mixson took charge of the wagons, women, and children and brought them to Denison. They were kept here for several days and then turned over to Bob Mayes, who was then sheriff of the county.

This incident happened twenty years ago. The strangest part is yet to come. One of the men has been recognized in Oklahoma and papers are now in the hands of the proper authorities for his arrest. This carries out the old saying, "The mills of God grind slowly but sure." Perhaps before this issue of the *Gazetteer* is out, the man may be lodged in the Sherman jail.

Since this was written, Officer East has visited the *Gazetteer* office and tells of his narrow escape during the battle. He was standing behind a small hackberry tree, and a number of balls lodged in the tree, and one ball passed through his collar, grazing his neck. East has been an officer here for many years, and this was about the closest call he ever had.

No. 72
Hunting in the Boggies

Sunday Gazetteer, July 2, 1911

We frequently wish for a return to the old Choctaw grounds that border the clear and the muddy Boggies. Why it is called the Muddy Boggy, we could never discern. After heavy rains, both streams look alike. We have been all over the Indian country in the outdoor life, but no place visited has so much sentiment for us as the Boggy. It seemed to me as the jumping-off place of civilized life. There were dense forest and wild animals, and it was very seldom that a strange face was seen. The Indians that live on the hill bordering the great woods would sometimes visit our camp. They had the scent of an epicure and were always very punctual at mealtime, and we made a point to give them a hearty welcome, for there were occasions when they were very useful.

On our first trip to the Boggy country, an old Negro, whose feet were shoeless and his coat composed of as many colors as Joseph's garment, rode into camp on a mule who, he declared, had passed through the war with Van Dorn's command in Arkansas. He said that he thought the animal was over fifty years of age. He led the mule to a tree and left him, and the mule never stirred in his footsteps from early morn until the hoot of owls which announced the approach of night.

Being strangers, we asked him about the game, and he told us of a big buck that roamed the forest. It was, according to his story, as big as a steer, and so wild and alert to danger that no hunter had yet been able to kill him. The big buck had roamed the woods for several years and seemed to bear a charmed life. While telling the story, the old man's eyes dilated, and he seemed to be worked up into great enthusiasm, saying, "If you stay here long, you are sure to see him, as this is the running season, when the bucks chase the females."

A few nights afterwards, we marched down to the old sawmill crossing, the road where the teams used to cross to the old mill that had long been abandoned, as the business was not profitable and in bad weather the highway was so bad that hauling did not pay. The distance to the railway where the lumber was received was about fifteen to twenty miles. There used to be at the crossing a very large log. Here the teamsters used to tie up for the night and go into camp.

On a very quiet night, seated on this log, you could hear the very sweetest of music coming from the blue waters just below you, singing a forest song as they rippled over the white pebbles and stones—ever flowing on, for it was a running stream throughout all seasons. Sometimes [the waters would be] standing in large blue pools which in the fall were the haunts of wild ducks in their migration south. Deer used to love to come to these big holes and in the still night hours would steal down the banks and quench their thirst, splashing the water with their forefeet. In the running season, if the bucks heard a noise, they would whistle so loud that you could hear them some distance. These large water holes were a great resort for coons. They would come in large numbers and fish with their paws, quarrel and fight and roll in the water.

On one occasion when the harvest moon was at its full, we saw a mother deer and her offspring come to the big hole. The fawn was so young that it was unsteady on its feet, just like a child that is learning to walk. Nature never held out to man a prettier or more innocent picture. The fawn followed its mother to the water's edge and stepped in, beating the water with its forefeet. It then turned and ran a few feet and laid down in the sand. The mother followed it, and with every demonstration of affection, licked its mottled skin until it shone in the moonbeams which were beating down on it. It was a pretty picture: maternal love on one part, and happy trust on the other.

There is no spot in the world where all the conditions are so perfect for reflection as in the forest. There is no other loneliness so deep and solemn, or that so haunts the imagination.

One night, on our first trip to the Boggy forest, we stopped at the old sawmill crossing for rest and reflection. The moon was full and flooded the forest with light. There was such stillness that it was almost oppressive. We heard a splash in the waters below, and going to another log for a better view, we saw a huge misshapen object in the bed of the creek. It seemed as if small trees were growing from its head. We had never seen such antlers before. It had become aware of our presence and turned to flee. When it dashed up the mountainside, we fired, but it disappeared in the dense woods. The next day the old darkey rode into camp, and we told him we had seen the big buck, and he replied, "You no kill him; nobody ever kill him."

On our next visit to the woods, we learned that an Indian hunter had slain the big buck and that cowmen and Indian rangers said that it was the largest deer ever killed in the Territory, and they based their opinion upon the fact that they had for many years been traveling through the Five Nations and had been present at the killing of many large bucks, but they had never seen one like the big buck of the Boggies.

Twenty-five years ago, when we first visited the Boggy country, it was essentially an unbroken wilderness. It was penetrated by but one bad road. The free range of the forest suggested endless possibilities of exploration. Then you could never travel without seeing deer and wild turkey, and the streams were swarming with wild ducks, especially the wood duck with its gorgeous plumage. We were always crossing the trail of lurking animals. The appearance of a human being was startling. We describe conditions when we first visited it. It had but little been spied out by hunting parties. In the foothills there lived a few Indians and Negroes, but they were not hunters. In the annual roundups, a party of cowmen might now and then be encountered, but it was rare.

But civilization was creeping slowly and irresistibly into this hunter's paradise—this lovely land. The Frisco built the road east from Durant, towns sprang up, and it was not long before white faces with dogs and guns put up their tents, and the slaughter of game began, until at present not a deer or wild turkey is left in all the land. The forest has been despoiled; sawmills are in operation, good roads established, and the creak, creak of traveling wagons salute the ear at almost any hour of the day. Farms have been opened, and brawny men are slashing away at the forest, letting the sunlight in on the open fields. This state of affairs may be all right but we can never reconcile ourself to it.

The last trip to the Boggy woods, we heard the firing of guns all around, the yelling and shouting of hunters, and we cursed the change that had come. Still, we would like to see the old country again and look down upon the stream that in the years gone by brought joy to our heart, for in the long tramps we never failed to stop now and then and drink its pure waters. Civilization could never change that country, but that we can [I wish we could?] go and pick out the spot where we used to go and loiter on moonlight nights and listen to the song of the water, and there review the old scenes, which might come back, and with them the old faces—Will Senter, Morris Crooks, China Joe, Fred Bogar, Tom Reardon, Bud Andruss, John Williams, Ellison the great fox hunter, James Senter, and Mrs. Senter, who was the kindest and most companionable woman we ever met in the woods. And then we would like to build a great fire and tell stories of the past, and listen to the demonic laughter of the owls, the cry of wolves, the most dismal sounds that ever disturbed midnight and silence.

Every year in the fall and winter, the old feeling returns, and we long for the real old Boggy woods, missing it like a dear old friend.

No. 73

Denison's Growth

Sunday Gazetteer, July 9, 1911

People say that Denison hasn't grown much. Denison has spread over a great deal of territory and covers a wide extent of land. We can recollect the time when a person would have been laughed at to say that the town would push out to the old Miller's Spring. In the seventies [1870s], when the foundation for the high school [Educational Institute] was being laid [in the 700 block West Main], a protest was made that the building was too far out.

We recollect a ride with Dr. [Alexander W.] Acheson in the western portion of the city, which was then covered with forest trees. There were cow paths but no regularly outlined streets. We said to the doctor, "Do you think that Denison will, in our time, expand to this section?"

The doctor smiled and answered, "Where we are now standing will contain hundreds of beautiful homes and well laid out streets." The doctor was right, but we did not believe it at the time.

Denison has grown miles and miles—east, west, north, and south. No particular section has outstripped the other. East Denison has perhaps shown a little more of the building spirit than any other section. It is a pretty portion of the city, the only drawback being so many railway tracks to cross. We recollect a sale of town lots over there about ten years ago. Every lot sold then has doubled its value.

Southeast Denison contains more vacant lots than any portion of the city. Within the past year, hundreds of lots have been purchased for speculation, the price paid being about $250 per lot. That it will prove a splendid investment no one can doubt. The Traction Company [Interurban] has promised to extend their line to that section, and then property over there will go off like hotcakes. The building of the subway [East Crawford Street underpass], which is an assured fact, will greatly help that portion of the city. Southeast Denison will build up very rapidly with beautiful homes.

Northwest Denison will always be the most aristocratic part of the city, as the owners of the property there are well-to-do businessmen who seem to vie with one another in building improvements.

Denison due north is a drag; it is the Negro portion. A large number own their homes and are too poor, and are contented to live in shacks. That portion of the town has shown no improvement of any consequence in many years. Every city must have its "happy hollow," and Denison is not exempt from the incubus. Wherever you find a Negro home, there you will find poverty and contentment, for the Negro is always satisfied to accept conditions as he finds them, living from hand to mouth. The Negroes are community people and live together.

Denison covers more territory than Sherman and has more houses. The public buildings of Sherman, however, surpass ours greatly.

We who have lived here since the seventies and eighties can only realize how much the town has grown. It is today the best laid out city in the state. Our magnificent wide streets are the wonder of visitors, and we really have the prettiest town in Texas. Denison will come to her own after a while. Its natural business advantages and geographical location are bound to make a prosperous and large city. Our present troubles will adjust themselves. What we need is more business sympathy, and that people get together and do something.

There has always been a lack of harmony, and the Board of Trade [precursor to the Chamber of Commerce] in its best days was never a happy lot of boosters. They got down on Tom Larkin, who worked day and night to keep things moving along, then he left and went to a larger city where he was appreciated. They owed him about one and one-half year's salary, which we do not believe was ever paid. The Larkin successors never amounted to a hill of beans.

Many people appreciated Larkin. Some said that he was a blow-hard. A man in his class must blow and "toot" his own horn.

We have sat with Larkin many times, and nobody knows the tremendous amount of work he performed. His office was always crowded with a lot of people who had a grievance to air. The croakers were largely country people who thought the Denison Board of Trade was neglecting them. Larkin started the Good Roads Movement. He set on foot our sales day, which drew more business for Denison than any other action in our history. He was frail in health but stuck to his post, and if he ever went away for a few days, it was for the good of the city.

Larkin has been secretary of the Board of Commerce at Beaumont (a city of 30,000 population) for over three years. They know a good man when they see one.

It is a great mistake to say that Denison is not growing. More homes—good homes—have been erected in the past year than any previous period in our history. Thirty years ago, two blocks in any direction from Main Street was a forest of trees; think of this when you make unfavorable comments. We have grown miles and miles beyond the woods. South Denison has pushed almost to the cotton mill. Every section shows amazing growth. A million dollars or more in public improvements have been accomplished in the past two or three years.

There is a class of merchants, common to Denison as well as to all cities, that cry hard times, poor business, etc., and yet they are all making money; and when you get them down to hard-pan, they will admit that this year's business was better than last. The banks of Denison are more prosperous than ever. Look at their quarterly statements. The banks are the best criteria to judge what a city is doing; and according to them, we are going some. When the season sends us plenty of water, Denison will move forward. In the matter of water, we will surpass any city in Texas.

The industrial advantages of Denison cannot be overestimated. We have coal at our door, and do you know that Denison has more passenger trains in and out every twenty-four hours than any city in Texas? We are the railway metropolis in North Texas. The agricultural conditions are no worse here than in other portions of the state. We will pull through—it is so written. Denison is all right.

No. 74

She Would Take Him Back

Sunday Gazetteer, July 16, 1911

There is a woman who lives in Denison who was bereft of her husband in a singular manner one cold, disagreeable Saturday night in the winter. She said to her man: "John, we have no groceries, and you take some of the money you have and go down to the store and get something for the Sunday dinner."

John, who was not in a very good humor, grabbed the basket and went out into the storm, muttering to himself. He left the house about seven o'clock and it was a late hour before he returned. He laid down his basket and pulled up his chair to the open fireplace. The wife remarked, "It took you so long that you had better stayed away for good." John said nothing at this rebuke, but put on his overcoat which he had hung up in the hall as he entered the house.

That was the last his wife saw of him for eight years. She was receiving the rent from two houses and owned the one she lived in and managed to get along. She adopted a little girl.

One Saturday night, just eight years from the time when her husband left, there was a knock at the door, and in stepped John. His reception was very cold and indifferent, and the wife began to ply him with questions. He hung his head and said nothing. They seemed to get along very well after the incident. He worked at the Katy shops for about a year. He was very much attached to the girl that his wife had adopted.

One night the wife said, "John, I want you to go to the butcher shop and get some meat, but don't stay away as long as you did before, but I got along very well without you."

John requested the little one to go along, and she put on her bonnet, and, taking his hand, they disappeared in the street.

The wife waited and waited, but John and the girl did not return. The next morning she visited the meat market and was told that her husband had been there and paid for the meat, which was ordered to be sent to the house.

That incident happened twenty-five or more years ago, and the man and girl have never been heard of since. No clue, no letter, has ever reached her. The woman is still a resident of southwest Denison and is living with her brother, who went to Australia and made considerable money in the sheep-raising business.

The woman still has hopes that John and her girl will come back to her.

There was a fortune teller who advertised in the Denison papers, and the woman consulted her, but she was told nothing new. She went to St. Louis several years ago, and a spiritualist medium startled her with what purported to be information concerning her missing husband and girl. She stated that the couple were living at Portland, Oregon. When the woman returned to Denison, she set an inquiry on foot and wrote to the chief of police and mayor of Portland. They answered that they had never heard of such a man and woman.

The wife is still hopeful and expects that John may step into the house any hour or day. She is old and bent with age. She has acquired the habit of peering into the blackness of the rainy nights, for, she says, it is on such a night that John and the girl will come back to her.

The silver is thickening in her hair, and deep lines of thought have furrowed her brow, but nothing but death, which is not far off, will quench the hope that John will come back, and she says, "When he comes I will keep him."

No. 75

Ed Lane, Outlaw Newsman

Sunday Gazetteer, July 23, 1911

There appeared in Denison in the eighties a young newspaperman by the name of Ed Lane. He dressed elegantly and was a handsome young fellow, and would come under the name of "a lady killer."

Lane arrived in Denison with a reputation. He had been city editor of the *Sedalia Democrat,* and one day on the capital steps at Jefferson, Missouri, slapped Gov. Crittenton in the face. [Thomas Theodore Crittenden (1832–1909) was a Union colonel during the Civil War and governor of Missouri from 1881 to 1885.] This incident compelled him [Lane] to leave Missouri, and he drifted down through the Indian Territory to Texas, stopping at Houston. While doing newspaper work there, he had trouble with the chief of police which ended in a shooting affair, both men discharging their weapons at one another while down in the gutter. The officer was badly wounded in the hip.

Lane went from Houston to Alexandria, Louisiana, where for some irregularity he was placed in jail. He broke out of jail, and, armed with a Winchester, defied the whole police force. How he escaped we never learned. From Alexandria he returned to Texas and did newspaper work. He was a brilliant writer, and it was easy for him to obtain employment.

Lane finally turned up in Denison. Tom Linn was at that time publishing a paper, and Lane was the city reporter. The paper ceased publication, and Lane revived it. He became very dissipated, and while in that condition wrote some articles which gave mortal offense to our Jewish merchants. He called names and declared that they were a detriment to the town and made their money by cheating farmers. His articles created a sensation, and the whole town got down on him. His reputation as a fighter made people afraid of him. He always went armed and would fight at the drop of a hat. He was a genuine bad man.

At that time the Scholl brothers [Charles and Mortimer], who were publishing a paper in the Nolan Building, went to the defense of the merchants. This made Lane mad, and one evening in his paper appeared an article that stirred the fighting blood of the Scholl boys. In fact, it was a challenge to come and fight it out. Charley Scholl accepted the gauge of battle and, procuring a Winchester, left his office at an early hour hunting Lane. Lane arrived with a .44 Colt, walking calmly down the south side of Main Street until he reached the Porter grocery store, where he stopped and called for a cigar. He then passed into the next store, looking across to the Scholl boys' office. Charley Scholl had caught sight of Lane and crossed over to the Porter's grocery store—and then the balls opened. Both were protected by iron awning columns. Scholl would fire, and Lane would return it. Mort Scholl ran across the street and got behind a dry goods box. He was unarmed. Lane fired one shot at him, which perforated the box but missed Mort. The police arrested both parties. When the battle was over, it was discovered that a country man passing down Main Street had the heel of his boot shot off.

For the want of patronage, Lane's paper suspended. In a few days afterwards, Lane and a man named Rhea had a drunken row in the hall upstairs in the Muller Block. Col. I.M. Standifer, who was present, saved Rhea's life. Lane had leveled his pistol at Rhea, when the colonel grabbed and disarmed him. If Colonel Standifer had not showed nerve, Rhea would have been killed.

Lane went from here to Oklahoma City, where he got into trouble over a girl and was sent to the penitentiary. The trouble was unquestionably a conspiracy, and after awhile Lane was released.

We heard that he professed religion and had turned preacher, but we cannot vouch for the story.

Lane was without doubt one of the most desperate men that ever lived here at the period of bad men. It was said that he was a graduate of the University of Virginia. He certainly was well educated. When sober, he was a splendid entertainer and a gentleman. He was very fastidious as to dress and put on a clean shirt every day. With him, money was as free as water. He borrowed money from Colonel Standifer to leave here to go to Oklahoma, if we mistake not. At that period, Colonel Standifer was a freelance, hail fellow well met, and would give up his last cent to a friend.

No. 76

"Save the Forests"

Sunday Gazetteer, July 30, 1911

Fifty per cent of the woods within a radius of ten miles of Denison has been cut down and brought here for stove wood. If the present vandalism is persisted in, this section will be treeless in a few years, and serious results will follow. A country without trees is the most barren, forlorn aspect in the world. A country dotted with groves is always inviting—always inspiring. We can recollect a few years ago that every Sunday we used to proceed down the line of the Bonham branch of the Katy and spend an hour or so stretched out on the ground in the cool shade of beautiful forest trees. It was pleasant to indulge in daydreams and gossip with our friend, Colonel Reardon. Now every tree is gone, the land put under cultivation, and the trees converted into cordwood. This depredation has extended to all sections of the country around the city. There used to be plenty of shady drives, but they have gone with the rest.

The very moment that a renter gets on a place, his first impulse is to attack the trees. There is not a farm around Denison that is free from large gaps where the trees have been cut out for stove wood.

Everybody knows that the rainfall is seriously affected when the forests are cut down. This has been demonstrated more seriously in the Adirondack region of New York State, where many lakes have gone dry and streams dried up. There legislation has stepped in, and no more sawmills are allowed, and a great many have moved out. That entire region is now in the hands of capitalists who go there and spend their summer vacations and have shut out the despoilers. That is one good thing, at least, that trust holders have done. This feeling has spread all over the United States, especially in the West. "Save the forests" has entered largely into political life. The government has employed hundreds of forest riders to prevent the spread of fire and keep the wood thieves out.

We can recollect that the old Boggy country in the Choctaw Nation used to be the ideal country for all kinds of wild game—a veritable hunters' paradise. The sawmills got in there, the game is all gone, and the forests have disappeared.

When the city of Denison was first laid out, a portion of the town site was covered with forest trees. They were cut down, but many of them could have been spared and made ornamental to the streets and yards. Civic pride is a new thing in Denison, but it is wending on. Thousands of trees are being planted annually, but the drought has done serious harm, and at least 75 per cent of the shade trees planted have died.

The question is to prevent the indiscriminate slashing of the woods contiguous to Denison. A great deal of the farming lands are owned by Denison people, and they can prevent the vandalism if they see fit. A few years ago, you might ride for miles in the shade of beautiful forest trees that kept the ground cool and shut out the scorching rays of the summer sun, at any point around Denison; but you can't do it now. The trees have disappeared—cut down for fence posts and cordwood.

When the writer lived east of the city about one mile and a half, there was a beautiful grove of trees on the southeast portion of the old Pete Lynn place. The Lynns had plenty of land to cultivate, but the beautiful trees seemed an eyesore, so Pete turned two or three Negroes in there with axes and had every tree cut down. Cattle used to stand in the shade of the grove during warm weather, and birds gave concerts in the branches. We thought of it as one of the most beautiful spots in that whole section.

Perhaps a quarter-mile east of the Lynn place, reaching up to the old [Howard] racetrack, there was a continuation of woods that made it pleasant for people passing along the Carpenter's Bluff highway to look at, but every tree has disappeared.

The average farmers, especially renters, have no idea of civic pride. We know of many farmhouses around Denison that were in a grove of trees, but now they stand in the barren open; the trees have been cut down. A little southwest of Denison, there used to be a two-story suburban home. The house was painted white, and it looked like a gem in a setting of emerald green. There were about two acres of forest trees, nearly all being of uniform growth. There was a lane that led from the highway to the house, and the pathway was graveled with small white pebbles. It was shaded on either side with great post oak and cedar trees. The owner sold the place and went back to his former home in Missouri. And what did the possessors do? In about two or three years, every tree had been cut down except in the lane leading up to the house. They seemed to have escaped. The well now stands in the sun. Many unfavorable comments were made on the desecration.

The time is coming when what has been done will be regretted. You can't place those trees back, for the majority were here long before Denison was on the map.

Spare the trees; ponder long and well before you use the axe. They are the noblest objects of Nature, the playgrounds for hundreds of children, and grown people also. The ravage has gone so far around Denison that our stove wood is nearly all coming from Oklahoma.

No. 77

Camping in Kiamitia Country
(Episode 1)

Sunday Gazetteer, August 6, 1911

The first trip that I ever made to the Kiamitia [also called Kiamichi] country, in the eastern portion of the Choctaw Nation, was about 38 years ago. My companion was John Collett. At that period the Kiamitia country was little known, and it was a very rare event to meet a white face, and the Indians were few and far between. Those mountains and the hundred-mile woods shut us out from any semblance of civilized life. We can recollect being in camp a week and then traveling for two or three days without seeing any other living object except the wild denizens of the forest that now and then crossed our trail and, seeing us, would stop and look—at one time a monster buck, in an attitude of battle, with head lowered to the ground and acting as if he intended to dispute our passage.

One night we heard a noise that made our flesh creep. It was a wail and cry like a woman in distress. We discovered next morning the padded footprints of a panther that had circled the camp but was kept at a respectable distance by a large campfire of pine knots that illuminated the forest for many yards distant.

In these woods the isolation was complete; it was a trackless forest. We saw no evidence that man had been there. The road we traveled was so rough that only several miles a day was possible. Along the creek bottoms, where travelers usually stopped to rest for the night, there were no signs of extinct campfires. There is no land so lonely that has not its graves. We saw a mound covered with rough split pine boards that told the story that someone slept there. On the grave were piled rocks to prevent wolves and bears from disturbing it. We were in that country two weeks and never saw a human being or habitation.

Descending the mountains to the settlement in the gorge of the hills, there was a deserted sawmill, the houses of which had rotted and partially fallen to the ground. Many years previous, the owner of the mill had been called to the door and was shot and killed.

The mountain streams were literally alive with game fish, principally bass. The very first cast that we made with hook and line, a five-pound bass was secured. The streams were as clear as crystals; the water was supplied by springs that gushed out from surrounding hills. Our principal enjoyment was fishing; in fact, our principal food was fish. We had been to the woods before but had acquired little experience in woodcraft. Our camp outfit was very plain—a sack of meal, a sack of flour, a side of bacon, some navy beans, jug of molasses, sack of salt, and a box of matches; no canned goods, a luxury which we enjoyed on every visit to the woods afterwards. The fish were spitted on sticks and broiled; they were delicious, fried fish being no comparison.

At night the stillness of the pine forest was remarkable, the least sound was alarming, and uneasy glances were turned now and then toward the darkness. One night we received a great scare. A black she-bear with two cubs stopped on the trail and then deliberately walked into the glare of the campfire. I cautioned Collett not to shoot, as a wounded bear is a dangerous neighbor. We scrambled into the wagon and held the mules, which had been secured to the wheels. They had started the wagon down the mountain, but fortunately it struck a big pine tree and hung up. When we again looked up, the bear and cubs had disappeared in the surrounding gloom. One of the mules broke loose but hung around the camp until morning, when it was secured.

The virgin forests had not as yet felt the impress of the woodsman's axe. Back behind our camp was a big peak with a small clearing, perhaps an acre; and in the morning, while the shadow of the sun was chasing the shadow out of the forest, we saw several deer. Some were standing and others lying on the ground. When they discovered our camp, they disappeared as if the ground had swallowed them up.

While in camp on a small mountain branch, we saw a troop of at least a hundred wild turkeys marching majestically out of the recesses of the forest. They were getting their morning feed and picking the ground as they moved on. Such a sight will never again be seen in the Oklahoma woods. At that period (November), the woods were full of mast. About two hundred yards up the creek was a number of pecan trees, which induced us to make our camp nearby. They were loaded with nuts, and here the gang of turkeys lingered, scratching and making the leaves scatter in every direction. They paid no attention to the camp. The distance was too great for gunshot. There was a burnt hole in the tent and we took turns looking at them. They soon fed out of sight up the mountainside, and we saw them no more. We saw many turkeys, but they were in small bands. Deer, turkey, and bear signs were noticed every day.

The deeper we penetrated into the forest, the more lonesome it became. There is no other loneliness so deep and solemn as that which haunts the imagination, and is so full of joy and fear as the far-away loneliness that is felt in the gloomy, trackless wilderness, especially when you have but one companion. We have often thought of the pioneer, who alone penetrated the forest and led a solitary life for years, surrounded by wild beasts and savages.

One morning early, we broke camp. We didn't know the country, but a dim road that had at some remote period been traveled led in the direction of the mountaintops. We were free travelers of the wilderness, sleeping where night caught us—buoyant, healthy, and happy. We found new worlds opened up to us in the virgin woods. We were companions of forests, mountains, and wild animals; lords of the wilds, as Jack London would have expressed it, had he been there.

As we roughed it along, Collett remarked, "What would we do if the wagon should break down or the mules stampede?"

"Do?" we answered. "Foot it back to the settlement and return with a rescue party, or desert the outfit."

At night we met face to face the delight of the whole trip—a lake. If I live rational to my dying day, I shall never forget its appearance. The azure waters had a perfect setting of green woods, in which the shade of the pines, post oak, and cedar were perfectly blended. It was very evident that the lake had never felt the caress of the fisherman's line. The waters were actually boiling, and game fish would now and then roll up and show their brilliant colors. We struck camp and explored the lake, and discovered a number of springs.

No. 78
Camping in Kiamitia Country (Episode 2)

Sunday Gazetteer, August 13, 1911

We cannot recollect a more delightful night than the one passed on the shore of the beautiful lake. At night the wolves howled dreadfully. It was so dark that we could not see them, but from the din, they must have been very close to the camp, and we saw their tracks the next morning in the soft mud at the lake. We also discovered many deer tracks and the signs of coons and o'possum. We agreed to remain in camp at the lake for two days. Thinking the matter over in our present frame of mind, we could now make those virgin woods and the beautiful lake our stopping place for weeks. There was probably not a human habitation within a day's travel of the lake. The game was very tame, which confirms the belief that no hunters had ever been in the country; and the roads— or, more properly, the trails—had not been traveled in many months. No wagon or horse tracks, or any signs of a camp, were discernable. In traveling we had no objective point and were lost most of the time. We had no compass to direct our course. The truth is, that is the proper way—or was the proper way at that period—to enjoy an outing.

We were early risers, and the sun never caught us in bed. At early morn is the proper time to hunt and see game, which is always on the move. But the hunter must not move around. The still hunter goes to an old log, takes a seat, and waits. If he is a good hunter, he is patient and will sometimes tarry at one spot for hours. His patience is usually rewarded. The novice is always on the move and steals through the woods like a shadow, but in nearly every instance, the game sees him first, and the novice is always a disappointed hunter. In the open woods of a pine forest, still hunting is the only remedy. The country around can be seen for a long distance, and if you are walking, it is almost impossible to get a shot. The man who seats the log and hardly blinks his eye is the man who brings in the game.

We can tell you another fact: the most successful wild turkey hunter goes to a large tree and sits in front of it in the open. He is immovable; there is not the slightest motion. Gangs of wild turkeys will very frequently feed up to within a few feet of the still hunter. Old Man Bozarth, a great hunter that lived in the Territory woods, hunted turkeys in front and not behind a tree. The tree must, however, be sufficiently large to cover the entire body. Still hunting for deer is carried on in the same manner. The man who sticks to his log, and the wind is in the right direction for the quarry, is sure to get a shot if there is any deer in that section.

As we stepped out of the camp, we said to Collett, "Old man, this is lovely, but what shall we call the lake?"

"The Unknown," he answered.

While proceeding to the lake to wash our faces, we saw at the other end a dim object. It was hardly light, and ponderous shadows were stretched across the water. The object moved, and, looking more intently, we made out the outlines of the biggest buck that we ever saw in the Choctaw woods. He was as big as the biggest steer that we have ever seen. He had caught a glimpse of our tent. In a few minutes, the sun had crested the treetops, and the big buck was in plain view; his feet were deep in the brown sands, and his antlered head lifted as if in proud challenge into the air. His position was one of haughty interrogation as to what the dim object at the upper end of the lake was, and, as if in superb defiance, he twice lifted a foreleg and drove his pointed hoof into the sand, displaying lordly impatience at the ignorance or audacity of those who dared to disturb by their bold presence, his royal privacy. Twice he lifted his brown muzzle and blew a blast from his resounding nostrils that tore fiercely through the air and made the forest behind him ring again, while the mountains across the lake received the wrathful sound and passed it back. Once he started, as if some suspicion had for an instant broken over the ramparts of his courage and stormed into the very pavilion of his kingly spirit; but it was only a passing weakness. He gave one jump, then stopped, planted himself as if incapable of fear, lifting his nose high up, and blew again a wrathful challenge to the rude intruders, while the hair on the line of his back ridged in wrath and his feet smote the beach like hammers. Collett lifted his Winchester and fired. The buck had never heard a sound like that before. Collett fired again and made a clean miss. The buck turned leisurely around and disappeared in the forest.

The first day we were surfeited with fish. They would jump at the shadow of the bait as it dangled over the water. They carried away two flies. We landed several bass that weighed several pounds. The first were very partial to artificial flies, and other bait was not much of a temptation. A simple brown hackle was seized with tremendous energy when it touched the water, and the fish put up a terrific fight before he was exhausted and could resist no more.

That night the wolves were so bad that we feared an attack and made a great campfire, leaving the tent and making our bed in the wagon. The mules were secured with double ropes, and we made a sort of corral by passing behind them a large rope which was run from the front to the hind wheels. If the mules had broken loose, the wolf pack would have run them down and killed them. Now and then the pack would break into the light. They were very large, the fierce loper that will attack men when hungry. We did not dare fire a gun, as the mules might stampede. There was one big wolf, more bold than the others, that seemed bent on entering the corral and seizing a mule. A portion of the campfire was moved behind the corral, and the leader of the pack was seen no more. Pine knots were plentiful and would burn a long time. We snatched up brands of fire and hurled them at the wolf pack. Just at the break of day, we left the wagon and went to sleep in the tent, and the sun was near the meridian before we left our couch. We had slept none during the night.

We never saw so many deer tracks, the shores of the lake being literally tramped up, and we noticed what was either a bear or panther's track. A lively discussion took place; the writer stuck to the bear sign. When we got into the foothills, an Indian told us that bear and panther were quite plentiful.

In spite of wolves, bears, and panthers, we decided to remain another day. The fishing was superb. We have never enjoyed such sport since. Toward evening, a large flock of wild turkeys, numbering at least fifty, appeared. They were in a joyful mood and chased each other along the banks. All at once, they looked in the direction of the camp, and some flew and others ran into the woods. We saw several deer that came to quench their thirst as night was descending on the wilderness. Collett saw a black stump and said it was a bear. We were all wrought up over the night's experience and were in a frame of mind to magnify a stump into a bear. I looked at the mountains in the gloaming and saw a line all around the horizon; the rosy tint in the west made a broad band of pink along the sky above the treetops, and the evening star was a perfect circle of light—a hoop of gold in the heavens. I said to Collett, "It is time to go to camp, reel in our lines, and go home."

No. 79

Camping in Kiamitia Country (Episode 3)

Sunday Gazetteer, August 20, 1911

The last night at the lake, there was a slight rim of light in the sky. It was the new moon. It was like a bracelet studded with stars. Moonlight is very comforting in camp; it drives away the loneliness in a strange country and among strange people, and when you get up in the lone hours of the night to see how the horses are getting along, the first impulse is to look into the woods.

The night came on us with a few light clouds that seemed to drop down from the sky like lace curtains. As the night grew deeper, the clouds disappeared. We made the campfire broad and high—vast pine logs, eight feet long and two feet thick, which we had cut and rolled together, blazed high on the edge of the forest and poured a rich light over the lake. It was a night of frosty sparkle and glory. Millions of stars and bright constellations reflected their lights upon the bosom of the lake, and now and then fish jumped out of the water and made a great splash as they returned to their element. Wolves sent dismal cries through the arches of the forest, owls hooted in the treetops, and night birds were abroad and dashed through the great conflagration that lit up the forest.

That night we lingered so long at the campfire, which was so cheery and comfortable, that it must have been midnight before we sought our couches, made in the bed of the wagon. The mules were quiet and went to sleep. A great horned owl perched himself in a tree at the camp and made the welkin [the vault of the sky] ring with his "too-hoo!" We had thrown several fish in the woods near the camp, and a bobtail cat sneaked through the brush after them. We could hear him crunching the bones. We yelled, and there was a streak of tawny fur that flashed through the woods, and the beast was gone.

Of all the sounds in the forest, none is more harrowing than the cry of the wolf pack. It is so dismal that it makes the flesh creep, and the hunter wishes for home. During the night we could hear the wolves roaming the mountains, probably in pursuit of deer. We heard a great splash in the upper end of the lake, and knew that a deer had taken refuge in the water from the wolves, but it was so dark that we could not see anything, and then we had no inclination to plunge into the dark on a tour of investigation.

It is said that wild animals always give vent to cries at the break of day. We heard a wild and humanlike cry in the mountains. "That's a panther," said our companion. The next day we ascended the mountain and came upon the traces of the brute. He had killed a wild turkey, and the bones and feathers were scattered over the ground. I confess that my hair arose with the consciousness of his recent presence, as it is said to do when a spirit passes by. Just to think of being lost in such a wilderness. Nature is so pitiless, so unresponsive, to a person that is lost. Nine persons out of ten lose their heads and reason and travel in a circle. Fright unsettles the judgment.

Once upon a time we were in the woods with a veteran hunter named Bozarth. He was never surpassed at woodcraft and the knowledge of wild animals. We had chased a deer with hounds from Long to Wolf Creek. All at once the old hunter sat down on a log, pulled out his pipe, and began to smoke, and lapsed into deep meditation.

"Taking a rest?" asked the writer.

"No," he answered. "Just lost; trying to get my bearings."

We left the woods and went out to the prairie, and he began to laugh; laughed loud. "Well, come on; let's go back to the woods. I hear the hounds on Long Creek."

In thirty minutes he had shot and killed a young doe. When he arrived home, he told his wife about getting lost, and seemed humiliated and ashamed.

We could hardly tear ourselves away from the beautiful lake.

209

When the team was hitched and the tent and camp utensils placed in the wagon, I proposed to Collett that we remain a few days longer. While the proposition was being discussed, a lone hound was spied running along the shore of the lake with his nose to the ground, and every once in a while he would give vent to the cry of the wild. The old hound came to our camp and went to nosing around. When we started up the mountain, he followed under the wagon, just as if he belonged there. Where he came from we never knew. At Tuskahoma he disappeared, much to our sorrow and regret.

We called him "Wolf." He was a good watchdog and would circle the camp at night and give vent to howls that would make a loper wolf ashamed of himself. He was quite old, had poor teeth, and swallowed nearly everything whole. One day a deer passed near the camp, and Wolf took the trail and was out of sight in a moment. We could hear his cry in the mountains, and then silence prevailed. He remained out all night, and we were deeply concerned at his absence. Wolf put in an appearance about midday of the day following. His chops and head were covered with clotted blood, and we supposed he had caught the deer and killed it. After that, we secured him with a rope and turned him loose at night. We lost a whole day at the Indian capital trying to get some trace of him. He must have been stolen by Indians or campers and secured so that he would not escape.

No. 80

Camping in Kiamitia Country
(Episode 4)

Sunday Gazetteer, August 27, 1911

We had been in the mountains several days, irresolutely traveling from point to point, going into camp when night overtook us. While traveling it clouded, and a cold mist descended; the weather turned cold and very disagreeable. There was a light flurry of snow and sleet in the air. The road was glazed with a coating of ice, and the brake refused to hold the wagon, which skated over the ice. The mules were struck several times in the hindquarters by the wagon running into them, but they were docile and did not pay much attention to the wagon crowding them. When night was descending on the wilderness, we arrived at a little creek, the bottom of which was covered with a luxuriant growth of grass that was as green as in the spring. We agreed to camp that night and the next day, so as to give the team a good rest in the green bottoms. Light clouds scudded across the face of the sky, and the new moon gave a faint light. It was quite dark before camp was made. While securing the mules, there came to us the sound of voices so unearthly and terrifying that it seemed to freeze the very marrow in our bones. In the deep stillness of the forest, the sound was fearful.

"The wolves are abroad tonight," said Collett, our companion. The mules were feeding at the end of a thirty-foot rope. We pulled them in and secured them close to the wagon. That night we made the biggest campfire of the whole trip. The wolves were all around us. Never since have we heard such a din. The mules were restless, and we made a corral with the ropes to better secure them. It seemed that human voices could be heard. At times the wolf pack would advance right into the camp so that we could see them. The old hound was dead game, and with bristling hair he would dash out in the surrounding gloom, and the wolves would flee.

Collett with a Winchester rifle and the writer with a shotgun went about thirty yards from camp and fired into shadows that could be seen sneaking and darting through the woods. The shots were effective, for we could hear the cry of the wounded animals. We did not sleep that night, and never was daylight so welcome. Around the camp we saw bloody traces of the wolves that had been shot.

The pasture was so good that we agreed to remain until the afternoon and travel to water and go into camp. The trail was much better. It was the same monotonous march under the silent and somber shadow of the vast forest, there being no change. The mules traveled rapidly—the green pasture had worked a wonderful change. We were leaving the mountains and getting into the foothills. A good stretch was made before dark, and we went into camp in a beautiful bottom alongside a mountain stream that was as clear as crystal. I never saw a prettier campground. In my imagination I can look back through the vista of thirty-five years and see the greensward, the noble forest, and catch the music of falling waters that tumbled down over rocks from the surrounding hills. In noble symmetry and beauty were the post oak, the hickory, and pecan trees, which told us we were leaving the mountains and descending into the bottom lands. The signs were hailed with joy, as we hoped soon to see a human face or human habitation.

At that period the eastern portion of the Choctaw Nation was *terra incognita*—a vast wilderness stretching over two hundred miles, ending only at the Arkansas border. Wild and ferocious animals roamed this vast domain. Even the Indians avoided it and made their homes on the prairie lands near the watercourses. Where we had been, we will never know; and when we returned to civilization, no one could place the country or the lake. We now believe that we had got lost in what is at present known as "The Glover Country," that looks to be east of the state of Arkansas.

The wolves came back that night and were as noisy and numerous as ever. At that period, you could not escape the wolf cry. The old hound made a grandstand platy, and with his barking and howling and the cry of wolves and the hoot of owls, we got but little rest. In the morning we distinctly saw where a bear had crossed the stream going in the direction of the mountains. Deer and wild turkey tracks were plentiful, and while getting ready to break camp, a large gang, at least fifty, of wild turkeys were discovered moving through the bottoms. We also saw a big buck. We were evidently in the hunter's paradise, with a beautiful stream of water flowing past our camp door, and a rich bottom of grass and game in abundance, and perfect weather, as the skies had cleared. I suggested that we remain for a period, but our companion declared that he was tired and annoyed by the wolves at night, and that it would be an appalling event to get lost while wandering in the woods. For the first time, squirrels were plentiful—the gray squirrel, which is the liveliest little game in the woods. We saw that we could kill all the game we wanted in sight of camp. The weather was delicious. We noticed a wild cherry that the frost had not yet disturbed; it was intensely green, while all around the forest was tinted with gold. The hardwoods were very brilliant. The American forests in the fall of the year cannot be surpassed in colors. The gaily tinted leaves were an inspiration to the vision. Morning in the wilderness, when the weather is perfect, once experienced will never be forgotten.

I sat on a prostrate log, and a feeling of exultation pervaded my person; health was perfect, and I was young, in the perfect flower of youth, and the world was bright before me. I thought what a pity, what a calamity it would be when this lovely place must be disturbed by the presence of civilization. Our sun has passed the meridian, feeling has changed, but age will never wipe out our love of the chase and the beauties of Nature.

While getting ready to start, an immense lobo wolf trotted through the woods and stopped in its tracks and looked intently at our camp. It was as large as the largest dog, and we have never doubted that an animal of that size was able to pull down and kill a yearling, and we do not think any dog would be able to stand up in a square fight and vanquish the lobo. Its body was long and lean. There were no cattle in the country, and that accounted for their incessant presence at our camp at night, attracted by the smell of game that had been cooked at our camp, especially the skulls of dead fish. Had the wolf pack attacked our camp, they would have picked our bones in a very few moments. Old Wolf, the dog, made as much noise at night as a pack of wolves and no doubt kept them at a respectable distance.

Crossing the beautiful stream of water, I jumped upon a log and shouted, "Farewell, dear old camp spot; will I ever see thee again?" I said, "John, we ought to have remained here until famine drove us out."

We have made several trips to the mountains since but have never been able to locate the stream.

We turned to take a farewell look at the mountains that were clothed in clouds, the mists rolling to the lowlands. I verily believe that I never saw so many squirrels that were jumping from limb to limb or on the ground, looking for the morning repast. We saw the first covey of quail; in getting up close, several flew into the trees and were killed. A coon crossed the trail and seemed indifferent to our presence. He was a big fellow, and when Wolf went after him, he turned and showed fight, but finally escaped up a tree before the dog could close in.

The first sign of civilization was an old cabin that had rotted and been deserted probably for years. There was an old worm-eaten fence that had partly fallen down. At some time or other, the land had been cultivated. In the weeds, a large gang of wild turkeys were scratching and feeding. When they saw our wagon, it seemed that a hundred black heads popped up out of the weeds. The woods near the field were open, and the turkeys ran like racehorses through them.

No. 81
Camping in Kiamitia Country
(Episode 5)

Sunday Gazetteer, September 3, 1911

We had moved but a short distance from our camping ground when at least thirty deer dashed in front of the wagon and disappeared in the woods with old Wolf in hot pursuit. We could see the deer scrambling up the mountainside in the open pines. In a few moments, old Wolf could be discovered; his yelping was like a trumpet, and the way he would make the forests ring was an inspiration to the listeners. The dog did not return until night. He was so tired that he crawled under the wagon and was soon fast asleep.

About noon we saw a well-defined road. Judging by the sun, we were traveling south, but the road ran east and west. We stopped to debate which direction we should go. It was decided to go straight ahead, as I believed the road would lead us back to the mountains. The country ahead was open, and the trail was good traveling, and I judged from the woods that the prairie was not far distant. There was a remarkable change in the weather. It had become uncomfortably warm, and the team was covered in white lather. We were traveling in our shirtsleeves. The sun had disappeared behind the mountains, and cool puffs of wind followed. I remarked: "A norther."

Black clouds began to gather; darkness began to creep over the east, the wind howled and shrieked, leaves and withered branches swept through the air in wild confusion, and an ominous calm succeeded, while the low growl of distant thunder seemed forced from the caverns of the mountains.

The wagon was stopped, mules taken out, and the wagon cover stretched. The wagon was run between two immense trees, the tent pitched, and the mules secured near the tent.

"Now, let her come," we remarked. The storm seemed to have taken us at our word. Big drops of rain began to fall, and the wind sounded like a death dirge. The thunder was appalling. The effect was indescribable. The lightning began to leap in angry flashes to the earth. The trees began to rock and roar above us. The mules threatened every moment to break loose. We ran the wagon behind them and stretched a rope in front and talked to them like a human. The storm lasted about two hours and then cleared off very cold. By morning it was freezing, our tent was flooded with water, and the most uncomfortable night we ever passed in camp was experienced.

In the morning we hung out our blankets to dry. Everything in the wagon was drenched. By the afternoon everything was tolerably dry, and we struck camp. The whole country before us was covered with water, but it was sandy soil, and traveling not very difficult. I felt sorry for the mules. The feed had been gone some time, and the only thing was to turn them out to grass. At that period the writer was young and dauntless, and no hardship dismayed us. We could sleep on the cold, wet ground and get up in the morning with a song in our mouth.

John said, "The team is giving out," and just then a cow, the first cow we had seen, crossed the road, then another and another followed.

I remarked, "Old man, we are safe." We heard a shout, and looking out from a grove of trees, we saw an old-fashioned southern cabin. Smoke was curling in spirals from a chimney made of clapboards and mud. The doors were closed, and when we drove up to the gate, no one appeared. A yell brought a young man out to the porch. He was followed by an old man leaning on a stick.

The first question asked was, "Have you any corn for sale?"

The young man answered in broken English, "Just a little; 75 cents per bushel."

We took out the mule team and gave them about fifteen ears each. The corn was large, with no evidence of smut. It was a delight to see the mules go for it. The old man, a full-blood Choctaw, hobbled back into the house. We asked the young man if he could accommodate us for a day or so; that we had traveled hard and wanted to rest the team. "Mabee so" was his reply, which we accepted as favorable.

A bright fire was burning in an old-fashioned hearth, but the Indian never said, "Come in," so we took a seat on the porch, and the door to the room with a cozy fire was closed in our faces. There was an east and west room, separated by a large porch. We brought in our blankets and made a bed down on the porch. It looked as if another storm was coming up. The mules were placed in a lot and turned loose. The cabin was built of rough, unhewn logs, notched together at the corners, and the space between them filled with mud and sticks. A large chimney was built of sticks and plastered with mud, supported at the back and sides where the fire burned. The floors were laid with puncheons; no glass was used for windows. At night, calico curtains were dropped down. The day and night we stopped to rest, we saw no candles or lamps. The family went to bed with the chickens.

The next morning, our attention was attracted by a woman's voice. It was soft and sweet and lacked the Indian guttural. When the door was opened and the young Choctaw appeared on the threshold, we peeped in. We saw a young woman, but it was so dark in the interior of the cabin that we could not tell whether she was black, red, or white, and we didn't wish to rush matters by attempting to draw out the young Indian. The door was closed abruptly. We went out into the cow yard to see how the mules were getting along. While leaning against the fence talking, a woman crossed the platform between the two rooms, but whether young or old we could not tell, as her face was secreted by a sunbonnet.

The old Indian hobbled onto the porch. The day was warm and pleasant, and he took a seat in a chair, leaning on his cane. All the young Indian could say in English was "Mabee so." We hung around the house and soothed the old Indian with a package of smoking tobacco. The old fellow could not speak a word of English. Many of the full-bloods understand and can speak English but when addressed in that language are as dumb as oysters. Gov. Wilson N. Jones of the Choctaw Nation was one of that kind.

In the evening, the young Choctaw mounted his horse and rode away and did not return until noon the next day.

The disappearance of the young Choctaw changed the situation. The next morning the woman assisted the old man to enter the room across the passage. We saw her face very plainly and were startled. It was a white face and very pretty and impressive. We spoke to her, and she invited the writer into the room and moved a chair to the fire. After puzzling my brain in vain to start a conversation, I turned to the girl and asked if the old man was her father. She said: "No; I am a white woman."

There was a long silence, and I made another conversational attempt.

Perhaps it is better to describe this strange young woman. Her complexion, without having the sickly yellow hue of the ague country, was of that exceeding fairness so rarely seen. Her head was covered with a mass of dark auburn hair which fell in a golden shower about her neck. Her eyes were large and melting, over which closed long and equally dark lashes. No painter could have drawn a more perfect form. As she sat there in homespun dress, I must confess that I felt tender emotions tugging at my heartstrings. How many wealthy parents would give half their fortunes to have such a daughter grow up into beautiful womanhood by their side. It was sad to feel that, no matter what dormant beauties and excellencies of character lay concealed in that young creature, they would never awaken into life to bless and cheer herself and others. I floundered along in conversation, but she hung her head and said but little. I asked how many years she had lived there, and she answered, "Many, many years."

"Are your parents alive?"

"I was captured by the Indians and never saw my father or mother," she answered.

"I am a newspaperman, a reporter, and would like your history."

"What is a reporter?" she replied. "I can't tell you my history, only that I have lived with these people many years, and they are very kind to me. I speak Choctaw and get along very well. I have never been in a city. About once a year we go to the capital [Tuskahoma] to trade. Sometime I am going to a big city to see things."

"What is your age?"

"I don't know. . . . I call him my brother. He is the grandson of the old man, who is 90 years of age."

"Don't you want to leave here?"

"Where would I go?"

"Can you read or write?"

"Read a little, not much."

"Does anybody call to see you?"

"Sometimes. You are the first white man I have seen in many months."

"Will you ever try to learn anything of your father and mother?"

"How can I, out here?"

That night we sat at the big log fire. I was vain enough to think that the girl had taken a fancy to me. I saw her many times looking at my face, and at one time she smiled and seemed to be studying my thoughts. I got up to go out on the porch. She asked me if I did not need more bedclothes. I told her I had slept in my clothes for nearly two weeks and very frequently slept in my boots.

When I went to bed, I slept but little, and when I did sleep, a sweet face haunted my dreams.

In the next issue, I will give the history of the girl as I learned it at a sawmill.

No. 82
Camping in Kiamitia Country
(Episode 6)

Sunday Gazetteer, September 10, 1911

We did not leave the cabin and resume our journey until the afternoon. The mules showed plainly the effects of the rest and the plentitude of corn given them. About noon the young Choctaw returned. After putting his horse away, he approached the porch, and passed into the room where the girl was. The cold reception given us was natural; it was Indian. We have sat for hours at an Indian fireside without a word being passed. We could hear in the room a conversation between the girl and Indian in Choctaw. The team was hitched up, and the mules seemed eager for the journey. I didn't care the snap of my finger for the Indian, but I was determined to say good-bye to the girl. I knocked at the door, which was opened by the Indian. The girl was standing at the fireplace, looking intently into the small blaze on the hearth. I extended her my hand and said, "I am sorry to leave you." And she took my hand, answering, "I am sorry that you can't remain longer." It might have been a mistake, as the room was dark, but I thought I saw a tear in her eye. I wanted to say some things to her, but the Indian watched me like a hawk. I asked where the road would lead me to, but all the fool Indian would say was "Mabee so!"

I afterwards learned at a sawmill that he could speak English fairly well.

The girl said, "Keep right straight ahead, and by night you will probably reach the sawmill, and from there is a public road to Tuskahoma, forty miles distant."

I never hated to leave a place so much in my life. I was deeply interested in the white girl and her history. That little old log cabin in the woods is a delightful memory. Being young and of an ardent and romantic temperament, I recalled to memory the stories I had read of gallant knights, clad in armor, eloping with maidens fair from some high castle. Why should I not rescue this girl from her miserable life?

The sun was just going down, and the shadows of night were creeping over the face of the earth when we reached the sawmill. It was the most melancholy spot that I had seen on the entire journey. There were probably a dozen wooden shanties, the place being clogged with sawdust; ugly, dirty-looking faces peeping out of the doors, and rough men standing around. The mill was silent. It was the Sabbath. It seemed to me that everybody was saying, "Look at those men; wonder who they are?"

I said to Collett, "Let us travel to water and not stop here."

A great big red-faced, red-haired man stepped up and said, "Where you going, boys?"

"Traveling," I answered. "We have been in the mountains and are going home."

"It is getting dark, and if you wish you can come and stay at my house, and it won't cost you a cent."

He was so frank and outspoken, that he at once won my confidence, and I answered, "Thank you. We will take out the mules and stay."

We then drove down to a store, to which was attached a shed. The man helped us to take out the team, and after giving them a good feed of corn, we followed the man to his home. It contained two rooms and a shed. He introduced us to his wife, who had a baby at her breast and two strapping big girls, his daughters. They were dressed in calico and looked very tidy. The house was clean. The woman gave us a warm greeting and told us to take a chair. The family were Scotch-Irish, the best class of people in the world. The lady announced supper. We had warm biscuit, ham, and eggs. The lady was very sorry that she had no butter. There was a clean tablecloth. When I told them that I was a newspaperman, it seemed to raise me many notches in their estimation. The girls were very attentive and quite pretty, on the order of the robust beauty.

There was an organ in the room, and the old man called for music. One of the girls played while the other sang, and I was so delighted and enthused that I left my chair and thanked them, remarking, "Why, you young ladies ought to be in a city; that beats our city young ladies."

This compliment pleased the parents very much. It seemed that the man had been in that country about a year and was getting out lumber for a contractor. His family had lived several years at Sedalia, Missouri. The girls had attended school there. He was going back there in the spring. The girls had no society, and his wife was tired of the woods. There was a big sheet-iron stove in the room, and the old man kept firing it up until the heat was suffocating.

"Don't put any more wood in the stove. Don't you see the young men are sweating?" yelled the old lady.

It must have been nearly midnight before the party adjourned to bed. We slept on a comfortable bed on the floor and with clean bedclothes.

That night we learned a partial history of the white girl that lived at the Indian cabin. We will tell it in our next issue.

No. 83

Camping in Kiamitia Country (Episode 7)

Sunday Gazetteer, September 17, 1911

Many years ago, a war party of Comanches left their homes on the Canadian. They were young men and wished to distinguish themselves on some daring expedition, principally horse stealing, which, next to taking a scalp, was the highest ambition of an Indian. Instead of going to Texas, they turned their horses' heads in the direction of the Choctaws. They pushed their depredations as far east as the Sabine River. They stole a large number of horses.

On the return they skirted the Texas line. A party of Choctaws pursued and came upon them in probably what is now Red River County. In the battle, several Choctaws were killed or wounded. The Comanches escaped but lost nearly all the stolen stock.

The Choctaws determined on a reprisal, and the period set for the expedition was in the dead of winter. The party numbered about thirty men. They started with the first quarter of the new moon, traveling mostly at night. When seven days out, a scout sent ahead reported he saw a small encampment of Comanches on the Canadian. The Choctaws made arrangements to attack at the next morning at daybreak. There were only three teepees, and it was decided to surround them.

As dawn was creeping over the world, the Choctaws, with fearful yells, dashed into the encampment. Men, women, and children poured out of the teepees and started for the surrounding forest. Three warriors were killed and the rest taken prisoners. In one of the teepees, a very old woman was discovered, too old to attempt to escape. A buffalo robe was spread on the ground, and something moved; the cry of an infant was heard. The robe was thrust aside, and a child was discovered—a white child. The teepees were leveled to the ground and burned; the horses (about thirty in number) were started ahead. The weather was cold, and the child was wrapped in a buffalo robe and lifted to the saddle of the leader of the Choctaws.

After traveling a portion of the day, the prisoners were turned loose on foot to get home the best they could. The Choctaws reached their nation, and proceeded to their various homes. The child had been stolen from some frontier home by the Comanches. The leader of the Choctaws accepted the responsibility of adopting the little captive, and it was she that we saw at the cabin.

It was very probable that her parents were never found. During the great Indian Wars on the plains, many children were captured and carried into captivity. Many were ransomed, while many acquired the language and habits of the Indians, and in the course of time, were so wedded to the wild life that no inducement would allure them from it. It has been proven that, when they grew up and became warriors, they were more daring, more cruel, than the Indians themselves. This was illustrated in the early Indian Wars and up to the modern period. Captain Pike, when he was captured and taken into Mexico, saw a number of white girls that had been captured by the Comanches and sold to wealthy Mexicans.

The winter was now advancing, and the weather was getting very cold. Before passing to the closing scenes of this wilderness trip, we wish to extend our gratitude and thanks to the good people who entertained us at the sawmill. Where they are we know not, but our best wish is that they may all be alive, prosperous, and happy.

When we said adieu to our friends, we got our course to Tuskahoma. The mules had improved greatly in appearance and stepped lively over the road. In personal appearance, we were ragged, hair unkempt, and our wild and motley aspect had transformed us into suspicious characters who were traveling their country on no good errand. We were like the robbers of the black forests described in the novels. Our bodies were coated in dirt, as we had not washed in a fortnight and slept most of the time in our clothes, and often in our boots. We were dirty but happy.

It was two days travel to the Indian capital, and the roads were fairly good. The first night in camp, we had company. While getting a supper of wild turkey and venison, we saw coming through the woods a wagon propelled by ox power. The occupants presented a strange spectacle of abject poverty. Tow-headed, boggle-eyed urchins looked out from beneath the wagon sheet; across the shoulders of the man and woman was thrown an old blanket, tattered and torn and faded into many colors. The woman was gray-haired, wrinkled, and haggard, her dried limbs scarcely concealed by rags; and the man, the first word that escaped his dirty mouth was, "Kin you folks give me a chaw o' terbacker? I am out; h'aint seed any terbacker for a long time." And then the old woman wanted "Just a little corn meal or flour." Two half-starved hounds invaded our tent and were attacked by old Wolf, and a beautiful fight was pulled off and the little tent almost pulled down in the squabble. The two hounds had floored old Wolf, when I took a club and beat them over the head, and they escaped with cries that brought the old woman and children to the scene. We tied up old Wolf, and peace prevailed. The old man had gone into the woods with his gun to look for his supper, and brought home a swamp rabbit and several squirrels, which were cleaned and thrown onto a bed of live coals, with some of the hair left on.

"Stranger, whar you bin?"

"Oh, just traveling," was our answer.

We asked the old man: "Where are you going; where are you from?"

"We gist travel and hunt, and do a little work along the road; pick cotton sometimes. We have traveled from Arkansas to Texas several times. Just a little out of the way in this d—n country. Are going to Arkansas."

And we said to ourself: Here is a man who is destined to wander from place to place through life, unsatisfied, surrounded by his white-haired, boggle-eyed urchins, who were probably born by the wayside, and ever accompanied by the woman, whose troubles are cured by a cob pipe and whose amazing fecundity seems no hindrance to emigration.

To escape our neighbors, we retired very early, but were awakened frequently by the snorts of the man, who snoring was almost equal in volume to the wolf howl.

The next morning we pulled out early. When we wanted to feed at noon, it was discovered that half of our corn was missing, stolen by our neighbors. We had three sacks, and the one under the deer hide was half-empty. All that we could do was to curse—"The d—n thieves!" we shouted. The great business of these movers is stealing, and if they thought you were rich in possessions, they would murder you, but in appearance we looked about as squalid as they did.

It was another day's travel to the Indian capital and one night more in camp. We went into camp at a mountain stream with a beautiful bottom that looked like a carpet of green velvet. The grass grew along the edge of the water. There was not so much of it, and by morning the mules had cleaned it up. We heard the wolves running in the mountains, but they did not come near camp. Old Wolf barked all night. He was a dear old watchdog, and his disappearance at the Indian capital was one of the saddest episodes in a hunting experience of nearly forty years. A man can become just as much attached to a dog as a human. Poor old Wolf; he came to us from nowhere, and went from us to nowhere.

That night we rolled into the little dogberry town of Tuskahoma. It looked as if it might have been a hundred years old or older. There were two or three stores conducted by white men with Indian partners. Indians on horseback were coming into town. They nearly all carried Winchesters on the saddle, and some had pistols buckled at the waist. The season had been good, and corn was selling at 40 cents per bushel. There was a barber shop, restaurant, and hotel. The stores were large and well stocked, and, strange to say, there was a millinery shop with a few hats displayed at the door. We noticed on the street an Indian who was drunk, and we said, "This is civilization!"

We put our team up at the hotel barn, and that night we slept in a bed, and a very good bed, too. There were several pistol shots fired during the night, followed by whoops and the clatter of horses' feet on a dead run through the streets. We learned the next morning that a whisky peddler had been in town and that an Indian had been desperately wounded. Occurrences of that character were so frequent that it excited but little attention. Yet many an Indian vendetta starts from an incident of that kind and is prolonged for years, until whole families are wiped out. It is a characteristic of the Indian to never forget or forgive a wrong, and the killing of a near relative calls for reprisal. Of Tuskahoma we will have more to say.

No. 84
Camping in Kiamitia Country
(Episode 8)

Sunday Gazetteer, September 24, 1911

We lost a day at the Indian capital looking for old Wolf, who joined his fortunes with ours at the mountain lake. At that period, a lot of poor trash were traveling through the country from nowhere, going nowhere. They were the dregs, so low in the scale of humanity that they could descend no lower. This class of the genus *homo* are very fond of dogs, especially hounds. They no doubt enticed the old dog with a piece of corn dodger, slipped a rope around his neck, and carried him away. Where the old hound came from will ever remain a mystery. He was very watchful, and in the very coldest and most stormy nights he never ventured into the tent, but kept a watchful vigil on the outside.

The first half-day's travel we heard the cry of the wild in the mountains—a pack of hounds on the trail of the deer. We thought that we could distinguish the peculiar yelp of old Wolf. The hounds were streaming down the mountain, but the hunted quarry was lost to view in the thick underbrush. The very hills seemed to shake with the distant prolonged notes (bell-toned) shaking the air in smooth vibrations. A short, sharp yell, followed by a prolonged howl, was caught up and re-echoed by other bayings along the mountainside, and with the swiftness of a bird, a noble buck plunged into view! The deer was heading directly for our wagon but must have caught sight of us, for it turned and disappeared in the mountain fastness. It was a race for life, and we hoped that the noble animal would escape.

Two or three hounds, having no doubt abandoned the chase, appeared in the wagon road. We wanted to steal one, a noble fellow with long ears, showing plainly that he was a thoroughbred, but to steal a hound in those days was as great a crime as stealing a horse, and if we had carried our desire into effect, we would both probably have gone to glory at the end of a rope.

While we were watering the mules at the mountain stream that crossed the road, several mounted full-blood Indians rode up and stopped to water. They were followed by a large pack of hounds that waded in up to their bellies and lapped the water. We said, "Deer"? And one man replied, "No deer." We guessed that they had been in pursuit of the big buck, at least we hoped so. They commenced to talk in Choctaw and eyed us suspiciously. One of them rode to the back of the wagon and lifted the sheet and looked in. They then rode away, and we proceeded on our journey. In a moment we heard the report of a gun, and zip went the balls through the treetops. We put the whip to the mules and made good time.

"That must have been a farewell salute from the full-bloods," we remarked.

It was dark when we pulled up before a cabin and yelled, "Hollo."

A voice answered, "What do you want?"

We could distinguish in the light that shone from the cabin door the face of a white man. It was a welcome sight. We had only one sack of corn left and asked the man if he had any for sale.

"Corn is mighty scarce and d—n high. How much do you want, stranger?"

"Three bushels, and how much do you charge?"

"Fifty cents a bushel, and mighty good corn at that; going to stay all night?"

"Yes; we will pitch our tent and sleep in the yard. We have plenty of bedding."

The mules were taken out, watered, and turned loose in the cow lot. After the tent was pitched and beds made down, an old woman as ugly as the Witch of Endor whined, "You strangers come in to the fire." There was a bedstead, two old chairs, a box, and a trunk arranged around the fireplace for seats. On the mantelpiece was an old clock, to which was attached weights. The flooring had rotted away, and in the dark a person was liable to stumble into one of the holes and break a limb or his neck. There was in the cabin an Indian boy who had the most sinister face we ever looked at, and although he gave his age as seventeen, he had snaggled teeth, deep wrinkles about his eyes, and a terrible gash on his cheek that extended down into his bosom. His elk locks hung in dirty ringlets about his face. I said to Collett, "There is a face part wolf, part devil."

The old man and woman were inquisitive. I left the impression that we were poor and had just enough money to pay for the corn.

Bidding the old man and woman good night, we crept into our tent and went to bed. It must have been about midnight; I heard a noise, and the voice of a man in almost a whisper, calling the dogs. Then I heard the toot-hoo of an owl. It was a good imitation, but I was satisfied it was a counterfeit. I heard tiptoes on the porch, then a man said, "Who is in that tent?"

"Strangers traveling," answered a voice from the porch.

Then a voice said, "I'll bet it's a blind; they are revenue

officers."

I was so wide awake that I heard every word distinctly, and I think my hair was a little nervous, with a tendency to rise. The whispering was then carried on in such a low tone of voice that I lost what was said. Ah, I said to myself, "Once I was blind, but now I see a thing or two. That grizzly old rascal and woman think we are revenue officers." In a few moments there was a jingle, jingle of a cowbell, and a voice said from the porch, "Come in." The cowbell was a signal, and a second voice was heard. I did not sleep a wink, and with the break of day felt just as if witches had been riding me. At the gate I saw horse tracks and remarked, "You must have had callers last night?"

I knew that away up in the mountains somewhere, there was a still, and that the night callers were moonshiners.

We ate breakfast with our host, and a very good breakfast it was, too: a large plate of venison, hot biscuit, and plenty of sop and molasses. The venison was fine. After breakfast I gave the old man and woman some smoking tobacco.

We made an early start. The weather was cold, with a clear sky, but when the sun rose it was warm and pleasant. About two miles away from the cabin, a horseman dashed across the road. It proved to be the Indian boy, who must have cut through the woods to head us off. He was hatless with a flaming red handkerchief tied to his head. When we arrived at the point of woods where he had crossed, we saw him in the brush with a Winchester dallying in his hands. We spoke to him, but he essayed no reply. It was evident that he was watching us. I remarked, "I don't like this country; let us get out of here."

The rest and good feeds of corn had put new life into the mules, and they dashed over the road at a lively gait. We drove hard all day, the road being in splendid condition. Many deer and droves of wild turkeys were almost constantly in view. We had two venison hams and a big gobbler in the wagon, and we did not tarry to hunt. We crossed many watercourses, but the stage of water was very low and we experienced no trouble. While stopping to water, a buck walked majestically out of the woods. He was as big as a steer and must have stood in his tracks at least five minutes, shaking his antlered head. When we started, he gave a loud whistle and dashed into the forest.

In that whole day's hard drive, we saw only two cabins. The people thronged the doors and windows and looked at us. They were full-bloods, and when we stopped and asked the direction to the railway, they answered in grunts and shrugs of shoulders.

At night we arrived at another sawmill. It had been shut down, and only two families remained. They were a dirty, squalid lot. There was a well of water, and we took out the team, pitched the tent, and prepared supper. I called at one of the shanties and purchased several dozen eggs and a piece of sowbelly. We were surfeited on wild game, and the change was welcomed.

In one of the cabins was a man in the last stages of consumption, and while he was dying, another man was courting his wife in another room, and it was said the arrangement was agreeable to the husband.

At the sawmill we learned that the nearest point to the railway was thirty-five miles, that the roads were good, and that we ought to make the drive in a day. We stopped at a lake for dinner. I was never more struck by a scene in my life; its utter wilderness spread out where the axe of civilization had never struck a blow. The deep purple of the distant mountains, the silence and solitude of the shores, combined to render it one of enchantment.

About an hour after sunset, we saw in the distance several lights and traveled toward them, and soon we arrived in the streets of Caddo. The team was put in a wagon yard, and we stopped overnight in the hotel. We left Caddo without breakfast, determined to make Denison that day. We made Durant by daylight, where we breakfasted and gave the mules a feed of oats. Red River was crossed on the ferry boat, and about 9 o'clock we were home. Our friends said that we looked like wild men. Our clothing was in rags, our shoes out at the toes, hair matted on our heads, faces covered with whiskers, and dirt plastered on our bodies. It was several days before we began to look and feel natural.

We never heard what became of the white girl, but guess she married "Maybe so."

(The end.)

In the story running in several issues of the *Gazetteer*, John Collett is mentioned as our companion in the mountains. It is not John Collet the butcher, as many think, but a John Collett who was at Gheen's livery stable for a short time, and who was a civil engineer. After returning from the mountains, he sold his wagon and team to John Parr and left for Colorado. This was in the seventies.

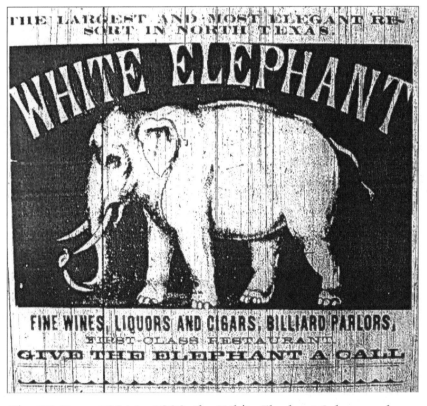

Fig. 19. From 1884 to 1892, the White Elephant Saloon and Restaurant was in business at 301 W. Main under a number of different proprietors.

No. 85

The White Elephant

Sunday Gazetteer, October 8, 1911

From 1878 to 1890, Denison was a gambler's paradise. People came here from all over the country to court the fickle goddess of chance. There were a half-dozen gambling houses on Main Street. In the eighties, the sentiment was so strong against them that they were driven from the ground floors to the second stories. You could get any game that you wanted, and the player was assured of a square deal. There was an air of respectability attached to it, and its votaries embraced almost every walk in life. We have seen on several occasions an ex-preacher hugging a card at a keno game, at the old White Elephant—of glorious and wicked fame.

The best patrons of the gaming tables were residents of the Indian Territory, largely cowmen. We have known cattlemen to ride a hundred miles to indulge their passion for gambling. They always had plenty of money and lost it without a whimper. The favorite games were faro and poker, and the winnings and losses sometimes ran into the thousands. There are several of the old faro dealers in Denison at the present time: Jerry Strait, the coolest and bravest man that ever pulled a card out of the box; old Bill Cooper, Theo. Tobin, Mike O'Brien, Enoch Hughes, and one or two others whose names we cannot remember. For many years, Strait has been an austere businessman. Theo. Tobin has an income sufficient to keep the wolf from the door. Enoch Hughes is rich. He has conducted a house in Hot Springs, Arkansas, for a number of years, but the authorities have closed out gambling there. Enoch now follows the racing circuit. Old Bill Cooper is still on the turf; it is his second nature, and he will never jump the game until the game jumps him.

The old-time gambler that flourished here in the seventies was the most romantic and picturesque character that ever lived in the wild and woolly West.

There was Alex. Reddick, Charley Clymer, Pink and Bud Fagg, Bill Tibbs, Joe Meadows, Foster, Sam Berliner, and old John Cox. The faro tables changed hands so often that it was hard to keep track of them.

The gamblers of the seventies were substantial men, and when Denison needed anything, they were about the first ones that the begging committees called on, and they always shelled out liberally.

When the Rev. [M.A.] Daugherty was building the old M.E. Church at the [northwest] corner of Woodard Street and Fannin Avenue, he did not consider it a breach of his clerical duty to appeal to the sporting fraternity, and they gave liberally.

When a poor, unfortunate devil drifted into Denison stranded and didn't know where the next meal was coming from or where to lay his head, it was the gambler who put food into his stomach and cheer into his heart, and if he wanted a drink, the first man to ask him to the bar was a sporting man.

It must be remembered that Denison was a great shipping point then. From every point of Texas, cattle were pouring in daily, in charge of men as wild as the horned kine they drove. The cowboy jostled you everywhere; you could not escape him, and he had money and spent it, too. Cattle from the Great Plains poured into the stockyards here. There never was a time in the seventies that thousands of cattle were not waiting shipment. At all hours of the night and day, you could hear the cry of the cowboy as he urged the cattle from the yards into the cars. And how they did die. We heard a cattleman once say that, out of a shipment of 2,000 head, he lost 500 between here and Omaha, where they were unloaded and driven to the Indian agencies of the west.

The cowboy is a natural gambler. Cards, whiskey, and women he has a weakness for, but gambling is the first consideration.

There used to be in Denison the White Elephant, at the corner of Main Street and Rusk Avenue, where Madden's store is now located. When it was opened, it was considered the handsomest resort in North Texas. The lower floor was devoted to saloon and eating purposes, and the upper story was given up entirely to gambling; it was never closed. The faro tables were in the front rooms overlooking Main Street, and in the rear was a large room devoted to keno. How many thousands of dollars have been lost or won on the second floor of the White Elephant, no one will ever know. There was a steady stream of humanity going and coming. They all had money, and they spent it. The faro tables were always busy. They commenced business in the forenoon, and in the afternoons the tables were crowded with patrons of the game.

What a study; the young and the old. Night stole into the morning, and they were still there—playing, eternally playing; hoping against hope. Then they would step out, others following. It was always so. One dealer would step down and out, but the game still went on. You could get a straight game. They were giants in those days; now they are pygmies—little bits of fellows who sneak around and play behind closed doors, taking the last cent you have in the world and never giving back a penny, even if you were starving. Fraud and cunning are so plainly written upon these fellows' faces that it is easy to believe that to defraud you was what they stayed and waited for.

There was another gambling house over the McDougall Saloon which never closed. Perhaps in twenty years, $500,000 exchanged hands.

There used to be a place over where the New York Barber Shop now is, conducted by Bill Tibbs; one over the Libbe saloon; and one over where the old Leeper hardware house was at that period. In fact, Denison was honeycombed with gambling resorts.

Reddick is dead, Foster is dead, Tibbs is gone, too; Bud Fagg is dead, Meadows too; Clymer is dead, Woods is dead; and, in fact, most of the old guard have been gathered to their fathers. Are they sleeping? What manner of life do they live? So many strange stories are believed and told of the dead. With all his faults, it may be justly said of him that he is a man that depends upon his courage, who has chosen his life; who is the fit and capable vidette who stands upon the verge of the mighty civilization which is destined to follow him, when he and his unconscious work shall have passed away.

No. 86

"She's Been Kind To Me"

Sunday Gazetteer, October 29, 1911

Now how would you like to sit down and think of a strong, healthy man courting your wife while you were slowly dying with consumption in the next room? Yet such was a fact that we learned some thirty-five years ago while traveling in the Indian Territory, and the courting was done with the man's consent.

We were rounding up our hunt to the Kiamitia Mountains and stopped for the night near a sawmill before we approached the Indian capital. We learned then the story which we are about to tell.

It was something like this: there was a cheerful light blazing on the hearth, and a man and woman were seated before it. The man was about thirty, the woman perhaps ten years his junior. They were laughing and telling the gossip of the day. The sawmill had closed down, and the man was just waiting for his friend to die in the next room. The woman was comely and coarse, while her companion was an athlete. It seemed that he had been hunting in the mountains and had met with good luck. There was a deer hanging outside the cabin, and two wild turkeys hung just inside the door; two hounds were dozing before the log fire. Every now and then, he would laugh and smack his lips. There was no light except the blazing light of the pine knots that lit up the room with a cheerful glow.

We passed into the room adjoining west, and the consumptive told us that it would soon be over; that the wife had been very kind to him. Of the man he said nothing. We asked him about the agreement, and all that he would say in return was that he knew that his wife would be taken care of, and that was something, as she had no place to go when he was dead. The man was dying with quick consumption, and the end was not far off, and yet in the next room sat his wife listening to the hunter, who was telling of his tramp in the mountains and the killing of the deer.

We retraced our steps to the wagon and were soon fast asleep. In the morning we laid in bed and thought of the strange things that happen in this world that the world knows nothing of.

No. 87

Loss of the Cotton Trade

Sunday Gazetteer, November 5, 1911

We can recollect when Denison was the most important cotton market in Grayson County. This was in the year of 1883 and continued until 1895. We have seen Main Street blocked from Houston to Mirick avenues. Cotton was very low then and did not command at the highest over 9 cents. Then we had a vast territory to draw from. We had Paul's Valley on the west and the entire Choctaw and Chickasaw nations, and cotton has been known to come here from the Creek Nation. There were many local buyers in the field in those days. Every dry goods house on Main Street had its buyer, and there were many who bought independent of the dry goods houses.

We have lost to a great extent all of our cotton business. Where there is at the present time only three or four bales that wander in, there used to be, in the period above mentioned, 300 and sometimes as many as 500 bales on our streets.

The loss of our cotton trade is attributable to the territory that has been opened up by the railways and the new towns that have sprung up, where as high a price is being paid, and it frequently happens that more is paid than on the streets of Denison—cutting off all that section of country that in former times paid tribute to Denison.

Fig. 20. "Views of the National Cotton Oil Company's Denison Mill, Crushing Capacity 120 Tons Per Day." From Industrial Denison, *compiled by Frank M. Robinson ([N.p.]: Means-Moore Co., [ca. 1901], page 21.*

The Industrial Cotton Seed Oil Mill is buying all of the cottonseed that it can get and is paying a good price. Durant and Madill have oil mills that are purchasing cottonseed, and we learn that Madill is paying a better price than Denison.

Probably Denison will never be recognized again as a cotton market. Others towns are paying just as much for cotton, and there is no inducement to bring their cotton here. And it must be remembered that Denison is a prohibition town, and people will not come to a dry town. The whiskey that is sold here is of a very poor quality and passes through the hands of bootleggers.

The loss of the cotton trade to Denison is a sad blow. We have the city payroll of the MK&T [Missouri, Kansas & Texas Railway], the MO&G [Missouri, Oklahoma & Gulf Railway], and H&TC [Houston & Texas Central] to fall back on. The strike has done Denison a great deal of harm, and there is no probability that the end is in sight. There are many things to discourage us, but the darkest hour has its silver lining.

No. 88
"Old Buck"

Sunday Gazetteer, November 12, 1911

If we should live a hundred years, we would never forget "Old Buck." Old Buck was a dog. He was a common "pocket licker," but he could stay longer on the trail than any dog that we have ever seen.

We first met Old Buck at a little cabin in the north woods of the Sassafras country. He was of the hound species. When we first struck the Sassafras country, thirty years ago, there was but one settler there. His name was Bozarth—Joseph Bozarth. He was a plain, unassuming man, who made his living by the chase. He was unquestionably the greatest hunter of the Choctaw woods. He lived just across the Choctaw line. He used to have his dogs—there was Old Buck, Brindle, Old Cute, and John—but Buck was the chief of them all. He never fluked his work but was always ready for the chase. He was a splendid animal; great long ears, tan color, and a melting black eye.

At the period of which we write, we lived in a little cabin that overlooked a portion of Allen Bayou. There used to be a deer there of enormous size. He was the king of the woods. We used to get up at daylight and look across the bayou—and there stood the old buck, tossing his antlers to the sky; then, giving a whistle, he was off. One day we put Old Buck on his trail, and it was a hot chase. He ran all day and all night and a portion of the next day. He got something, for when he came back to camp his head and chops were covered with blood. We said to the dog, "Say, Buck, did you get the big deer?" He wagged his tail, and that was all we could get out of him. We believe to this day that he killed the big deer, for it was never seen in that country again.

Our cabin was four miles distant from Bozarth's. Old Buck divided his time between the two cabins. One winter night the wolves were howling and making a fearful din. We heard a scratching at the door and asked who was there. We were in a partial doze and laid down again. In a few moments the scratching was continued. We then got up and opened the door, and Old Buck, covered with snow, walked into the cabin and laid down by the fire and was soon fast asleep.

He was the bravest, kindest, and most faithful of animals. It made no difference what time it was, day or night, he was always ready for the trail and was the best deer dog we ever saw. In the chase, he was a splendid animal to look at, long and lean, but he would "cut the wind" while he ran. There was nothing too difficult for him to do, and in all kinds of weather he was eager for the chase.

Perhaps a mile from our camp in the bottoms, there was a big slough, made from the overflows of Sassafras Creek. In the winter this slough was a great resort for wild ducks. We used to go down there and kill ducks by the hundreds, and Old Buck was never more delighted than when he was swimming around after the dead ducks. It made no difference to him how cold the water was.

I suppose (without exaggeration) that the dog had caught fifty deer. He would never give up the trail but would stick to it through thick and thin. He was not very friendly towards strangers. One day a Chickasaw Indian visited the camp, and the moment he saw the Indian he made a dash for him and would have devoured him had we not been present. He was very partial to white men but had no use for Indians and showed it on every occasion.

The last time we saw Old Buck was twenty-five years ago. He was getting old and showed it. He would sleep a good deal, which is a sure sign of old age in a dog, and he was not so alert on his feet, being very sluggish.

Poor Old Buck! His master died, and he soon followed. We never saw a better dog in camp.

No. 89

Woodlake and Other Outings

Sunday Gazetteer, November 19, 1911

A man said recently, "There is no scenery around Denison." The man is mistaken. We have plenty of scenery, and it is varied and beautiful to look at this time of the year when the trees are putting on their winter habiliments. If you will travel due east, the country affords a magnificent view of well-cultivated farms and hospitable homes. The country between Denison and Sherman and Woodlake is also worthy of a visit.

Woodlake, like a gem, sits in the bosom of emerald green. It is a beautiful spot to visit at any season of the year, and many people go out there every week to spend the day. We have a lake, and the grounds are laid out in a beautiful manner. We have a pavilion; in fact, everything conducive to the happiness and contentment of the visitors can be found at Woodlake. It is not an ordinary place to visit, as many thousand dollars have been expended to fix it up. Every day in the summer and fall, picnic parties with well-filled baskets go out there and spend the day in the shade of the noble forest trees. There we have boats for the pleasure of those who wish to go boating. There used to be theatrical performances at the large hall, but the many attractions in the city caused the show feature to be discontinued.

Great blessings are associated with Woodlake. Did you ever think of it—what would Denison and Sherman be without Woodlake? The scenery around Woodlake has a beauty of its own and will ever remain what Nature and art have combined to make it.

A little farther on, you come to the baseball grounds, which are patronized every Sunday afternoon by many hundreds of people from Denison and Sherman. All seem to meet there on common democratic grounds.

From the ball grounds to the city limits of Sherman, you pass through a beautiful country, dotted with large, cultured homes.

Now that we have been down south, let us return to the east. There you have the Carpenter's Bluff highway, which is certainly a beauty to look at since it was improved by the Good Roads people.

The railroad has penetrated all that country to the [Red] river. The MO&G [Missouri, Oklahoma, & Gulf Railway] is a magnificent tribute to Denison. If you follow the Carpenter's Bluff highway to the river, you will go through a beautiful country lined with farms; and down near the river, you will enter shady groves of forest trees that stretch away to the right and left until they are lost in the dim distance. The drive from Denison to the river is well worth taking. You will see well-cultivated farms that are a pleasure to look upon.

Take the east line of the MK&T [Missouri, Kansas & Texas Railway]; after going about one mile, you plunge into the woods primeval—a beautiful country at this time of the year, when Nature beckons you to come and see her, when she is changing into all kinds of colors. You cannot go to a more beautiful country than the country northeast. At this season of the year, "it is a thing of beauty and a joy forever." You will see farmhouses nestling in the valley; you will notice contented cattle, and you can get more of country life east and southeast than in any spot around the city.

Then take a stroll out to the dairy farms. You will notice the silos and large herds of contented cattle that are well kept and rolling in fat.

The man who said, "There is no scenery around Denison," is mistaken. He has not seen this country.

No. 90
Oakwood Cemetery and
More Outings

Sunday Gazetteer, November 26, 1911

We mentioned in the last issue of the *Gazetteer* that Denison was surrounded with attractive scenery. Not in recent years has this fact been more apparent than recently.

Now let us take the northwest with Red River and the Washita Railroad connections. If you stand with the writer, you will behold a scene not easily forgotten in recent years. For many miles there is a vast stretch of country ending only at the river. It is a magnificent country and would be called beautiful in any section of the land. You go to the river and cross the railroad bridge. You pass through the little town of Warner, which lies in the valley at the foot of the hills. While descending to Warner, you see the Catholic cemetery, a beautiful spot. Following the road you cross Duck Creek, where a geologist might pick up fossils that are a million years old. The whole country there is a rich spot for geologic study. While proceeding to the river, you see vast fields dotted with large forest trees that have stood there many years, before Denison was thought of; and then the MK&T and Frisco tracks cut a wide swath through the hills to the valley.

Between them lies the most beautiful scenery in the world. The Munson pasture, which is covered with trees, is where picnic parties go in early spring to pass the day. It is a lovely place. Down through this pasture in early days, the artillery used to rumble along, and the whole country was covered with the young people, holding picnic parties, etc. Al Hall used to have fish fries—and how dear to memory they are. At night you would catch the dulcet

Figs. 21–23. A few grave stones in Oakwood Cemetery, Denison.

242

strains of music, and the young people would dance until "the fairies come."

If you will go to a little further east, you will come to the Pawpaw Bottoms, which we declare are not surpassed in the whole section for beauty. The Pawpaw Bottoms are two miles in length; open woods for the most part, but where the sewer intersects them, they have been befouled. About two miles above the sewer, the water is as clear as crystal. Great hills shut in Pawpaw—vast rolling hills—where we have been lost in coming to the Carpenter's Bluff highway. There are many rugged paths there, composed of white rocks strewn along in confusion for a mile. In summer you have to comb through so many wire fences that you grow tired; and when you reach the top of the hills, you are willing to cry Eureka—and take off your hat and wave welcome to the fresh air that is always circulating at the top of the hill.

After you leave the Pawpaw and come up the river to Warner, you encounter beautiful scenery; and when you leave Warner and ascend the hill that leads to Denison, the ascent is gradual and you will have no trouble in climbing it. There are many places along this hill that will interest you, and you cannot miss them if you are an observing man.

Winding along, you will come to the greatest cemetery that Denison has. Many hundred sleep there. There are many beautiful monuments to attract your attention, and many sleep there whom in life you may have known. Oakwood is the burial place of some of Denison's most noted dead, and there they will rest when the present generation are dead and forgotten. You may linger there for hours and not grow tired; and you may go there at all seasons of the year to muse with the dead, plant flowers, and fix up the grounds. It is a beautiful place to visit, for the grounds are kept in order and never allowed to look untidy.

No. 91

Old Man Bozarth's Woodcraft (Episode 1)

Sunday Gazetteer, December 3, 1911

Woodcraft is a great thing, and without some knowledge of it, one cannot be a successful hunter. You can't live in the city nine months in the year and be a successful hunter. You have to live with the animals of the wild and study their natures and habits closely. You must understand the wind, the moss on trees, windbreaks, and many other things which you will never learn in the city.

That is why there are so many poor city hunters. If they kill game, it is because they stumble onto it.

You may not believe it, but woodcraft is an art—a well-defined art—that requires judgment, keen observation, and discretion. You must thoroughly understand the habits of wild animals—where they lie and when they get up to feed, etc.

Hunting against the wind is a bad practice and brings disaster to the person who indulges in it. A deer can smell the hunter at least a mile during the rutting season. All wild animals depend on their smelling power, except it be the duck.

Old Man Bozarth, the greatest of the old Indian Territory hunters, used to declare that wild turkeys could smell you, not in a direct line, but they could tell that there was something moving around in the woods that didn't belong there when you were perchance a hundred yards away—and that is what makes them so watchful.

A remarkable case of woodcraft was exhibited by old Bozarth one time on the north fork of the Sassafras country. He was going along on horseback when he suddenly stopped, alighted from the horse, and began to examine the ground. He remarked, "A two-year-old buck crossed here about two hours ago, and I am going to have him; he will never leave the woods, but will stay and feed around here. Wait for him; I don't think he is far off."

The old man carefully examined his gun priming and turned off into the woods. He told us to remain where we stood, and that he would be back in a few moments. We heard two loud reports, it seemed that they were not far. In about half an hour, he returned with a young buck secured to his saddle.

Now, that is what we call a very fine sample of woodcraft; and the man from the city would have gone straight ahead and seen nothing. Bozarth was trotting when he saw where the young buck had crossed the road. The man from the city will stumble around in the woods all day and kill nothing.

We have been hunting with Old Man Bozarth—still hunting, we mean—when we would get very impatient, sitting on a log an hour or two and seeing nothing, and then our impatience would be rewarded. We have killed four deer with the old man at our side, simply because we waited.

When deer are plentiful, they have a runway to the watercourse, and they never depart from this course. The true hunter knows this and lays in wait, killing them when they go to water.

On another occasion, Old Man Bozarth remarked, "Come with me, Polk, and we'll kill a deer tonight." This was about 9 o'clock. The distance to travel was about a mile. I asked him about 10:30 why he didn't start.

"About 11 o'clock will do; the deer will get up and feed, say for an hour, and then start for water." It was midnight when we reached the hole. "Take the north side," remarked the old hunter; "they always come from the south; it is dark over there, and they love darkness; never mind if the moon is shining."

About midnight we heard a noise. It was so imperceptible you could hardly hear it. The noise advanced and then stopped; the deer was taking in his surroundings; he was not sure that all was right. In a few moments he advanced and was in full view. He retreated and stood in the shade of a thick briar bush that grew on the edge of the water. He looked in every direction. Bozarth raised his gun. The deer was not ten paces from where we were concealed. He advanced boldly to the stream and drank his last water. The old man placed a whole charge of buckshot into his head, and that morning we had venison for breakfast.

We used to like to hunt with Old Man Bozarth. He never became excited or got frustrated. He was the law and gospel of the Sassafras woods. We do not believe he ever made but one mistake in his whole hunting career, and that was when he got tangled up over on Wolf Creek, while in pursuit of a deer, and that was corrected in a few moments.

We could give many extraordinary examples of his woodcraft. He could circumvent a deer to a dead certainty. No deer could escape him when he once got on his trail. He was a dead shot—and how cool he was—his aim true to the mark, cool, calm, deadly. He was the best shot in the Choctaw woods. His walk was slothful and indolent, but in the chase a new spirit seemed to animate him—he was all animation and spirit.

In the next issue we will tell more about his prowess as a hunter.

No. 92
Old Man Bozarth's Woodcraft
(Episode 2)

Sunday Gazetteer, December 10, 1911

In the last issue of the *Gazetteer*, we promised to give our readers something more of woodcraft, as illustrated in the person of Joseph Bozarth. Bozarth was a man who could neither read nor write. He was, to put it mildly, "half horse and half alligator."

There is an art that has no place among the sciences, which the schools cannot teach and of which the savants know nothing, and which is more wonderful in accuracy, more precise in its details, and more curious in its practices than much that Cavier [Georges

Cuvier] and [Louis] Agassiz have written. Its school is very far from the verge of civilization and its disciples are the ignorant sons of the wilderness.

Bozarth was a true son of Nature. He never mixed among men to any great extent, his companions being the denizens of the woods. He studied their habits and was as familiar with them as the very animals themselves. He would sit half of a day and look into the woods.

"What are you thinking about, old man?" we inquired.

"Why, I was just thinking about the many strange things that happen in the woods."

One day we went over on Wolf Creek and took a seat in a little ravine that looked down into the valley. "In a few moments a deer will come along; this is their runway to the bayou," said the old man. And in a few moments one did come along. Bozarth fired, but the distance was too great. He made a clean miss. In about an hour or so, another deer crossed over and disappeared in one of the numerous gullies that overlooked the valley. Bozarth got up and crossed to the gulley, but the deer was nowhere to be seen. It had scented us and was running away. Bozarth returned and sat down, saying nothing. "We got on the wrong side of him," he remarked a few moments later.

At another time we struck a fresh trail in the Sassafras woods. He alighted from his horse and said, "I will take this deer on foot; the brush is too thick to hunt on horseback." He told me to hold his horse; that he would be back in a few moments. He disappeared in the woods and was gone half an hour. We heard a shot; then another. He returned but had no deer.

"What is the matter?" we asked.

"I am a fool; my gun would not reach that far, but I took chances and fired."

He was a very silent man, and at times he would remain in the woods for an hour and not utter a word. Then he would become very talkative and would talk you to death if you would let him. It was only when he went out for a genuine hunt that he was quiet. We worked with him two hours once and not a word escaped his lips.

Bozarth had all of the hunter's dialect. He never spoke correct English. He said "wol" for "well," and there were many other notable examples of how he murdered "the Queen's English." We have frequently sat down and read to him. He was tall and gaunt, and remarked, "I feel just like a stovepipe put together."

The old man is dead these many years. He sleeps over in Oklahoma. Where we cannot say; perhaps in the Sassafras country, or, it may be, in the Allen Bayou region. He was by all odds the greatest hunter of that period—thirty years ago.

No. 93

In the Kiamitia Mountains

Sunday Gazetteer, December 24, 1911

You may have been to the Kiamitia Mountains. It is a great unbroken range of rocks, stretching east, west, north, and south, and nothing to be seen but rocks—the eternal rocks.

The first time that we entered the Kiamitia range was about thirty-nine years ago [about 1872]. Things have changed since then. Civilization has pushed its way to the very border of the rocky ledges, overleaping the caverns and forming homes in the valleys that nestle between the range of mountains. You will come to the range of mountains that overlook many of these valleys and wonder why people should live there contented and happy. They are mostly full-blood Indians, with a sprinkling of white people. They are rough and uncouth and, we might say, savage, and yet they are hospitable and will greet you in their native dialect: "Say, aren't you out rather late; git down and pass the night with we'uns." They are ragged and dirty, but if you are lost, you are bound to accept their hospitality. You enter the cabin through a door where you must stoop to gain admission, the outside being more acceptable than the inside. Inside the one room of squalid wretchedness, everything is topsy-turvy, and to pass the night in such a hovel is undesirable. The fleas bite you, the room is hot to suffocation, the bunks on the floor dirty, and under such conditions sleep is not to be thought of. About midnight you get up, stretch yourself, and go out into the fresh air, light your pipe or cigar if you have one, and, if not, creep in a corner and doze. You arise early in the morning and bestir yourself; drink a cup of black coffee and eat a piece of corn dodger for your breakfast. You then mount your horse, get your bearings, and start for camp.

We wonder how people in such surroundings live; they don't live, they merely exist.

It is a relief to breathe the pure mountain ozone once more. You sing a song as you go jogging along, just as if you thought the world didn't owe you anything, and perhaps it doesn't, but you assume that air of indifference which leaves the impression, and impressions are a great thing in this world—they count for much. If a person could have seen you on that bright October morning, they would have said, "There goes a man who doesn't care a fig whether school keeps or not."

You pick your way to camp but find no one there. There are two of you. But how cheerful and comfortable the camp looks. There is a bright fire blazing; you feel at home—"Home, sweet home; there is no place like home." Perhaps it is at a branch of pure mountain water that comes tumbling down, and there may be fish in it. So much the better. A mountain stream without plenty of fish is not a stream at all. You whip the stream and go to camp at night with a string of fine fish which is almost too heavy to carry.

"Hello, what luck did you have?" cries a voice from the camp.

"Pretty good," and you jangle the string of fish you have and throw them down at the camp door.

Fishing in camp is royal sport, but fishing in winter when the ground is frozen, twice royal—isn't it? The night is very cold, and you snuggle up to your companion and are soon wrapped in pleasant dreams; and that night you dream of the Christmas tree and the good things that it contains.

Obituary
B.C. Murray

Col. B.C. Murray,
A Resident of Denison for 51 Years,
Succumbs after Short Illness

[*Sunday Gazetteer*, February 10, 1924]

Colonel Bredette Corydon Murray, former owner and editor of the *Sunday Gazetteer*, a veteran newspaper publisher of statewide reputation, and a resident of Denison for more than fifty years, died Wednesday morning at 1:36 o'clock at the family residence, No. 1031 West Main Street. Deceased was 87 years old on his last birthday, January 14, 1924.

Funeral services were conducted at the place of death, Thursday afternoon at 2:30 o'clock, by Judge W.S. Pearson, and was attended by a large gathering of sorrowing friends. Around the casket were banked many beautiful floral offerings, mute evidence of the love and respect in which Mr. Murray was universally held. At the conclusion of services at the home, the long funeral cortege proceeded to Fairview cemetery, where a burial service, in charge of the Denison Typographical Union, was had. Mr. Murray had the distinction of holding the longest membership in this organization of any known man in the state.

The active pallbearers were chosen equally from among the Sons of Confederate Veterans and members of the Typographical Union, as follows: Charles H. Jones, Captain E.J. Smith, J.H. Randell, S.P. Willard, C.W. Chapman, and F.W. Miller.

Honorary pallbearers were men of long acquaintance with deceased, and among the number a few who came to Denison at or near the same date as Mr. Murray. These were Dr. A.W. Acheson, A.H. Coffin, Anthony Cuff, W.J. Scott, Richard Terrell, Nat Decker, Dexter Warner, James Cuff, J.W. Anderson, Tim Murphy, P.H. Tobin, Rube Taylor, A.W. Hewlett, J.H. Dunn, and Howard Hanna.

Deceased is survived by four children, Miss Dulce Murray, Mrs. A.A. Thomas, Mrs. E.D. Carter, and Mr. Edwin Murray, all residing in this city, and a number of grand and great-grand children. All members of the immediate family were at the bedside when death came.

Until about a year ago, Mr. Murray had enjoyed the best of health, frequently mentioning the fact that he had not taken a dose of medicine of any kind for more than thirty-five years. An attack of influenza, however, broke that wonderful record, the effects of which confined him to his home during the greater portion of last year. Recovering slowly, he gained sufficient strength to walk [illegible]. January 24, the date of his last visit downtown, he returned home and his exhausted condition caused him to take to his bed, since which time his strength had continually failed, until the end came Wednesday morning.

Colonel Murray, until advancing age, had been a member of numerous lodges and societies of the city, and the B.C. Murray Post, Sons of Confederate Veterans, upon organization a few months ago, named their organization in his honor. He was a charter member of the Denison Typographical Union and one of the organizers of the Texas Press Association.

Coming to Denison during the latter part of the year 1872, Colonel Murray soon became prominently identified with the civic affairs of this city. At this date Denison was a border community at the edge of Oklahoma and the vast territory to the west, which relied upon this point for supplies brought in by the Katy Railway, newly constructed into Denison. With the pioneers who came in with the railway, there were also many soldiers of fortune, gamblers, and the usual followers seeking the end of the rainbow and its pot of gold. As a natural consequence, lawlessness of all kinds was prevalent. Mr. Murray, through the *Denison Daily News*, which he established a few weeks after locating here, took up the fight for law and order. Soon he was elected to the office of Alderman, serving several terms under the early form of city government.

Deceased was born January 14, 1827, at Allegan, Michigan, the only son of Edwin A. and Roxana Murray. At the age of 22 he located at San Antonio, Texas, and a year later entered active newspaper work at Mesilla, New Mexico, continuing same until the outbreak of the Civil War. Soon after hostilities began, Colonel Murray cast his lot on the side of the Confederacy and assisted in the mobilization of a regiment of cavalry in the vicinity of Mesilla, serving throughout the period of the war. Following the surrender, Colonel Murray located at San Antonio, entering the employ of the *San Antonio Express.* Here, on October 7, 1866, he was married to Miss Amanda Swisher. To this union five children were born. A daughter, Mrs. Cora McMillian, died March 8, 1903.

Shortly after his marriage, he became one of the publishers of the *Austin (Tex.) Statesman,* this during the administration of Governor E.J. Davis, for whose removal from office Mr. Murray worked unceasingly, until that gentleman, referred to by all Texas pioneers as the "carpetbag executive," was returned to civil life by an overwhelming vote.

Disposing of his interests at Austin, he [Murray] came to Denison in the month of November 1872, beginning the publication of the *Denison Daily News,* the first newspaper published in this city. Later he established the *Sunday Gazetteer,* devoting his energies to this publication until 1904, when he retired from active newspaper work. From 1914 until a few months ago, he contributed a column of remembrances each week in the *Gazetteer,* under the title of "Twenty-Seven" and "Fifty Years Ago," which have furnished a fund of history as well as other interesting matter to the many readers of this paper.

Tribute to Deceased
by Judge W.S. Pearson
During Service at the Home

"Kind friends:

"This is a sad hour in life's experience. There is no time so solemn as the hour of death: no service so mournful as when, on occasions like the present, we meet to perform our last duties and show respect to a dear and honored and loved friend. It is not mournful because of any danger that may be thought to await him who has just left us, or, that he has passed into a state of suffering or unhappiness. It is not because we have a belief in any such chimera that we mourn at this time. Our sadness arises from the necessity of parting with one so manly, so free, so sincere, so amiable, so gentle and so kind as he whose remains now lie before us.

"It is, indeed, a loss painful in its nature that we are called on to sustain. Such men as he was, are, unfortunately, too scarce in this world of ours. Such men cannot be spared without exciting the deepest regrets and the saddest reflections. Our friend was one by whose deeds and services the world is made better by his having lived in it.

"Our departed brother was one who took great pleasure in the investigation of truth. He was an admirer of Nature—a student of the grand and unchanging principles of the Universe. His mind was unusually clear, and his reasoning power of the highest order. He was singularly free from the blight of superstition and the effects of an erroneous early education. He was fair and candid in an eminent degree. He accepted like an honest man, what his reason approved. He was no slave to mistaken dogmas, antique fables, nor mythological fictions. He accepted the teachings of science as the most reliable facts within the grasp of the human mind. He sought to know the truth and the right, and he embraced them with the full ardor of his nature.

"He was a kind and indulgent husband and father; a warm, a devoted friend; amiable in his intercourse with his fellow man, respectful of the rights and feelings of others, and attentive to all who had claims upon him.

"He yielded up the struggle, the current, the stream, the fire, of life, in ripe old age; he made a long, a plain, a good record; he has proven his faithfulness; he has borne himself manly. He hesitated not to avow his convictions. He has now passed from our sight, bearing with him our kindest memories and our highest esteem.

"He who leads such a life has no need to fear death, nor what may possibly follow after it. One who faithfully discharges his duty according to the sphere in life he occupies, has no need to recoil at leaving this state of existence. If his actions have been governed by the principles of right and justice toward his fellow-man, he neither fears to meet him in this life nor to part with him at the time of death. He dreads no angry being, no vindictive personage, from whom to expect vengeance and wrath. He is ever willing to meet the consequences of a well-spent life.

"Such was our departed friend and brother."

Biography

B.C. Murray was born January 14, 1837, at Allegan, Michigan, son of Edwin A. and Roxana Murray. He learned the printers' trade at Allegan, and in the fall of 1857 he left Michigan and went by the way of New Orleans to San Antonio, Texas. He worked in a printing office in that city for a year or more. At that time the government had established a post at Santa Fe, New Mexico, and L.S. Owings was governor of the New Mexico Territory. San Antonio, Texas, was the nearest trading point; and army supplies for the post were wagoned from San Antonio. In response to invitation from the Governor, Mr. Murray, in 1859, purchased a printing outfit and freighted it by wagon train from San Antonio to the Mission of Mesilla, New Mexico, and there engaged in the newspaper business.

When the Civil War began and it became imminent that the Mission was to fall into the hands of the Federals, Mr. Murray buried the printing plant for safe keeping and assisted in the organization of a cavalry company for Confederate service. As the war progressed, the Confederates fell back from time to time by way of El Paso, and at the close of the war the company had reached San Antonio. Immediately following the close of the war, the company with which Mr. Murray served was enlisted to preserve order in San Antonio and in that part of the State until the Federal army took charge.

At San Antonio on October 7, 1866, Mr. Murray and Miss Amanda Swisher were united in marriage, Miss Swisher being the sister-in-law of Governor L.S. Owings. In the fall of 1872, Mr. Murray, with his family, moved to Denison, the city then being in its infancy.

Early in the following year, he began the publication of the *Denison News*. Mr. Murray was a fearless as well as independent writer, and the *News* soon took its place as one of the foremost papers of the State. In that day, Denison was a typical Wild-West border town. The various forms of gambling were conducted in the open and in the first-floor store rooms the same as any other business. About the second year in this city, Mr. Murray was elected to the City Council, and his first official action was that of drawing [up], offering, and securing the adoption of an ordinance that resulted in driving all games of chance and all gambling from the public and from the first floors of the business houses of the city. Mr. Murray was a strong believer in, and an earnest advocate of, freedom and liberty, both individually and collectively, but he drew the line sharply and strictly against every species of vice. To him freedom did not mean license. He was ever on the side of civil and moral order.

For a long period of years, Mr. Murray participated actively in the affairs of the City, County, and State. An ardent Democrat, a liberalist, a detester of all shams, in religion as well as in politics and in economy, a student of history, a ready as well as versatile writer, Mr. Murray, in the very nature of things, during his long newspaper career, made many friends as well as many enemies. The enemies, however, practically all of them, belonged to the class of intolerance with its usual manifestations of hasty zeal and intemperate language. In his every relation, public as well as private, Mr. Murray was the soul of honor.

Mr. Murray was active in organizing the Texas Press Association; and, following such organization, he attended the annual meetings for many years, and did much of the work that resulted finally in the establishment of one of the strongest, if not the strongest, civic organizations in the State for public as well as for private good, for the general welfare of the State. As suggested, Mr. Murray was a tireless reader. His is, by far, the best general library in the city, if not in the county. His books cover a wide field of thought and endeavor. Early in life he became proficient in shorthand writing. For his work along this line, he was given a medal and a life membership in the Gregg Shorthand System.

Mr. Murray established at Denison the Murray Power Printing House and from about the year 1880 on to 1900 this was one of the leading printing houses of the Southwest. Show and poster work for billboard advertising was made a specialty, and business came in from practically all of Texas. As a newspaper man, Mr. Murray was ever fair with all opponents or antagonists. The columns of his paper were all open for discussion; he wished for the public to have all that there was to both sides of every discussion, in religion the same as in politics.

B.C. Murray and Amanda Murray were parents to five children, one son and four daughters. These children are: Miss Dulcie Murray; Mrs. Helen Thomas, wife of A.A. Thomas; Edwin Murray; and Mrs. Edith Carter, widow of E.D. Carter, late of Abernethy, all of whom reside in Denison. One daughter, Mrs. Cora McMillin, is dead; she died March 8, 1903. To Mr. and Mrs. Murray there are now seven great-grandchildren—three to Mrs. McMillin and four to Mrs. Thomas. Mrs. Amanda Murray died June 16, 1894.

——THE——

Sunday Gazetteer,

ESTABLISHED 1872.

B. C. MURRAY, PROPRIETOR.

MURRAY'S

Power Printing House

B. C. MURRAY, PROP'R.

No. 112 W. Main Street, DENISON, TEXAS.

Best Equipped Office for Poster Printing in the State.

Show Printing a Specialty.

A FIRST-CLASS BINDERY IN CONNECTION.

TERMS:

Per Year, - - $2.00 | Three Months, - - 50 cts.

The Largest, Handsomest and Most Widely Circulated Newspaper

IN

GRAYSON COUNTY AND THE INDIAN TERRITORY.

Fig. 24. Advertisement in 1891 Denison City Directory.

260